WORLD AFFAIRS
National and International Viewpoints

WORLD AFFAIRS
National and International Viewpoints

The titles in this collection were selected
from the Council on Foreign Relations' publication:
The Foreign Affairs 50-Year Bibliography

Advisory Editor
RONALD STEEL

SEA POWER

in the

MODERN WORLD

by

ADMIRAL SIR HERBERT RICHMOND

ARNO PRESS
A NEW YORK TIMES COMPANY
New York • 1972

Reprint Edition 1972 by Arno Press Inc.

Copyright © 1934 by Reynal and Hitchcock, Inc.
Reprinted by permission of Harcourt Brace
Jovanovich Inc. and G. Bell & Sons Ltd.

Reprinted from a copy in The Wesleyan University Library

World Affairs: National and International Viewpoints
ISBN for complete set: 0-405-04560-3
See last pages of this volume for titles.

Manufactured in the United States of America

⌒◟◝◠⌒◟◝◠⌒◟◝◠⌒◟◝◠

Library of Congress Cataloging in Publication Data

Richmond, Sir Herbert William, 1871-1946.
    Sea power in the modern world.

    (World affairs: national and international view-
points)
    1. Sea-power. 2. Naval art and science. 3. Dis-
armament. I. Title. II. Series.
V25.R5 1972   359   72-4293
ISBN 0-405-04585-9

SEA POWER
in the
MODERN WORLD

SEA POWER

in the

MODERN WORLD

by

ADMIRAL SIR HERBERT RICHMOND
K. C. B.

VERE HARMSWORTH PROFESSOR OF NAVAL HISTORY
CAMBRIDGE UNIVERSITY

REYNAL & HITCHCOCK

NEW YORK

PRINTED IN THE UNITED STATES OF AMERICA
BY WAVERLY PRESS, INC.
BALTIMORE, MD.

CONTENTS

MAHAN AND SEA POWER

MAHAN, in the preface of the first of his great works on the influence of sea power, explained that the definite object he had in view was an examination of the general history of Europe and America with particular reference to the effect of sea power upon its course. That effect, he remarked, had passed unnoticed, or insufficiently noticed, by historians. The connection between the operations at sea and the events passing elsewhere appeared to him to have been unrecognised except in particular cases when a naval action determined the fate of an invasion or the possession of an oversea territory. The control of the sea had exercised an influence, not merely in deciding some such particular issue, but in giving a definite direction to the whole course of events. Hence he aimed at making an estimate of the effect of sea power on the course of history and the prosperity of nations.

With this purpose in view he made those monumental studies which have caused the expression "Sea power" to be associated pre-eminently with his name. The studies in his first work[1] embraced a period from 1660 to 1783. In his second work[2] he carried the study up to the end of the Napoleonic Wars. Thus his analysis of the capacity of sea power to influence the course of events was confined to the

[1] *The Influence of Sea Power upon History*, 1889.
[2] *The Influence of Sea Power on the French Revolution and Empire*, 1892.

period when ships were moved by sail. Steam navies, he then remarked, had as yet made no history which could be quoted as decisive in its teaching; hence, theories about the naval warfare of the future must be almost, if not wholly, presumptive.

In his yet later work[3] published a score of years later he found that such experience as had been acquired in the wars fought in later times added little to his earlier analysis. The Spanish-American and the Russo-Japanese Wars had taken place; but the lessons to be distilled from them were mainly of a tactical or minor strategical order. Like the war between Chile and Peru they demonstrated certain facts which were obvious—that an army could only reach an oversea territory if the line of passage was secured by fighting strength. But no great problems either of international policy in war, or of those economic results which might follow sea command, to which he had drawn so much attention particularly in the final chapters of his *French Revolution and Empire*, had as yet made themselves clear, for the struggles were too limited in their character and entailed no vast international upheavals of commerce and economics. The influence of sea power upon the relations between England and Germany, and the consequential effects upon the grouping of the Powers, were at that time (1911) in full progress; but the information available as to how sea power was affecting policy was still insufficient, and the events were as yet too close for them to be brought within focus of the historical eye.

The introduction of steam was not the only new element

[3] *Naval Strategy*, 1911.

in the problem of the exercise of sea power and its capacity to influence events. The torpedo-boat had already reached a considerable stage of development in 1911. The *Blanco Encalada* had been sunk by torpedo attack in 1891. Torpedo-boat attacks had taken place in the Chino-Japanese War; and torpedo-boats had attacked ships in harbour and been attached to a great fleet at sea in the Russo-Japanese War: but, as yet, the part they might play in the future was not discernible, nor could their further development then be foreseen. The chief rôle of the torpedo-boat, Mahan considered, would lie in attack upon a fleet attempting to blockade. The vast increases in the flotilla which proved necessary in the late war, and the tactical part which torpedo craft would play in battle, were still to be experienced.

Still more was the submarine in her infancy. Though she had been invented over twenty years earlier and Lord Brassey had expressed the belief that she might some day prove "a terrible adversary to the ironclad,"[4] Mahan did not attempt to forecast a greater future for her than that she would prove a serious factor in blockade, by placing a greater strain upon a blockading fleet and compelling large ships to keep at a greater distance from a port. That she should possess so extended a range of action, and be capable of being employed against merchant ships in such a manner as gravely to threaten the existence of the greatest Sea Power, allied as that Power was with other great maritime nations, and almost to prove the deciding element in a world war, was beyond the vision of even this great thinker.

[4] *The Naval Annual*, 1893, p. 62.

The twenty years which have passed since the war began in 1914 have added many new features to the material of sea power. The torpedo-boat, whose rôle appeared then so comparatively limited, has become a far larger, faster and more powerful craft, with a greater endurance; her capabilities are vastly increased; her size has reached that of the lesser cruisers of forty years ago. The submarine, whose utilities hardly extended beyond a certain participation in local defence, has become a sea-going vessel, capable of seriously interrupting communications at sea, and of influencing both policy and budgets not only by her own cost but also by the demands for defence to which she gives rise. Finally, a new carrier of explosive missiles has come into existence—the aircraft. The bomber in naval warfare is a flying gun-boat, the torpedo-carrying aircraft is a flying torpedo-boat.

Finally, great increases have been made in the size of the principal fighting units of navies. The so-called "battleship"—an inaccurate term, since all ships fight battles—has grown from the 10,000 to 14,000 tons of the time of Mahan's first book, and the 20,000 tons of his later, to 35,000 tons. Her cost has increased ten-fold. The numbers which any country is able to afford become correspondingly reduced. War, whether on sea or land, is an affair of distributing the available force between the "mass," which has the function of opposing the "mass" of the opponent, and the detachments which secure communications, threaten communications, feint, or otherwise endeavour to produce diversions of force from the mass of the enemy. It is these detachments which furnish the means of strategical manoeuvre. The object of manoeuvre is to acquire a superiority, at the spot at which, and at the time when, a decision is aimed at, sufficient to ensure a victory.

The "mass" of the navies from the history of whose struggle Mahan drew his conclusions was composed of what were then called "ships of the line." In the phrase of a writer in the early nineteenth century, those ships were the "infantry of the sea." It was between those navies composed of this sea infantry that the battles at sea, which decided the fate of the national communications, took place; and it was by means of detachments of these that manoeuvre was conducted with the object of creating superiority at the decisive time and place. Thus, comparative strength between navies was measured in terms of this, the infantry. So, when the French fleet numbered some seventy ships of the line and the Spanish not far from the same number, the British, whose force was determined by the strength of those two Powers, numbered about a hundred and forty: and not only were the principal fleets in home waters composed of these ships but also those squadrons abroad in the Mediterranean, the East and the West Indies. A great change has taken place in this respect. Today, in consequence of the growth in the size and cost of these fighting units, the number of the "capital" ships has been reduced to about one-tenth of those figures. The "infantry" in the outer seas in the war of 1914–18 was composed of smaller types of vessels; it was they that fought the battles in those parts.

Armed force has, as the final reason of its existence, security. It constitutes a weapon which defends some vital interest in the form either of territory or of national communication. War at sea consists in a struggle between armed forces, the result of which is to enable the victor to command and control the communications of its opponents at sea. As the importance of the control of these communications will vary according to the activity of a nation's existence, so the quantity of naval force which a nation requires depends upon the extent to which its national existence, territorial or economic, is dependent upon the maintenance of its external communications.

The changes which have come into existence as the result of the increased size of the ship have altered the character of the mass. Whereas the main bodies of the navies from the history of whose operations Mahan drew his conclusions were furnished by vessels in great numbers, to-day they can be composed of a few only. In the wars of which he wrote the British or French, Spanish or Dutch forces which provided the fleet and squadrons—the "forces in concentration", which, like armies in the field, produced the decision—were drawn from a total available force numbering between one hundred and fifty and two hundred sail.

The relative importance of naval strength varies therefore between nations according to the degree to which their security is dependent upon the maintenance of those sea communications. Hence, as will be illustrated later, those nations which, by force of circumstances or because the national characteristics of their people have led them to expand their interests territorially or commercially overseas, have perforce been those which found it essential to develop their forces at sea for the security of those interests: in the old phrase, they are the "Maritime Powers."

That which determined the size of the ships of the line was—apart from cost and knowledge and skill of shipbuilding—the size of the principal ships whom they had to meet in battle. Size was determined by function, and function was not determined only by considering the ship as an individual unit but as a portion of the whole force. Mobility, adaptability to go wherever a force might be needed, flexibility in the mass, were all factors in determining the size. So we do not see the fleets of the past composed exclusively of the largest ships which the skill of man could produce, the "first-rates," but of ships of such size as made the whole fleet a flexible instrument, apt to the needs of the country. Nor had the size of the ship any reference at any time to the size of ships of lower classes. The theory that the size of the "ship of the line" was determined, in any way, by a military necessity for unquestioned superiority over what to-day is called a "cruiser," is a pure figment of the imagination, wholly devoid of any historical foundation. The sizes of both the greatest and the lesser fighting ships were determined by no rules, either abstract or Pythagorean, but by the very commonsense doctrine of making them large enough to do that which they had to do and no larger. The ship of the line had to be a suitable unit to form one of the "infantry" forces which were required to oppose the concentrated bodies of the opponent, composed of similar vessels, the most powerful with which that opponent had chosen to furnish himself. The lesser ships had to be of a size to perform the duties which fell to them, mainly detached duties, in which the opponent they would have to meet would be of a size considerably smaller than that of the largest ships. In a word, size was determined by function. "Size" and "force" are, in this respect, almost synonymous terms.

While the number of the principal heavy units has thus been drastically reduced, another very marked change has taken place. Navies have always comprised a large number of smaller vessels, necessary for the almost innumerable demands that arise in war which can be performed by ships smaller than the largest of an antagonist. They scouted for the great fleets, they took part in operations with the army in rivers, they were the third line of defence against invasion, they conducted continuous sporadic warfare, and defence against such warfare. It was they that worked in shore and stopped the coastal communications; that were flung widespread over the seas to capture shipping, or were used, on the other hand, as a guard to that shipping. But they had, except in particular circumstances, no "battle value." Given sea room, no number of sloops or gun-brigs, or gun-boats, could endanger the security of a great ship. Only when fitted as fireships, in that time, did they constitute a threat to be reckoned with in battle, and that threat was seldom effective: but in no phase in all that series of wars treated by Mahan did the flotilla affect, and much less govern, the course of operations of the great ships. At a later period, when developments in artillery had led to the construction of larger guns than hitherto, the flotillas armed with such guns became, as the torpedo-boat and submarine later were to become, a threat to an investing fleet. The Russian gun-boats in the Baltic in 1854-5, armed with 8-inch shell-firing guns, outranging the guns of the British ships of the line, were then flotilla craft whose presence had to be reckoned with in the confined waters off Cronstadt.

One of the great changes that have taken place since Mahan developed his thesis is that the "flotilla" of to-day has a definite fighting value, whereas the only vessels that counted in a fleet or squadron of the past were the "ships of the line," the heavy frigates which might be employed either in the line or as auxiliaries to it, and the fireship— and her importance dwindled as the numbers of ships of which fleets were composed dwindled from the four score or more of the seventeenth century to the score, or two score, of the Napoleonic Wars. To-day, a fleet is no longer a fighting force of one arm only. The torpedo-boat on the surface, the torpedo-boat under the surface, and the torpedo-boat or gun-boat in the air may be brought into action against the ship of the line.

Again, the fleet of battleships of the past could lie at its ease off an enemy port, so long as it was equal to meeting the force of similar ships within: no flotilla could dislodge it, though, as remarked earlier, a flotilla of heavy gunned craft could hinder it. To-day, it must lie in a harbour protected either by distance, by obstacles, or by other means of defence, against the flotilla in its various forms. A convoy, escorted by a great ship, had nothing to fear except from a superior force of great ships. To-day, wherever a fleet may be operating within the range of action of either of these new types of torpedo-boats and gun-boats, its largest vessels may be disabled, and, if not sunk, put out of action for a prolonged period.

These are great changes; and it is proper to consider whether, in the new conditions which they have introduced into that struggle for control which constitutes naval warfare, it is now, or will continue to be, possible for a nation to possess such a measure of sea power as will be capable of exercising the far-reaching influence which Mahan showed sea power to possess in the periods on which he founded his "doctrine of influence."

What was that influence? What form did it take?

When a great struggle between groups of nations took place like those of the past century from which Mahan drew his conclusions, or that from which we emerged in 1918, a large number of men were employed and the cost of war became a double burden. Armies and fleets had to be maintained and paid for, the industries from which a nation draws its wealth had simultaneously to be denuded of men, transferred from producing wealth to producing the means of its security. The Seven Years' War cost Great Britain directly £111¼ millions, an average of £14 millions a year; the American War cost £115¾ millions, an average of £14½ millions; the war from 1793 to 1801 cost £200 millions, an average of £25 millions a year.[5] The sources of revenue required to be expanded to meet this additional cost. Trade was then of great importance, and each belligerent endeavoured, to the utmost of its power, and consistently with the means available, to strike at the eco-

---

[5] *Parliamentary Debates*, vol. xxxv, pp. 611 *et seq.*

nomic resources of its opponent. There was a difference between the methods employed by the superior and the inferior at sea. The stronger Power, either driving the enemy main fighting forces into their ports, or reducing them in battle to such an extent that they could not contest the control of the sea, reduced the volume of its sea trade; and added to its opponent's difficulties of conducting its trade by capturing those colonies or overseas settlements, which, at that time, were great sources of national wealth. The weaker Power, unable to contest the "command," either threw its energies into a commerce-destroying war, or, by diversionary attacks on commerce or colonial possessions, endeavoured so to disperse or weaken the main body of its superior opponent that a battle could be fought with an expectation of victory. In the first of these forms of strategy the general principle observed was to "fix" the greater forces of the superior by a threat either of invasion or against a crucial spot in the communications of the enemy, who must necessarily maintain a constant vigilance demanding the use of greater numbers. This threat could be met only by the maintenance of superior forces both large and small. Lesser vessels in great numbers, or detachments of the greater vessels in small numbers, were thrown out by the weaker Power in all the oceans of the world to destroy the commerce of its opponent. Great losses were caused by this "sporadic" warfare, but they never fulfilled the sanguine hopes of those who conducted it. The average losses of the British merchant marine in the eight years of each of those wars quoted reached a figure of between three and four thousand vessels. But while British shipping suffered in these wars, the trade of her opponent was virtually destroyed: and though British trade was thus injured it prospered; for captures from the enemy reached figures nearly as high as its losses, and shipbuilding added to its strength. Thus, in the four years between 1744 and 1748 British exports to her North American colonies rose from £640,000 to £830,000, though they fell slightly in the West Indies, where privateering was particularly active. But in the war which followed, even before command had been effectively established by the victories at sea, the exports to the North American colonies rose from £1,246,000 to £1,832,000 and to the West Indies from £655,000 to £877,000.[6]

This is by no means to say that Great Britain, superior though she was at sea and expanding her commerce, did not suffer. She suffered severely. But so long as she could trade she could obtain credit and continue the struggle. Speaking of the Napoleonic Wars, Mahan remarked that "while Great Britain was making appalling drafts upon her future in her ever-mounting debt, France was exhausting a capital which no forcing power could replace by her conscriptions." It was a struggle of endurance.

The credit of France was gone and her people could not bear any added burdens until the sea, over which Great Britain moved unresisted, was open to them. The people of the continent had become bitterly hostile through the sufferings caused by the blockade and the Imperial power could only be maintained by an army which was itself filled

---

[6] *The Cambridge History of the British Empire*, vol. 1, p. 535.

by borrowing on the future; its capital, its reserve, was fast
being exhausted."[7]

Mahan thus interpreted the influence of the British sea
power in the Napoleonic Wars. "The directly offensive
use of Britain's maritime resources made by the ministry,
in order to repress the French system of aggression, consisted in throwing back France upon herself while at the
same time cutting off her resources. The continental armies
which begirt her on the land side were supported by subsidies; and also when practicable, as in the Mediterranean,
by the co-operation of the British fleets, to whose influence
upon the Italian campaign in 1796 Bonaparte continually
alludes. To seaward the colonial system of France was
ruined, raw materials cut off from her manufacturers, her
merchant shipping swept off the sea. . . . At the same time,
while not denying the right of neutrals to trade with ports
not blockaded, every restriction that could be placed upon
such trade by stringent, and even forced, interpretations
of international law was rigorously imposed by a navy
whose power was irresistible. Even provisions were deemed
to be contraband of war on the ground that, in the then
condition of France, when there was a reasonable hope of
starving her into peace, to supply them contributed to
prolong hostilities."[8]

A vast chain of circumstances was linked to this action
at sea. Though the long struggle between the years 1806
and 1813 involved many powers—Prussia, Russia, Austria,

[7] *The Influence of Sea Power on the French Revolution and Empire*, vol. 11, p.
343.
[8] *Ibid.* p. 395.

Sweden, Turkey—it had its roots in the contest between England and Napoleon. The Berlin and Milan Decrees, which were the measures of boycott sanctioned by the armies of Napoleon by means of which Britain was to be forced to surrender, were answered by those retaliatory acts, the British Orders-in-Council. The Continental System in its integrity was essential to Napoleon's success. But the Continental System gravely injured Russia. In 1810 she had been forced to prohibit many imports in consequence of the low rate of exchange, the rouble having fallen to barely half its value, and the restrictions on commerce were severely felt by a nation whose products, largely agricultural, were beyond its own needs, and were too bulky to export by land.[9] Thus, even a great self-supporting continental country was shown not to be independent of the sea; and a corresponding situation arose in modern war when, owing to the shortage of shipping and interruption in sailings caused by the "U" boat campaign, foodstuffs for export were piling up in New York, to the serious inconvenience of the producers in the West; and for the same reason cargoes of produce blocked the storage space in Australia and New Zealand.

In his examination of the war against commerce after the Berlin Decree, Mahan pointed out that although Britain had been unable to blockade all the individual French and continental ports—"an inability due more to the dangers of the sea than to the number of the harbours"—she could render their approaches so dangerous that it was

[9] For much information on the Russian situation and Napoleon's attitude towards the Czar, cf. *Mémoires du général Caulaincourt*, 1924.

more to the interest of the trader to observe than to evade the Orders. In a few illuminating sentences he draws a picture of the situation that arose: "The battle between the sea and the land was to be fought out on commerce. England had no army wherewith to meet Napoleon: Napoleon had no navy to cope with that of the enemy. As in the case of an impregnable fortress, the only alternative for either of these contestants was to reduce the other by starvation. On the common frontiers, the coast line, they met in a deadly strife in which no weapon was drawn. The Imperial soldiers were turned into coastguardsmen to shut out Great Britain from her markets: the British ships became revenue cutters to prohibit the trade of France. The neutral carrier, pocketing his pride, offered his services to either for pay, and the other then regarded him as taking part in the hostilities."

Many sentences in Mahan's work have become household words; "Those far distant storm-beaten ships upon which the Grand Army never looked stood between it and the dominion of the world" is familiar to all. Less familiar, but no less worthy of being as widely known, is that picture of an economic warfare. The contestants "met in a deadly strife in which no weapon was drawn." A war truly; but a war, to use the words of Dana, that took no blood and imperilled no household; but it touched the tender spot of the pocket, and its effects were felt in varying degrees by all the citizens. Some, mistaking the nature of war, believing that it is synonymous only with bloodshed and the destruction of property, treat this process of economic restraint as though it were distinct from military action.

25

Thus Signor Nitti in his *The Decadence of Europe* remarked that "Germany laid down her arms, overcome more by famine than by military force." Yet what provided the condition from which this distress arose? Military force which controlled the communications at sea. "To call the measure of either [the British or Napoleon] not military," wrote Mahan,[10] "is as inaccurate as to call the ancient practice of circumvallation unmilitary, because the only weapon used for it was the spade,"—the spade, working under the protection of the spear and sword.

The conclusion to which Mahan was brought by his studies, and in particular by his final studies, of the Napoleonic Wars, as to the part which sea power played in that great struggle—a part, it is necessary to observe, which it may not be able to play in a lesser—was that the economic results which it produced, slow-acting though they may have been, were in the end decisive. Bonaparte had the resources of the continent at his disposal but not the resources of the world. He needed these also. He exhausted the "stored up aggressive strength of France" while Britain, preventing him from refreshing the dwindling vitality of France, was nourishing her own by a constant opening of new markets and breaking through, by every means in her power and with the willing connivance of France's dependent allies, the ring Napoleon tried to draw round Britain. "The eloquent derision poured upon his [Pitt's] predictions of failure from financial exhaustion, from slack-

[10] *The Influence of Sea Power on the French Revolution and Empire*, vol. 1, p. 290.

ening of enthusiasm, recoils from the apprehension of the truth."

The instruments of sea power have changed. The means by which goods are carried into and out of a country have been extended. A new means of invasion, imperilling lives and households, has been brought within the power of man, and appears to have received acceptance as both proper and appropriate for the purpose of compelling compliance upon a people. In this changed situation how does sea power stand? Does it still possess the power which, in Mahan's analysis, saved the world from the dominion of Napoleon? Are the nations of the world to-day—not this country alone but all countries, for all are equally concerned for their own security, for peace, and for economy—pursuing such policies, or such community of policy, as promises to achieve those results, each of which is interwoven with the other two?

To consider this it is not enough to limit one's vision to the present-day national needs, or what those needs appear to be in the light of the transient policies of the moment. They are factors, and factors not to be disregarded in a practical world. But we need also to look further, into the abstract reasons, the fundamental necessities, which have brought sea power into existence, to extend the horizon of our vision, freeing it from the fetters which almost necessarily constrain and hamper one when one seeks inspiration solely in the present. Those who now are devoting their resources to the creation, development and maintenance of sea power are not the first who have done so. Earlier nations have furnished themselves with power at sea. What caused them so to act? Were they driven by compelling necessity of some kind? Was sea strength the outcome of a spontaneous need, or was it the result of a calculated policy, with conquest, either of market or of territory, as its ultimate aim?

The words "defensive" and "aggressive" are open to very wide objections. A policy of expansion may well be considered as "aggressive" by those at whose expense the expansion is proposed to be made: while to those who undertake it under the pressure of insecurity from troublesome neighbours—a cause of Rome's expansion across Gaul and Britain's expansion from her settlements on the coast of India to the territories of the British India of to-day—it will appear unmistakably "defensive." Nevertheless, recognising the existence of these different interpretations of the words, we may still use them to express certain broad conceptions: namely that a "defensive" policy is one of noninterference in the affairs of other nations, and of security for that which one possesses; and an "aggressive" policy is one of interference in other nations' affairs or of taking—whatever or however justifiable the claims of necessity may appear to be—something which another nation or nations possess.

We have to consider the present and the future, not the past. We see programmes for expansions of sea power in all parts of the world, supported by comparisons with the strength of other nations, by assertions based upon the presumptions of necessity, by references to the importance of sea communications and to the influence which sea power has exercised in the past. It may be that we can find something in the nature of a ruling principle in the history of sea power of times so far behind us that we can study them without the national prepossessions which are almost inevitable when our eyes are fixed solely on the problem of to-day. What was it that caused certain states or nations in the past to create what we call "sea power?" Was that power something without which national existence would be imperilled, or the people unable to exist as they had accustomed themselves to exist? In a word, did it arise specifically from a need to defend that which the people had created and possessed? Or was the sea power created in order to acquire something which the nation did not possess, to put the nation in a position to dictate its will to other nations, irrespective altogether of whether the nation would be in any danger of loss of its territory, its prosperity, above all its liberty, if it lacked power at sea?

These questions are fundamental.

THE GENERAL OF THE CITY

"Your wine is excellent, Don Francesco, I will really so—— that all ——say for knowing whether Horace would—— religious—— are fundamental."

Don Francesco was a wealthy landowner in southern Italy whose vineyards in the Campania produced a superlative white wine. But he had got it into his head that his wine was the Falernian of Horace. He had collected all the Latin works about the famous wine; and, with the help of these, he endeavored to establish the glorious genealogy of his cellar. Having heard that I was passing in the neighborhood of his lands on my way to Sicily, he sallied forth to meet me, brought me into his domain, and called upon me to acknowledge that he was giving me the true Falernian. As a historian of Rome, it seems that I was especially competent to decide. It was in vain that I sought to convince him of the impossibility of comparing a wine that is drunk today with a wine whose merits were sung by a poet twenty centuries ago. Later I learned that he was the terror of the local archeologists; every expert on antiquity was forced to prove his knowledge by in-

CHAPTER I

THE CAUSES OF SEA POWER

THE causes which impelled or compelled states in the past to develop sea power may be very broadly divided into two categories. In the one there are those nations for whom the development of sea power was the result of natural or spontaneous economic or social movements. Thus trade and colonies were the definite expression of a national spirit, of the genius, character and activity of the people themselves, needing no lead from their rulers, and definitely individualistic in origin. Sea power, in its full expression of a form of national strength capable of giving weight to national policy, was the result. It was a natural, not an artificial or political, growth. In the other case are those nations who, themselves not dependent upon trade or territory but desiring it for the added wealth and strength and influence which it would confer, strove to acquire that which others had established.

The characteristic of the "natural" Sea Power, as opposed to the Sea Power artificially created for political purposes, was want of territory in which the people dwelt, and therefore of the wealth which the possession of territory confers. A small state perched upon a seaboard could not acquire wealth through pastoral and agricultural production, the sources of the wealth of greater inland states. It had however one outlet: the sea. A seafaring population was a natural element of a city built upon a harbour or in a

river which gave access to the sea. Merchants created a
business of transport, not only carrying goods for themselves but also performing the useful function of carrying
for other peoples, who either for want of the stimulus of
necessity, or of natural capacity or skill, could not or were
disinclined to perform the arduous work for themselves.
Trading became the principal activity of such people, and
the influence of the mercantile class grew as a result of its
wealth and power in a state. Settlements and colonies also
came into existence, either as forerunners of the trade, as
in Greece, or as the result of the needs of trade, as in the
Phoenician state. Both the trade and the colonies offered
prizes to the pirates, and hence, as the cargo carrier could
not be a match for the pirate, so ships specially adapted
and furnished for fighting were found necessary for her
protection.

Several rich trading cities grew into existence, and with
that came rivalry and conflicts between those several
states; and, with the rivalry, came the national concomi-
tant of an increase in the strength of the warship, each
seeking to build a weapon more powerful than that of its
rival. Thus the fifty-oared galley developed in the eighth
century B.C. into the bireme and the trireme, not because a
galley was not able to fight the galley of a rival or a pirate,
but in order to meet the larger ship which the other was
able to produce. As the trading state had all its interests
concerned in the preservation of the trade, so for the reasons of its existence it was forced to develop stronger sea
power than the purely predatory state, the pirate: and as
its wealth arose from trade, and was greater and better

assured than wealth derived from booty, so it was better able to support a larger force: a true "Sea Power" was one whose existence depended upon sea traffic, created by the energy, ability and enterprise of the citizens.

But though sea power had its origin in the need for defence, it furnished at the same time a means of aggression. A democracy is not necessarily of a more peaceful nature than an aristocracy. In the Athenian state it was the trading democracy which stimulated the policy of aggression, and sent its army, the principal instrument of aggression, to conquer Salamis and to establish permanent stations on the shores of the Hellespont. Realisation of the utility of the possession of bases in regions remote from the metropolitan state brought with it an extension of settlements. One form of bringing pressure upon another state was the blockade of its commerce, and the power to exercise blockade depended upon ability to maintain a fleet in the close neighbourhood of the enemy state. The Athenians could not blockade Corinth from a base at the Piraeus, but the capture of Naupactus, a sheltered port on the north of the narrowest part of the Gulf of Corinth, gave them a position in which their fleet could lie, and from which its vessels could intercept the commerce, which was the principal source of prosperity of the Corinthians. The revolt of Naxos in the same century was subdued by blockade, and, when Cimon had defeated the Thasian fleet, Thasos succumbed to blockade.

In epitome, and so far as any generalisation is permissible, this is the story of the rise of maritime Powers and of the use to which sea power was put by them. The need for security of an interest upon which the life and fortunes of the peoples depended brought it into existence; the needs of defence could be furnished only by possession of superiority of the fighting force at sea; and capacity to employ those forces in all those parts where the interests were threatened required secure harbours. The forces which the needs of defence had brought into existence were capable of offence and the forms which offence could take were two-fold: armies could be carried by sea to conquer on land, or trade could be stopped by blockade and capture at sea. The danger to which a nation possessing this power was exposed lay on the land. However great its strength at sea, it might be overwhelmed by a Power which could bring strong land forces by land against it. It must therefore eschew all commitments tending to increase its liabilities on land which would require armies capable only of being maintained at the expense of its sea power. "If we were islanders," said Themistocles, "we could defy the world." But the temptation to adopt a continental policy proved too great on more occasions than one: and misfortune followed.

When the various maritime city states of Greece found themselves threatened by the Persian Empire, they saw the need for co-operation, however greatly they disliked the process. They drew together, forming the Confederacy of Delos. The common need of security demanded community of action and community of effort.

"It was a league of sea states, and therefore the basis of the contract was that each state should furnish ships to the common fleet. But most of the members were small and poor; many could not equip more than one or two ships; many could do no more than contribute a part of the expense to the furnishing of a single galley. To gather together a number of small and scattered contingents at a fixed time and place was always a matter of difficulty: nor was such a miscellaneous armament easily managed. It was therefore arranged that the smaller states, instead of furnishing ships, should pay a yearly sum of money to a common treasury. . . . From the very beginning the Confederacy consisted of two kinds of members, those who furnished ships and those who paid an equivalent in money. . . . As leader of the Confederacy, Athens had the executive entirely in her hands and it was of the highest importance that the treasurers were not selected from the whole body of Confederates, but were Athenian citizens. Thus from the first Athens held in her hands the means of gradually, and without violent revolution, transforming the naval union into a naval Empire."[1]

For two reasons this union was weak. It was weak in consequence of the spirit of extreme localism of the several city states. None would make any sacrifice of what it deemed to be its sovereignty. "In the face of a common danger cities might be ready to combine together in a League, each parting with some of her sovereignty to a common federal council but preserving the right of secession . . . but even such a voluntary and partial surrender of sovereignty was regarded as a misfortune." When the danger was past, full independence was instantly and eagerly resumed. Thus the sea power of this Thalassic Empire suffered gravely from the want of a permanent common policy of mutual support. The second cause was the reten-

[1] J. B. Bury, *History of Greece*, vol. I, pp. 353-4.

tion, by the principal member, Athens, of the whole control. If the Athenians had had the breadth of vision to bring into the Central Council the representatives of the lesser states, though it will not be said that this would have dissipated altogether this intense love of local independence, it would at least have operated in its mitigation.

Thus one of the principal problems which affects so profoundly the modern successors of the Athenian maritime Power existed two thousand four hundred years ago. A means was devised by which the whole strength of a scattered set of communities could be brought together; but the League lacked the wisdom, both at the centre and in the extremities, to make certain minor sacrifices of what they regarded as their "rights": and Athens, after reaching, through her sea power, the very height of her greatness, fell. Her fall was not the consequence of any want of skill of her commanders or of her seamen, or of superior design in the ships of other Powers. It was due in part to over-reaching herself in operations on land but more still to the want of a wise policy of mutual support and mutual sacrifice in the maintenance of her sea power.

Athenian sea power had grown partly out of the needs of trade defence, partly out of the spirit of adventure which sent men to seek new countries, and partly out of social legislation which drove men from their own land to lands where greater freedom was to be found. Phoenician sea power on the other hand arose out of trade. The people of the city states of Tyre and Sidon were traders because there was no other development in the landward direction. Phoenician trade produced Phoenician colonies and Phoenician fighting ships to defend their trade and their colonies. The need then arose for more ports where trade and the fighting ships which defended it could meet, or from which the latter could operate. Ports in Sicily were necessary for the defence of the trade on its way to the Carthaginian ports in Western Italy. For Carthage, as it was for Greece, trade, a fighting fleet and colonies or bases were the three essential elements in her sea power.

In her time and turn Venice arose, for similar reasons, from a population of fishermen into a Sea Power. The land being closed to the activities of the dwellers on the sandbanks, they sought their fortunes in the only direction possible—the sea. From a fishing community she developed into a community of traders, and was already a rich trading state when the union of the Eastern and Western Emperors caused the removal of the embargoes which had prohibited her trade with the Western Empire: hence came a great expansion of her trade in the eighth century. But she did not yet possess sea power. For the security of her commerce she depended upon the imperial fleet at Byzantium. But when that fleet, engaged in other tasks dictated by the policy of the capital, failed to give protection to her commerce, Venice proceeded to provide herself with a fleet of her own. Rendering herself independent in all but name from the Empire, she then became a true Sea Power. In the middle of the ninth century she built her first ships of war; her complete independence soon followed. Thus, the growth of her sea power was a natural growth of a defensive character. It was the result of a national life depending on sea trade, colonies essential to that sea trade, and, finally, of a fighting fleet to preserve both the trade and the colonies.

The Hanseatic League was in like manner a true Sea Power, within the range of its influence. It was the northern counterpart of those Mediterranean trading states, and its sea power originated from the same causes. German colonisation landwards towards the east along the shores of the Baltic created towns wherever a river or a bay gave facilities for shipping. German trade developed in the Baltic, and, as elsewhere, pirates preyed upon it. But it lacked one element in sea power. Trade and bases there were: but the fighting forces, adequate though they were to deal with the individual pirate, lacked unity, even more than those of the Mediterranean city states. Internal dissension, the jealousies and rivalries of the several communities—in fine, the localistic spirit that had undermined the Greek sea power—for long hampered the League and hobbled its sea power. The apogee of its power corresponded with the period at which the process of unification had made its greatest progress: but though it possessed the two essential primary elements of trade and sea ports, the territorial possessions of the League were confined to the Baltic area; and the traders were dependent for the existence of many of their marts upon the good will of other powers, or upon such economic forms of pressure as they might possess with which to retaliate against discriminations or injury to their commerce. They lacked an organised and co-ordinated fighting force capable of being centrally directed. For want of unity the Hanse League did not become one of those Sea Powers whose influence played a part in the great Euro-

pean struggles which succeeded each other from the time of
the Reformation onwards. As a number of armed men does
not make an army, so the number of armed vessels possessed by the several Hanse comptoirs did not make a
navy. By the beginning of that time it had already lost
most of its powers: and its extinction—for though its name
survived for another two centuries, it was dead as an effective force—had already taken place before those struggles
began. It furnishes with Athens a classic example of the
effects of the localised spirit which, mouthing the word
"co-operation," in practice refuses to make those minor
sacrifices of local sovereignty which are as necessary for co-
operation as the sacrifice of individual wishes and freedom
are necessary for the individual fighting man.

Dutch sea power arose in trade. The inhabitants of the
barren tracts of unfruitful sandy sea coast of the Nether-
lands must perforce look seaward and to manufacture for
their livelihood, in place of producing the fruits of the earth.
The materials for the manufactures must come, and the resulting goods must go, in the main, by sea. Freed, through
the decisive defeat of the Spanish sea power in 1588, from
attack by sea, though many years were to pass before freedom was to be achieved on land, the Dutch were able to
expand their commerce by sea. Their East India Company
was formed in 1600, and Dutch sea power grew in the form
of fisheries, then trading ships, settlements and colonies
and, eventually, an organised fighting fleet: or, more properly speaking, an organisation of fighting ships belonging
to the seven separate provinces of the Republic. The difficulties of obtaining a real unification of effort, experienced
in one form by the ancient Greeks for which the agreement

reached by the Confederacy of Delos was the cure, were found also in the Dutch Republics; and the want of unity of direction was a contributory factor to the weakening of Dutch sea power. It is however the origins rather than the reasons for decline which at this stage concern us. The origin lay in the necessity for a small people, without rich territory, to find a means of livelihood. The land alone could not provide their needs, and they turned, as other peoples have turned, to the sea because there alone could they find an outlet. Once that outlet was found, prosperity followed: and, as sea power grew in the making of that prosperity, so it was a necessity for its maintenance and for the life and liberty of the people.

I have called the acquirement of sea power of such states as these—Carthage, Athens, Venice and the Mediterranean city states—and the Dutch Republics a "natural" growth. Its origin was economic: it was forced upon the peoples in question by the sheer necessities of geography and the national characteristics of the people themselves. It was not a growth stimulated by some policy imposed by a ruler or ruler's authority, except to the extent that policy —as in the case of Athens—was consciously directed towards the creation of a commercial, as contrasted with a military, foundation of the national life. Though the eventual possession of power in this form might—as it did in the democracy of Athens—prove a temptation to put it to an aggressive use, it was in neither case an expression of a deliberate aggressive conception. Fundamentally, it was the outcome of a need for security for that which was a necessity for the peoples' life.

But sea power has originated otherwise, unconnected

with any national economic necessities, but in accordance
with a definite and calculated national policy of extending
influence, obtaining and exercising power in the world. The
causes of Roman sea power differed profoundly from those
of these essentially trading states. The Roman peoples
were not maritime; they were under no pressing economic
need to seek their fortunes at sea. That which brought
Roman sea power into existence was the political question
of who should rule in Sicily. Whether the Mamertines
should be supported against the Carthaginians affected in
no way whatever the individual life of a single citizen of
Rome. Political intervention in the internal affairs of another state formed the occasion—whether such intervention was imposed by a conviction of a moral necessity to
to give justice to an ill-governed community is immaterial.
To intervene required a force capable of obtaining control
of the waters between Sicily and Italy, in order that an
army might cross the sea. Though the Romans of the fifth
century B.C. possessed a navy it was one whose strength
was far below that of the maritime Carthaginians. Her sea
power began by the creation of a fighting fleet capable of
meeting that of Carthage; its object was to impose the will
of the Roman Senate upon Carthage. Trade and colonies
were not the first begetters of sea power; they were begot-
ten by the fighting navy which crushed a rival out of
existence.

The sea power of the Mussulman Turks had a similar
origin. In the height of Turkish power it dominated the
Eastern basin of the Mediterranean. It was the means by
which the instrument of Turkish conquest, the army,

moved to subject the islands and coasts from the Black Sea to Malta to Turkish rule, unopposed effectively until the battle of Lepanto because of the jealousies between the several Christian states—that same want of unity, in another manifestation, which had weakened the Athenians and was later to weaken the Dutch. The Mussulman Turk was not a trader. Indeed, when Constantinople fell into his hands its prosperity, as a sea port with which the Turk had had commerce, disappeared. Nor was he driven to the sea for want of lands: the territories he acquired were not colonies or trading settlements. His sea power was not the outcome of a need for the security of the national existence of his people, but of the purely aggressive spirit of expansion by conquest. In so far, also, as the successors to the Turk, the "Barbary States," were Sea Powers, though minor only, they were so for reasons of plunder, not from necessities enforced upon them by the conditions of national life to use the sea for trade.

Spanish sea power was not of what I have called "natural" origin. Spain was a poor country, but its people were not driven to sea to find their livelihood and found their existence upon fisheries and commerce. With possessions acquired by marriage and conquest, with a foreign policy which required the employment of military force, her need was an army; and the need of the state was money to pay that army. The beginnings of her sea power lay neither in colonies, in trade, nor in fighting ships, but in conquests of territories from which the precious metals could be obtained—wealth, in its most simple shape; a shape in which it was understood. Of trade, in the true sense of exchange of goods, Spain had little. She imported bullion in its various forms. As the ocean was used by none but her, in the early stages of her Western Empire, her treasure fleets moved in security. Roads that are unthreatened demand no defence; fighting ships in the oceanic trade were not needed. Her ships on the ocean were traders or transports, while in the Mediterranean she maintained fighting vessels, adhering to the as yet unchanged and purely military galley type, proper for the functions they were called on to perform.

The true fighting fleets on the ocean came into existence when the need for security arose, and in this respect her sea power followed the natural course. As it had originated in the development of interests over sea, in the form of territorial possessions and the transport of oversea products, it became necessary for Spain to furnish herself with the fighting strength essential to the security of these interests: interests which, however different from those of the Sea Powers to whom reference has been made, had become an essential in the maintenance of her power as that of the other states had been to their existence. But as she formed great territorial interests in Europe which brought her into collision with neighbouring continental Powers, it was incumbent upon her also to maintain great land forces. Her revenues would not suffice to provide adequate defence on land and at sea, and her sea power suffered in consequence.

French sea power found its origin in normal needs. Fishing and trade on the coasts developed the interest in the sea. The same spirit of adventure which had sent the early Greeks into the Black Sea sent the French seamen across the Atlantic to found colonies in North America and the West Indies, and, at a later date than the Dutch or English, in India also. But whereas the smaller sea states were forced by necessity into the sea, having no other resources, France, as a country, was not similarly forced, for she possessed a territory rich in every respect, whose products were her support. The inhabitants of her coastal cities had the impulse: but the capital, Paris, lay far from them, and the ruling caste was not the merchant but the soldier. Commercial elements did not possess the power behind the Government they possessed in Venice or Genoa, in Holland or London. The Crown discerned that there was profit in the oversea trade, Eastern trade became state-managed, but not by the traders. The French East India Company became dependent on patronage, and it not only lacked the vitality of a national impulse which drove forward the sea commerce of other nations, but was itself devitalised by the policy of state control. Speaking of the French East India Company, Sir Alfred Lyall contrasted the conditions of its existence with those of the English. "Official patronage proved gradually fatal to the Company that depended on it. . . . The English Company . . . were an independent and powerful corporation trusting not to official favour but to parliamentary influence in transacting business with the Crown."[2]

But if France as a whole had not the same pressing need, regarded as a nation, to seek her fortune on the sea, those in her maritime districts were as fully aware as any Hollander or Englishman that their own prosperity lay on the

[2] A. Lyall, *British Dominion in India*, p. 77.

water. All the necessary elements were there—trading ability, manufacturing ability, a brave and adventurous seafaring population. Once the internal divisions of the country were healed under Richelieu and Mazarin, trade expanded, colonies were formed. What was wanting was fighting strength both to maintain and to expand these elements. The Roman Senate made no more fateful decision when it determined to intervene in the affairs of Sicily, which led to Rome becoming a Sea Power, than Louis XIV made when he gave his preference to the policy of Louvois instead of to that of Colbert. Thenceforward, though rivalry for colonial empire in the great age of expansion from the late seventeenth to the latter part of the eighteenth century led to struggles at sea between the contending powers, the orientation of the policy of the Bourbon kings was landward and continental, not seaward and economic and French sea power held a place secondary to land power, and suffered accordingly. Thus French sea power was of what I have called a definitely "natural" character. It sprang from trade and colonies and the needs of their defence as distinct from the efforts of the rulers. But because the efforts of the rulers were not, as in the other sea states, directed with an exclusive aim to prosperity by way of commerce and colonies, so French sea power was limited in its scope by what could be spared for the sea forces after the needs of the land forces which implemented the policy of her rulers had been satisfied. But the sea power which France created was at no time of an "artificial" nature. It represented a definite need. When the energies of her people, however curtailed by her rulers, had created interest on and over sea, the fighting forces were as essential for their preservation as the possessions over sea were themselves essential for the exercise of the power to defend them.

I have endeavoured in the preceding outline of the origins of the sea power of various states to show that there is a distinction between "a navy" and "sea power." A navy is a constituent—a primary constituent indeed—in sea power. But a state which possesses a navy will not necessarily possess sea power—power, that is to say, consisting in the ability to exercise control over the maritime routes to the markets of the world, and thereby of influencing the course of world events. Though a militia may preserve a state from invasion, that state may nevertheless have no influence; except to the extent that it is able to prevent contending nations from making use of its territories, it will not be one which possesses "power."

Though there was an English navy before the Norman Conquest, English sea power, though adequate for the security of the coasts and, to a lesser degree, of the trade round the coasts of England, did not exist as a world force. The Saxon navy was a force purely for coast defence, called into being when occasion needed. After the Norman Conquest a need for a more extended navy arose. The kingdom of the Norman kings was no longer an island; it embraced the territories of its rulers in two countries, England and France, between which, like a wide river, ran the Channel. The Channel connected the two like a bridge so long as that bridge was secure for the passage of armies. The situation was indeed analogous to that of modern France, whose

territory lies in France and Africa, connected by that wider
river the Mediterranean so long as the passage of the Mediterranean is secure: or of the Japanese Empire with possessions on the mainland of Asia and in the islands,
connected by the Straits of Tsushima.

Sea trade, though important always, bulked less in the
eyes of the Norman and Plantagenet ruler than the preservation of what he regarded as his territories. In the succession of wars of the fourteenth century the maintenance
of a navy was necessary in order to transport armies across
the Channel and hold the territories in France to which
claim was laid. The navy was an armed transport service.
Though, as the *Libel of English Policy*[3] shows, it was recognised that strength at sea was a sharp weapon for use
against the Flemish states, who for their livelihood and
prosperity must send their goods by sea, there seems little
reason to assume that the navy was, in itself, looked upon
as an instrument of policy. The army was that instrument,
and the navy was the means by which it was used. There
was a need to deal with piracy, which was rampant, and
though Royal ships or ships hired for the purpose might be
used in dealing with it, the remedy for injuries suffered
from the pirates was placed principally in the hands of the
aggrieved merchants, who, by means of letters of marque
and reprisal, were given liberty to reimburse themselves
for the losses they had suffered.

So long as English kings claimed the sovereignty of portions of France, England was necessarily a land power. It

[3] A small book in verse written about the middle of the fifteenth century,
expounding the importance of the sea to England.

was her army which fought at Agincourt in 1415, though her navy must be strong enough to make it reach France. To maintain an army at the needed strength absorbed so much of the revenues that the sea forces suffered, and piracy consequently increased. But simultaneously with the loss of the French provinces in the early fifteenth century a new oversea interest was developing. Trade and shipping were increasing. The weakening of the Hanse, as in the wars with the Danes, afforded an opportunity for English ships to carry English goods to the Baltic, and the English trader also found his way into the Mediterranean. With the development of trade the political power of the merchant increased as it had in Athens and in Venice, and he became able to make his voice heard and to insist that proper steps should be taken to guard his interests. The King must no longer look on the navy as his personal possession, to be used to guard his personal property and interest, but as an instrument for the protection of his subjects. Naval strength, arising out of the need for intercommunication of two territories between whom a comparatively narrow waterway ran, was making the beginnings of the transformation into sea power in its wider significance. Interests were becoming more widely diffused, contact, and consequently the possibility of friction, with states far removed from the Channel were yearly increasing. The English ship of war was becoming, as the vessels in the old Mediterranean states had become, definitely differentiated from the trader: larger and specifically designed for the particular purpose of fighting.

English sea power made itself manifest as an interna-

tional factor in the Elizabethan struggles with Spain, for
the fate of the Low Countries depended in the last resort
upon whether the Spanish armies could be maintained by
sea and whether the fisheries and external commerce of
Holland could continue to furnish her people with the will
and power to resist. But it had a wider significance in the
establishment of that tradition of action against the external sources of an enemy's wealth which was never after
absent from the minds of her statesmen.

New responsibilities, and a new necessity for strength at
sea, arose with the founding of colonies in North America,
in Newfoundland and the West Indies, and of trading settlements in India. But if these imposed an added burden
for their defence they added also the essential element of
increasing sea power. Many of the needs of the fighting
ship could only be furnished in harbours where anchorage
and shelter were to be had, where supplies could be accumulated and repairs performed. When such footholds were
obtained it became practicable to conduct sustained operations of large forces where previously no more than sporadic or temporary operations by small ones had been
possible.

England, like others before her, experienced as they had
experienced the need for establishments over sea. If she
was to be able to give security to her interest at and over
sea, her navy must possess mobility. It was not enough
merely to reach a particular area, which is the first need of
a navy; it is necessary also effectively to conduct operations until a decision is reached. In particular circumstances the needs might be furnished by an ally. Her fleet

could have at different times facilities available at Lisbon, at Toulon, at Maddalena or Palermo. But this implied not only the existence of an ally but also of one so situated that his ports would serve the needs of the navy. So we see Cromwell sending Montagu in search of a harbour in the entrance of the Mediterranean which the fleet could use as a base, Charles II readily accepting and reluctantly abandoning Tangier, the captures of Gibraltar, Minorca and Malta: and when proposals were made to return Gibraltar to Spain, notwithstanding the political advantages of Spanish friendship and a share in the Spanish trade, which were urged by Stanhope, Chesterfield and Sandwich, we see the steady refusal by Parliament on each occasion to countenance this weakening of Britain's sea power.[4]

As trade and colonies steadily developed in the middle and later part of the seventeenth century, sea power was fostered to meet the demands of their security. Colonies, shipping and a fighting sea force were the interlocked parts of a single whole. The result was sea power in its widest sense—ability to send the ships of the community or of the state carrying cargoes or armies where they were needed, and to prevent or hinder an opponent from a like freedom in war. It was the need for the security of the acquired oversea interests, created by the people, which obliged Britain to intervene in continental disputes, often contrary to the wishes of many of her statesmen, and in the merits of which she was uninterested. Thus the union of Bourbon Powers under one crown would produce a sea power pos-

[4] Viz. in 1714, 1718, 1721, 1727, 1748, 1756.

sessing the three elements of naval force, colonies and shipping in such measure as would give that crown the law at sea. So early as 1746 there were Englishmen who discerned the possibility that the hegemony of a single state on the continent could be employed to close the harbours of all the states who came under the military heel, the Continental System eventually established by Napoleon. For the security of her own interests it was felt to be essential to resist such a domination, and her sea power was her instrument.

Thus, although Britain in the early stages of her existence was not forced to sea for her livelihood, as the small trading states whose territories could not support their people had been, she grew in stages into that condition. She needed naval force in Saxon times for the security of her coast: in Norman and Plantagenet times to connect her continental and island territories: in Tudor times for security against invasion of her own country or the occupation of territory across the narrow sea from which invasion could be facilitated. Trade and colonies brought with them the need for fighting strength at sea. In illustration of one manifestation of sea power, it was the growing trade of the Dutch, with the growth in Dutch sea power which accompanied it, that was one, though not the only one, of the causes which brought her into collision with a people with whom from every point of view the closest and most friendly relations should have existed. Finally, when her transformation from an agricultural and pastoral into an industrial state made her absolutely dependent upon assured ability to receive the raw materials of her industries and the food of her population, sea power became an essential condition of her very existence.

Thus there are two conditions which may originate sea power. Either its origin is due to an intrinsic need arising out of an inability either to find a livelihood for a people or to be secure against the domination of others: or it is due to a desire to conquer or to enforce the will of the state upon others. If, without sea power, the existence of the state and the life of its people is exposed to destruction, sea power constitutes its legitimate means of security. The criterion of the character of a state's sea power is to be found in the relation between the vital needs and the force which defends them. Sea power which merely satisfies those needs is defensive. The state which lays claim to a "right" to sea power on any scale would appear also to be under the obligation to demonstrate that its vital needs of security require that power: that its people would suffer such injury if its oversea commerce were circumscribed that they would be forced to surrender to a foreign demand: or that it is exposed to the danger of invasion by sea conducted by forces superior to its own. The words of Mahan,[5] written nearly half a century ago, indicate this differentiation of the origins of sea power:

"The ships that thus sail to and fro must have secure ports to which to return, and must, as far as possible, be followed by the protection of their country throughout the voyage. This protection in time of war must be extended by armed protection. The necessity of a navy, in a re-

[5] *The Influence of Sea Power upon History*, p. 26. Mahan is speaking of the ships conducting the country's commerce only.

stricted sense of the word, springs therefore from the existence of a peaceful shipping, and disappears with it, except
in the case of a nation which has aggressive tendencies, and
keeps up a navy merely as a branch of the military establishment."

CHAPTER II

THE ELEMENTS OF SEA POWER

WHILE the so-called "Sea Powers" of the world have been nations whose sea power was the outcome of the necessities of the national geographical situation, and of the ability and characteristics of the peoples, other nations have possessed "sea power" but in a different measure and with a different meaning. There is an obvious distinction between the possession of strength at sea sufficient for the security of interests circumscribed within a restricted area or zone and the possession of such strength at sea, as renders its possessor an influence in international affairs—one whose word carries weight in all the great problems with which the nations of the world are constantly confronted. Thus both the Chileans and Peruvians possessed "sea power" in their struggle in 1879–81. Their respective strengths at sea were represented by the two 3500-ton battleships and seven smaller vessels of Chile, and the four armoured vessels of from 2000 to 1100 tons and four smaller craft of Peru. The territory which was the cause of the dispute between the two nations was separated from both by desert regions and by the sea. As armies could not cross the desert, the sea was the only route, and control of that route was thus obtainable only by sea power. Those navies, with their capital ships of 3500 and 2000 tons, were the expressions of the "sea power" of the two countries. Small as they were, both in numbers and size, they were adequate for their purpose. But the forces of neither country were of any weight in world affairs.

Thus in using the term "sea power" we need to realise that we may do so in more senses than one. We may use it to refer to the strength of a nation at sea in regard to a particular situation or area, which is a relative and restricted sense: or we may use it to express a capacity to exercise an influence in the problems of the great nations of the world. "A Sea Power" is one whose power at sea is of the latter nature. It is in that latter sense that, in the past, reference has earlier been made to nations which possessed sea power. These "Maritime Powers" were always to be reckoned with as factors, in world affairs, whose attitude towards any great international problem could not be disregarded: for they were able to control not local movements at sea only, but movements extending over the broad areas of world commerce.

Considered in that connotation, what are the elements of sea power? What are those constituents which render its possessor able to speak with a voice which will receive an attentive hearing?

In the preceding sketch of the origins of sea power an attempt was made to show that a definite purpose informed the national will of those peoples who, in the past, became Maritime Powers: and that that purpose was either defensive or acquisitive. Three elements entered into the composition of sea power—oversea trade, oversea possessions and fighting force. Oversea possessions in the form of colonies or settlements might be the forerunners of trade, as they would appear to have been in Greece and were in both the

English and French North America: or trade might produce settlements as it did in the Phoenician state and in British India. Again, possessions are acquired for purely military reasons, as is the case with some of the British and American possessions: while again the needs of increasing the personnel of the fighting forces has had its part in the development both of trade and colonies. "The Plantacon Trade is one of the greatest nurseries of the Shipping and Seamen of this Kingdome," wrote the Commissioners of Customs to the Lords of Trade in 1678.[1] It is in fact hardly more possible to establish an order of genesis of the three elements than to say which came first, the hen or the egg. The men of the seventeenth century, remarks Mr. Beer, argued in a circle of navy, commerce and colonies. The navy enabled England to expand and to protect her foreign trade, and the increased commerce, in its turn, augmented her naval strength. Colonies were both dependent upon, and necessary for, the exercise of naval strength. "Your Fleet and your Trade," Lord Haversham is reported as saying in the House of Lords, "have so near a relation and such mutual influence on each other, they cannot well be separated: your trade is the mother and nurse of your seamen: your seamen are the life of your fleet: and your fleet is the security and protection of your trade: and both together are the wealth, strength, security and glory of Britain."[2]

Thus sea power in its true expression as a natural national growth arising out of the life of the people them-

[1] G. L. Beer, *The Old Colonial System*, vol. I, p. 17.
[2] *Parliamentary History*, vol. VI, p. 380. Quoted by G. L. Beer, *op. cit.*

selves will rest, like a three-legged stool, upon three supports—shipping, colonies or oversea possessions, and a fighting force capable of overcoming the opposition of an enemy armed force and of exercising control over the movements of sea traffic. It must do this in accordance with the recognised laws which have been evolved to govern conduct at sea, and in a manner which will be acceptable to nations not engaged in the dispute, that is to say, in accordance with what is called the Law of Nations: for unless it does so it will bring recruits to the forces of its enemy.

MERCHANT SHIPPING

A nation which needs strength at sea to defend its shipping needs it for the simple reason that shipping is vital to its own national life, and in itself beneficial to the community. Shipping, except when artificially stimulated into existence and maintained, is a branch of trade and source of revenue; it performs services, both for the nation and for others, from which a definite return is obtained, which constitutes a part of the exports with which that nation pays for its incoming supplies. Its constriction is a loss to the revenue, as well as the destruction of an important national industry. Whether the stoppage of a subsidised shipping which constitutes a charge upon the people would be an injury may be left to the economists, but one thing is plain. If a large proportion of the goods of a country, which by the nature of things is dependent upon foreign trade, is carried by its own bottoms, the stoppage of the sailing of its shipping will be bound to produce a serious situation.

If the national ships which normally carry a very high proportion of the nation's goods are unable to sail, the deficient tonnage must be procured elsewhere. Except in very prosperous times there is a margin or "pool" of spare tonnage available: but while there will not improbably be a sufficiency to meet a comparatively small demand, it is unlikely that so great a demand could be met as the laying up of all the shipping of a "natural" sea power would involve. The supply of so large a quantity of tonnage as would be needed from other sources might not be forthcoming, and such a nation whose life, by hypothesis, depended on her external trade, would be liable to find herself reduced to a degree of isolation which could not be borne and must therefore compel surrender. During the European War, when British tonnage was being lost faster than it was being replaced, Lord Lansdowne pointed out the seriousness of the situation;[3] for the country was becoming increasingly dependent upon neutral tonnage, the supply of which, he remarked, could only be precarious.

The survival of Germany, through four years during which her own shipping could not sail except within the Baltic, illustrates the wide difference which separates the circumstances of a "natural" Sea Power and one whose fighting strength does not derive from an inherent and pressing necessity for reasons of security at sea. Germany's needs were met during those years of seige of the Central Powers and their Allies in two ways. By conquest on land she obtained the use of the products of the territories occupied by her armies—Luxemburg, Belgium, Poland, the in-

[3] In November, 1916.

vaded territory of France, the Ukraine, Rumania: and the territories of herself and her Allies were capable of producing food stuffs and other raw materials. By means of the help of neutral tonnage she was able for this long period to meet her needs of those goods which the Central Powers and conquered territories did not produce, and, but for her having antagonised neutral opinion, she might have continued to do so, provided her credit could have remained. A nation possessing powers of resistance, for so long a period, is not one of whom it can be truly said that the possession of sea power is an essential condition of her security. A "natural" Sea Power which cannot use the sea would be driven to surrender within a few months. Therein lies a true criterion of a nation's necessities for strength[4] at sea: Would the nation be obliged to surrender if its sea communications were interrupted? Is the nation exposed to the danger of having those sea communications interrupted, to an extent sufficient to produce distress on a scale which will create an irresistible demand for peace? Or, short of that, would the nation suffer so severely as to oblige its surrender if its own shipping were unable to sail, and it were to be dependent upon supplies across its frontiers from its neighbours on land, and upon such quantities of goods coming directly by sea to its own ports as could be brought by neutral tonnage? These are very important questions if the many burdens which now oppress the world, caused by economic nationalism and armaments—causes closely re-

---

[4] I use the word "strength" with a full realisation that strength is relative, and that a nation may need sea forces for reasons other than its necessity for security against economic isolation.

lated—are to be reduced. They are, clearly, not the only questions. There are others concerned with the security of lines of military communication which are of high importance, and are particularly difficult of adjustment owing to their being relative to the strength of other nations at sea in the areas concerned.

A considerable shipping is an element in sea power in another respect. It furnishes a reserve of seafaring officers and men. No nation can maintain in peace the force which is needed in a "great" war. The personnel of the British navy in the late war rose from about 146,000 to 407,000; and altogether 640,000 officers and men served at sea during the war.[5] In the War of Secession, the Northern States began with 7640 men. In December, 1864, this number had increased to 51,500 men; and the officers had increased four-fold.

Mahan, in discussing this fact of the problem of sea power,[6] remarked: "The whole question of the value of a reserve, developed or undeveloped, amounts now to this: Have modern conditions of warfare made it probable that, of two nearly equal adversaries, one will be so prostrated in a single campaign that a decisive result will be reached in that time?" Sea warfare, when he wrote those words, had given no answer. Since then it has given a partial, but still no conclusive, answer. In the Russo-Japanese War the adversaries were, in a material sense, approximately equal at sea. No decision was reached in a single campaign. When

---

[5] *Naval Operations*, vol. v, p. 433. The Royal Naval Division is included but not the Mercantile Marine Reserve.

[6] *The Influence of Sea Power upon History*, pp. 48 *et seq.*

the war was brought to an end Russia, though driven back and defeated in Manchuria, was not crushed. If the will of the country had been behind its rulers she would have been under no necessity to make peace. The war had not seriously injured her credit. Japan, victorious both on sea and on land, was however reaching the end of her resources. Her credit had declined more than that of Russia, and for financial reasons peace had become necessary to her.[7] But the decisive stroke which terminates a war rapidly had not taken place.

In the last war there was no decisive stroke for four years. Certainly, if the anticipation of that school of thought which forecasts a sudden decisive blow brought about by the destruction of the people and their cities from the air are correct, there will be no such prolongation of war in the future. But these forecasts cannot be admitted as being more than an hypothesis, and we cannot be blind to the numerous occasions in which equally confident prophecies have failed in the past. There seems no reason to suppose that a rapid decision is more likely to be obtained in a great war in the future than in the past by an overwhelming defeat at sea. The two phases which have characterised many of the great wars of the past may be expected to be reproduced. The first is a phase in which command is in dispute between the main bodies of the navies, the first trial of strength in battle not uncommonly being indecisive.[8] When a superiority on the part of one fleet has been

---

[7] Cf. E. Cramond. Paper read before the Institute of Bankers, April, 1910.

[8] Beachy Head (1690), Malaga (1704), Toulon (1744), Minorca (1756), Ushant (1778), First of June (1794), Round Island (1904), Jutland (1916).

established so markedly that the inferior fleet ceases to dispute command, recourse is had by the inferior navy to an effort made directly against the shipping of its enemy by cruising forces. Large numbers of vessels of the smaller, even down to the smallest types, or small squadrons of the larger, are launched in every possible combination against trade, while a respectable main body continues to exercise a threat which obliges a larger force of the superior navy to be kept in concentration for the purpose of keeping it under control. A great expansion of cruiser and flotilla forces becomes necessary to meet this form of attack. There is indeed a close resemblance between the anticipations of Vauban in 1706 and those of the German Staff in 1917. "If we were to be quit of the vanity of great fleets, which never can suit our needs, and to employ the ships of the navy partly on commerce warfare and partly in squadrons to support it, we should bring about the downfall of the English and the Dutch within about two or three years, in consequence of their great trade in all parts of the world."[9] Such a warfare inflicts great losses, as its protagonists have correctly expected. So it was after the battle of LaHogue (1692), after Trafalgar, and in the last war. The value of a reserve of seamen to the country whose life depends upon its commerce then makes itself felt. The three-fold increase in the personnel of the British navy in the late war was, to a large degree, rendered necessary by the needs for meeting the attack upon trade by submarines and by the cruising forces composed of a few armed auxiliary vessels.

The size of a mercantile marine is an element in sea

[9] De la Roncière, *Histoire de la Marine Française*, vol. VI, p. 406.

power for another reason, particularly to a nation dependent upon the sea, whose shipping, irreplaceable from neutral sources, must continue to ply. Losses are inseparable from war, however great may be the strength of a fighting fleet, and the power of standing punishment, of surviving heavy losses, depends to a very great extent upon the number of merchant vessels: for, the more numerous a merchant fleet, the smaller is the percentage of any given loss. Replacement of losses is made up by new building, but new building implies a great shipbuilding industry which is itself both a cause and a result of a healthy shipping industry and will not exist without it. But there is bound to be a definite lag of production behind loss, through the period of which the shipping must have vitality enough to live. That vitality resides in its numbers, and in the existence of seafaring men who are ready to take the risks of the sea.

Further, a nation which is dependent upon trade is, above all others, constrained to draw its needs from all parts of the world. In the "conclusions" of the Royal Commission's Report on Food Supplies in War (1904), the commissioners remarked: "We look mainly to the strength of the Navy, but we rely in only a less degree on the widespread resources of our mercantile fleet and its power to carry on our trade and reach all possible sources of supply wherever they exist." The truth of this was amply displayed during the war of 1914–18 when the needs of the Allies had to be supplied from every quarter of the world. A bad harvest may render it impossible to draw supplies from one producing country; shortage of shipping may make it necessary to economise tonnage by supplying needs from the nearest sources of production. Experience then illustrated to the full the high degree of organisation which is needed in order to obtain the full services of any given quantity of tonnage,[10] and such organisation, though it may regulate the use of neutral tonnage in very exceptional circumstances, is possible only if there is a great national tonnage capable of being freely used wherever it is needed.

Since the late war the world has been swept by a great wave of "economic nationalism." The merits or demerits of this movement in an economic sense must be left to the economists. Shipping is among the industries which have been affected by this wave, and it has been calculated that, directly and indirectly, a sum of not less than £100 millions has been spent by Governments in subsidies to their merchant fleets since 1918. While it seems plain that a desire to construct "the self-sufficient state" has had its influence in this movement, it may also be that it owes something to the part which a mercantile marine plays as an element in sea power. It is however to be observed that those benefits which have been quoted accrue only to a nation which possesses at the same time a fighting navy of strength sufficient to give such security to the sea routes it uses as will permit its shipping to sail, and territorial possessions so distributed about the routes as to enable that navy to operate wherever her shipping is required to trade. A reserve of ships to replace losses is of no value if the mercantile marine, confined to harbour for want of adequate protection of fighting ships, ceases to sail and hence incurs

[10] Cf. Salter, *Allied Shipping Control.*

no losses to be replaced. A reserve of seamen to give protection to the ships against the sporadic warfare of cruisers
and flotilla craft is similarly of little value where there are
no base positions from which the defending cruisers and
flotilla craft can operate. Thus while these reserves are of
obvious value to the shipping in those waters in which it is
possible for commerce, though threatened, to continue to
ply, they can fulfil no defensive purpose when the other
fundamental elements, fighting strength and bases, are
lacking.

But may they not enable an effective offensive at sea to
be undertaken by a weaker state? If there be a large reserve of seamen may not a weaker Power be able to fit out
commerce-destroying vessels, as privateers and corsairs
were fitted out in the past, which would be of value to the
state, and justify the expenditure incurred in building up,
by uneconomic measures, a mercantile marine?

In what situations does commerce attack by sporadic
action play an effective part in a war? In wars in which the
decision must be made on land, wars, that is to say, in
which the invasion, conquest, subjugation and occupation
of a territory is the aim, commerce attack in this form will
be likely to play but little part. In the wars between France
and Germany (1870–1), the United States and Spain,
Russia and Japan, Italy and Turkey, commerce attack did
not affect the course of operations. Command of the line of
passage of the armies at sea was the object of the naval
operations. The only purpose which, in these wars, an attack by the weaker Power upon the commerce of the
stronger might have served would have been to effect such

66

a diversion of force from the main theatre as to weaken its control there, and therefore to expose its armies, whose line of communications was at sea, to danger on their passages. Some such an aim did indeed enter into the minds of the Russian Staff, who hoped that the powerful cruiser squadron which they stationed at Vladivostok, would make diversionary raids upon the Japanese coasts or coastal trades and oblige the Japanese to weaken their forces in the Sea of Japan: a hope that was disappointed, the Japanese rightly refusing to weaken themselves in the decisive theatre in order to provide security against injuries which, however unpleasant they might be, would not affect the result. But in any case the need, if need there appears to be, for making use of this form of diversionary action, implies the superiority of the opponent: and that superiority in turn implies that the shipping of the weaker power is largely unprotected and cannot sail: and that, in consequence, those seamen who are normally employed in sea trade are without employment and are available for any other form of work at sea. So it was in the old wars between France and England. When French shipping could not sail there was always an ample supply of bold and experienced seamen to man the commerce-destroying vessels. The very fact of a lack of employment in the trading fleet set free the seamen normally employed in it for service in commerce destroying; and these sufficed to cause great injury and to impose a strain upon the resources of the enemy country. But the strain was not enough to produce a decision.

So, too, sporadic attack by means of submarines undoubtedly brought the Allies within measurable distance of defeat during the late war: but it needs to be recollected that that form of war was not undertaken until there was no further hope of reducing the superiority of the Allies' main fleets by attrition. When that hope was abandoned, the men for manning the new submarine construction were available both from the large ships which were no longer intended to seek battle, and from the crews of merchant vessels which could not sail. The successes of the submarines ceased however when the Allies adopted the proper measures they had so long deferred adopting, for various reasons, to defend their shipping.

Thus, while an extensive mercantile fleet is an element in the security of a nation whose existence depends upon the sea—a true "Sea Power"—it is very open to question whether money is usefully spent, in a military as apart from an economic aspect, upon artificially creating a mercantile marine in the belief that it constitutes military strength. Wars between continental Powers affecting the possession of some territory or the enforcement of some policy are almost certainly decided by armies: and if some of those armies cross the sea, the struggle at sea must necessarily lie, not excentrically upon the trade routes but in a concentrated effort to master the main naval forces of their opponents in the area of passage. Wars between "maritime" and "land" Powers will certainly be marked by action against commerce, in one or other of its forms. But as a mercantile fleet, however large, cannot sail in the face of superior force, so a land power desiring to effect a blow at sea by the only means open to it—sporadic action —will always possess in a mercantile marine of natural unstimulated growth a supply of seamen for this offensive. Finally, if military advantage constitutes the reason for state expenditure upon shipping, it would seem proper that the sums so voted should appear in the national budgets as naval expenditure.

One form in which a numerous merchant fleet is sometimes considered to constitute an element in sea power is that the vessels are capable of being turned into fighting ships. Objections have, for example, been made to effecting a reduction in the "Washington" tonnage of 10,000 tons for "cruisers" for the reason that by so doing the value of the merchant navy of a sea-trading nation, as a fighting auxiliary of the fleet, would be greatly increased: and that hence the nation which possessed the most merchant ships —Britain—would profit by the reduction in size of the cruisers.

This supposition is based upon two errors, one technical and the other strategical. The technical error lies in the belief that a merchant vessel is a match for, or a threat to, a man-of-war smaller than 10,000 tons. No such idea ever entered the heads of any sea officers at the time when the "cruiser"—the vessel to whom the duty falls of direct control of shipping on the sea—was a vessel of 5000 tons and even smaller.[11] These vessels were deemed, and rightly deemed, competent to engage any merchant vessel, however she might be armed. A very good judge, Admiral Sir Edward Seymour, who commanded the armed ship *Oregon*

[11] *E.g.* The *Medea* class, 2800 tons, *Latona*, 3400 tons, *Forth*, 4050 tons (British); *Jean Bart*, 4160 tons, *Davout*, 3027 tons (French); *Baltimore*, 4413 tons, *Charleston*, 3730 tons (U. S. A.).

in the mobilization of 1885, expressed the unqualified opinion that no merchant vessel could be a match for a man-of-war. The passage of time has not only added nothing to the relative fighting value of the merchant ship: it has reduced it. It was never imagined that the British cruisers of about 5000 tons were not able to give the law to any merchant vessel. The German commerce-destroying cruisers (Emden, etc.) were all smaller than this, and there it is certain that not one of the armed liners, fitted out with 6-inch and 4.7-inch guns in this country, could have fought the smallest of the German cruisers with any prospects whatever of victory. Since the early seventeenth century the armed merchant vessel has never been a vessel capable of meeting any but the very smallest types of men-of-war: for the man-of-war had by then become specialised for fighting and therefore too powerful for the merchant vessel to fight her. Some merchant vessels, such as the East India ships of France and England and the Register ships of Spain, were armed because they sailed in seas infested by pirates against whom they must furnish their own defence. But fine ships though the largest of these were, they were not a match for the contemporary frigate of the medium size.

The strategical error lies in the fact, to which the introduction of this book drew attention, that those nations which develop sea power in the natural course of their growth (differentiating, let it be repeated, from those whose sea power is the result of a policy imposed for purposes other than defence) are those who need it for the security of their interests at sea. The nations with numerous merchant vessels are those, therefore, which also possess, because they need them, the most numerous fighting forces. The nation which is most powerful at sea does not achieve its aim in sea war by sporadic action against the commerce of an opponent. It endeavours to prevent that commerce from sailing. Its aim is prevention of traffic, not capture, and its success is most complete, not when it has a long tale of captures at sea to show, but when it makes no captures whatever because there is no trade at sea to capture. Trade, as all experience shows, is unable to sail when the fighting forces are unable to give it protection. Further, the Sea Power probably needs all its merchant ships for their proper purpose of the conveyance of cargoes.

While the arming of a merchant ship does not render her able to engage a man-of-war, it gives her strength enough to arrest an unarmed merchant ship and of course to engage one of her own kind, similarly armed. The rôle in which the armed ship finds her principal occupation is that of a commerce destroyer engaged in sporadic operations against trade on the ocean routes. As such she is effective. It is not, however, to the stronger Sea Power that this advantage accrues, but to the weaker, which is driven by its weakness to abandon the struggle for command and to adopt in lieu the lesser form of offensive warfare. A nation, however, which adopts a policy of an artificial increase of its mercantile marine by subsidies and other forms of discrimination, on the score of the military value of the armed vessel and the reinforcement she consequently represents to the fighting navy, cannot with propriety assert that she does so on the score of her needs for defence. Defence and offence are admittedly so inextricably intermingled that it is, in practice, quite impossible to draw a distinct dividing line between them, and one who should attempt to do so will infallibly find himself pleading a special cause which regards what appears to him to be his own advantage. Two things, however, are certain in this matter of the military value of the merchant ship and merchant navy. One is that, as already mentioned, the sea-going man-of-war (as apart from such small vessels as may be used for purely coastal work) of the smallest class is a match for the armed merchant vessel of any size. The other is that if the merchant navy has the military value which is claimed for it by some of the subscribers of a policy of subsidies, those subsidies should in propriety figure as part of the naval estimates.

OVERSEA POSSESSIONS OR BASES

The second element in sea power is that of oversea possessions. That no fighting forces can operate without bases is a truth established by long experience. The modern fleet, however large the ships may be built with a view to increasing their endurance, is no more able to conduct a continuous campaign in waters in which it has no bases than the fleets of galleys and triremes of Greece and Carthage and the two- or three-decked ships of the seventeenth and eighteenth centuries. Reference has been made earlier to Cromwell's recognition of this fact, which induced him to seek a suitable position in the entrance to the Mediterranean—Gibraltar, Oran, Tetuan or Buzema—a sheltered and secure port in which a squadron could be maintained, and afterwards caused Parliament uncompromisingly to reject the many attempts made either by the King or by influential ministers to restore Gibraltar. It was this too which gave an importance to Britain's friendly relations with Portugal, without the use of whose harbour in the Tagus a British fleet could not be maintained in the approaches to the Mediterranean. To-day the assemblage of convoys and their escorts is impossible without friendly harbours in which that assembling can be made. One of the causes indeed which contributed to the delay in the establishment of the convoy system in the war of 1914–18 was the very fact that certain neutral powers could not allow the military processes of assembling and organising convoys to take place within their national harbours. The military operations in the Dardanelles, and later in the Balkans, could not have been conducted without harbours for the fleet, the flotilla and the supply services. Thus the arm of sea power of a nation stretches precisely so far, standing by itself, as its ships can conduct the operations of sea warfare from the harbours under its own control.

A deficiency of bases may, it is true, be supplied if a nation is acting with an ally who possesses adequate ports, suitably situated. But the needs of endurance are then satisfied if it can reach these bases. We are apt to forget how greatly the existence of an almost ubiquitous British Empire contributed to the task of affording security to the sea traffic of all kinds of the Allies. If we should imagine that there had been no friendly harbours in Australia or New Zealand, at the Cape or Halifax, at Dakar and Sierra Leone —to mention a few only—but that these had been the territories of neutral states taking precise and strict views as to their obligations as neutrals; that there had been no establishments outside the home territories of the Allies, where ships could repair or refit beyond limits of time which international law permits; we shall realise that it is no more than the plain truth that oversea possessions—call them colonies or dominions or territories—are an integral element in sea power, if that power is to be the influence in international affairs that the term implies. Bismarck had good reason for his statement to the Danish Ambassador in 1865 that without colonies Prussia could never be a great maritime nation:[12] and the inability of the German Chancellor to give an undertaking that no annexations of the French colonies would be made if Britain in return should remain neutral, may well indicate that this third "leg" of the stool of sea power was intended to be provided by the acquisition of those colonies.[13]

This element of sea power is very far from being a "mere" matter of abstract principles. It has one particularly practical application, which affects the cost of navies to-day. For three reasons the United States has opposed a reduction in the size of the "cruisers" to a figure well below that so unthinkingly adopted at Washington. First, that a reduction in size would render ships of the cruiser type unfit to deal with the armed merchant ship. Second, that the result of this would be that the strength at sea of a nation with a great mercantile marine would be thereby increased, its merchant vessels becoming effective fighting vessels: a supposition which falls to the ground if, as it is, the former assumption is incorrect. Then, there is the

---

[12] Quoted by Lord Morley, *Life of Gladstone*, vol. II, p. 320.
[13] Sir E. Goschen's telegram, July, 1914.

third claim that a nation which has no oversea possessions requires these large ships in consequence of the great distances across which naval action has to take place.

This last assumes two things. First, that vessels smaller than those of 10,000 tons cannot make these long ocean passages: second, that continuous operations can be conducted without bases. For neither of these is there the slightest justification. It never was supposed that the cruisers of the United States navy of the 'eighties and 'nineties were incapable of crossing the seas, though their tonnage was well below this supposedly necessary minimum tonnage of 10,000 tons:[14] nor that when ships were of the smaller dimensions, the United States was ever in any danger at sea. The increase in the size cannot enable the present ships to act effectively in defence of the national interests in Europe unless the United States should either place itself in possession of a European harbour by armed force, which may be rejected as impracticable, or should have an ally whose base she could use; in which case she would not, by hypothesis, need ships of great tonnage provided they could perform the voyage across the Atlantic. But no greater mistake could be made than to imagine that defence could be given to trade in the Mediterranean, the Bay of Biscay and the Northern waters by a fleet of ships, however large its units, unless it had the use of harbours. The matters of assembling convoys, to which reference has been made earlier; of awaiting at sea, exposed to attack by flotilla craft of all types, the convoys while they assemble

---

[14] *E.g. San Francisco*, 4083 tons; *Philadelphia*, 4413 tons; *Olympia*, 5800 tons; *Salem*, 3500 tons.

in harbour; of furnishing escorts, a succession of each of strength sufficient to meet the concentration of force which could be brought against them—all of these render the conduct of the familiar operations of defence of trade utterly impracticable without bases. And what is true of a war with a European Power is also true of war on the western side of the Pacific Ocean.

It is essential to bear in mind that colonies are one of the elements of sea power, once that power is required to be exercised beyond the operating range from the ports of the country, for one very practical reason. One of the burdens which the nations have to bear to-day is that of the costliness of the individual fighting ships. To act upon the erroneous belief that navies can render themselves independent of oversea positions by the mere process of increasing the size of the ships is to add vastly to the cost of all naval armaments in the pursuit of an unattainable object.

THE FIGHTING FORCE

The third element in sea power is the fighting force. This is so obvious a factor that it may well seem that no more than a reference to it is needed. There are, however, some points to which notice needs to be drawn. I use the words "fighting force" of set intention in place of "fleets" or "men-of-war" for reasons which will appear.

The fighting forces are the executants of sea power. The merchant fleets and the oversea possessions are the means which enable the fighting forces to act, furnishing them with the elements of endurance and mobility. I have compared sea power at an earlier stage to a three-legged stool, all three legs of which are interdependent for its completeness as an effective instrument.

I may make another analogy. A boxer requires to be in condition to stand blows, ability to move nimbly and place himself where he desires to be, and hitting power to overcome the resistance of his opponent. The mercantile navy which can stand punishment or furnish reserve strength is the analogue to the boxer's condition. Oversea possessions and bases, which give mobility to the fighting fleet, form the analogue to his ability to move. Finally, the strength needed to overwhelm or dominate the enemy fleet is found in the strength of the boxer's muscles and his skin. And, I might add, behind all, directing all, is the brain, an organ whose training is occasionally overlooked.

What have the fighting forces to do? They have a specific and plain function, which is, in the final analysis, to obtain and exercise the control of the communications at sea. The means by which they attain this final object is by overcoming the resistance of the armed forces of the opponent. These ultimate and immediate objects are attained by the use of instruments capable of fighting armed force and controlling unarmed force, at sea. The instruments of which this fighting force is composed are a part of the navy because they serve this one function. The means by which they are propelled, their shape or their size, the manner in which they move from one place to another, and the weapons with which they are armed, may differ to any extent. However different these may be in their various types, all, since all have one function and object, are units of the naval service.

This fundamental truth has been lost sight of in recent years. Several nations—though not all, some being wiser in this respect than others—have imagined that because a vehicle carrying artillery, or artillery whose projectiles move under the force of gravity instead of under that of some chemical propellant, and moves above the surface of the water, it therefore belongs to a different service from one which moves on the surface of the water. The same erroneous idea affected the French Chamber of Deputies in 1917, when, in consequence of discontent with the result of the operations against submarines, it established a special department of submarine warfare, in the belief that the submarine was so specialised a vessel as to require a separate Ministry. "Public opinion, Parliament uninstructed persons in general, measure problems of military organisation on a purely subjective basis. They have an instinctive tendency to gather under one directing authority everything that relates to a *subject*, to an engine, to a settled order of affairs: they either eliminate or do not perceive the end, the *raison d'être*—in a word the object. . . . It would be somewhat the same if, in war on land, everything which related to action against enemy artillery, or cavalry, or aviation were separately grouped under one direction."[16] This separation of one part of the French navy from the remainder lasted, however, a short time only, for its error was soon perceived. Objectivity, not subjectivity, is the true principle which should inform and govern the constitution of a fighting force. All of those instruments which have the common function of operating at sea with the ob-

[16] Castex, *Synthèse de la guerre sous-marine*, p. 156.

ject of obtaining and exercising control of the sea are instruments of the sea service.

The fighting forces which constitute the "executive" of sea power are of three principal types—that of those composing the massed body, or bodies; that of the major detached services needing considerable endurance; and of the flotilla, a force of small craft, mainly of restricted endurance. The flotilla in turn is composed of three main types: those which navigate on, below and above the surface of the water. Thus torpedo-boats which attack large vessels may be either surface craft, submarine craft, or aircraft. Gunboats which attack these torpedo craft, or bombard land positions, may work on the surface or above the surface—the utility of submerged gun-boats is small. The creation of a separate service in the air, even if it may have some advantages in the realm of administration or supply, has no justification on the grounds of strategy and can only prove disadvantageous in the conduct of operations.

Both the sizes and the numbers of the larger types—the "cruiser" and the "battleship"—are capable of being determined by function.

When two sets of combatants oppose each other, the aim of each is to overcome the other. Hence, the normal and natural procedure is to collect as great a force as possible into one mass and employ it against the similar mass of the opponent. Into this mass all those vessels which are capable of playing an effective part in combat are gathered. Vessels whose armaments do not enable them to stand in the ranks in battle find no place there, and the mass is therefore composed of ships fit to lie in the battle formation and of vessels which, though they cannot "lie in the line," possess weapons of offensive value: such were fire-ships in the past, and torpedo craft to-day. This mass requires a scouting force: and as the services of scouting can be performed by vessels smaller than those needed in the line, so smaller vessels suffice for the scouting services: and provided they in their turn are of such a type as will enable them to gather the information either by overcoming any resistance of opposing scouting forces or by circumventing them, they are large enough for their purposes. These vessels are the "cruisers."

Cruisers are needed also for another service. The communications of the fleet, and the communications of the nation, both economic and military, whose security is the ultimate object of the operations of a navy, need defence. The massed body gives a general protection but cannot give protection in detail, any more than an army in the field, though it may dominate, defeat, or hold in check an opposing army, can prevent detachments from that army from attacking its communications. In addition, therefore, to the general protection, or "distant cover," which a mass provides, it is necessary to give individual protection, or "close cover," to the units moving, either singly or in bodies, on the lines of communication. Sufficient vessels are needed of a type suitable to meet whatever vessels the enemy may elect to detach to attack the communications. Normally, the ships employed to conduct this sporadic attack are comparatively small vessels of respectable endurance: hence the calculation of cruiser strength, apart from that part of it needed for the service of the main body, was always made by the experienced men of the past on the basis of the number of places where such vessels would be wanted. If trade sails in convoys, the number of cruisers must suffice to give defence to all those convoys, in any areas in which it is reasonable to estimate that there is risk of attack. The number, in fact, is not relative to the number of cruisers of an opponent, but to the number of places in which cruisers are needed. Each nation has its own absolute needs in this matter. Each requires enough cruisers to furnish the means of defence of a scattered trade in those areas in which it is possible to give defence—it would have been idle, for instance, to calculate the number of cruisers needed by Britain before the late war on a basis which included the defence of trade in the Baltic, an area in which Britain had no bases and where the enemy must possess such a superiority that trade defence would be impossible. It is therefore to the interests of every country which possesses sea-borne trade that the cruiser's size should be kept down to the smallest limit compatible with the functions she has to perform.[16]

Finally there is the "mass." There are two elements in the mass—the total strength and the size of the individual unit. If the nations of the world are to solve the problems of sea power with satisfaction both to their security and to their revenues they cannot too closely investigate the fundamental problems of qualitative and quantitative size. I shall not attempt to go into these in detail at this point, but shall confine myself to an indication of their nature.

[16] I have discussed at some length the factors affecting the size of a cruiser in my *Economy and Naval Security*.

Taking first the individual unit of which the mass is composed, the so-called "battleship" or "capital ship." What is her function in the use of sea power? Her function is to act as a unit of a body of vessels of different types called a "fleet," which vessels possess the attribute of fitness to take an active part in the fighting. In the past the fighting units were the ships of the line and the fireships: their auxiliaries, for scouting, for repeating signals, for carrying messages and for giving aid—such as towing wounded ships into safety or intercepting fireships—were frigates. To-day, the fleet consists of ships of the line capable of engaging the ships of the line of the opponent and torpedo craft of various types—surface, submarine and aircraft: their auxiliaries which obtain information, repeat signals, intercept torpedo attacks are cruisers.

The "capital ship" is merely the most powerful ship. To speak of the "abolition of the capital ship" is to lose sight of the fact that however small the ships of a navy may be there must always be some that are the largest: these largest are the "capital," principal, or most important ships. If we should imagine a war between two Powers each of which possessed no vessels larger than what we call destroyers, these destroyers would be the "capital" ships. Thus, the "capital" ships of the navies of Chile and Peru, referred to earlier, were those armoured battleships of 3500 and 2000 tons.

The main fighting body of fleets, from the earliest times of which we have any knowledge, has been composed of vessels whose size has been determined by various considerations. This "infantry of the sea" must be fit to meet the opposing infantry. Size, therefore, depended partly upon the contemporary skill in shipbuilding and the material available, which determined the maximum possible limit of construction, and partly upon strategical policy. The nation which found itself unable to compete in numbers tended to counteract its lack in numbers by larger ships.[17] But this policy was not pursued under any belief that naval warfare was not possible unless ships were of that size, but because it was believed that in the competition of armaments the particular nation's necessities could best be met, within the limits imposed by the purse, by a smaller number of ships larger than those of the possible opponent. The British view in the eighteenth century was that the service of the country would be most effectively performed by ships of medium size. Both France and Spain took the view that they obtained a better value for their expenditure from larger ships. The large ship had relative advantages which were perfectly recognised, but these advantages disappeared when both nations were provided with ships of the same size. A French writer of 1772 observed that "the service done by these enormous ships is by no means proportioned to the great expense which they occasion. . . . The English themselves say they have them only because France chooses to have them: and that they will lay them aside as soon as she thinks proper to set the example."

Of recent years a belief has arisen that there is an intrinsic necessity for "battleships" to be of a great size. Opinions differ as to what this size must be. According to the

[17] *Vide* the Italian policy, p. 109.

views of American authorities, 35,000 tons is needed, while the Japanese appear to consider it impossible for a ship to be of less than 28,000 tons. The British authorities think a ship may be of 22,000 tons but cannot be smaller. There is truly a great diversity of opinion, a diversity so great that one can but conclude that the various bodies who have come to these conclusions cannot have been engaged in solving one and the same problem. Their answers must surely be answers to different questions, their terms of reference cannot have been the same. For it would seem impossible that even "experts," set the same questions to answer, could arrive at conclusions differing to the extent of sixty per cent.

The naval estimates of the Great Powers have risen phenomenally in the last forty years. Many causes have contributed to this increase, some historical, some economic, some purely material: but presumably every nation which has made its own individual contribution to the increase in this third element of sea power, fighting strength at sea, would give one reason why it has pursued the courses of political and material policy that it has pursued: that it has been necessary for its security. The idea which has compelled each nation to provide fighting strength in the quantity and of the types that have come into being in these years has been that, without so many ships of such sizes, they would have been insecure. If the policy was sound, all the nations to-day would be at least as secure as they were when ships were smaller: though one might hope that an increase of from three-fold to some vastly higher proportions might be expected to render some proportionate increase in security. Which nations are more secure than they were forty years ago? What dangers to which they were then exposed have been removed by this extra expenditure? It is sometimes said that these great sizes are rendered necessary by the development of new weapons— the bomb, the torpedo and the mine. But it is to be observed that the ships had already reached very great sizes before any of these new weapons had become so developed as to give rise to anxiety for the great ships: and that the increases in the ships from 10,000 tons or thereabouts, which was deemed adequate by the authorities of all nations for all purposes of speed, endurance, offence and defence in the later part of the nineteenth century, had taken place purely as a result of the competition between guns and armour. No nation was made more secure in consequence of the introduction of ships of great tonnage, but all paid vastly more for their sea power.

CHAPTER III

THE LIMITATIONS OF SEA POWER

SEA power, by the nature of its action, necessarily interrupts the economic and commercial intercourse not only of nations engaged in war but also of others who have no part in the dispute or the struggle. Hence it was recognised, even in the earliest times, that it was necessary to establish some principles which should govern action in regard to commerce in war: principles which should receive a general assent and could do so only by harmonising the consequential conflicting interests of the belligerent and the neutral.

The interest of the belligerent must be to deny, to the very utmost possible, the use of the sea to the opponent. The interest of the neutral must be to contrive to conduct the normal[1] trade he has been in the habit of conducting with both belligerents, and, human nature being what it is, to take advantage of the abnormal situation which war brings into existence to extend his own commerce of all kinds. War affords the neutral manufacturer of goods, the producer of food and raw and war materials, the trader and the shipper, a great opportunity to do an increased business. Hence a state possessing sea power almost of necessity finds itself in conflict with the private interests of neutral states, and the Governments of those states tend

[1] I stress the word "normal."

to place such interpretations upon the Law of Nations as will further the interests of their citizens.

In the long series of wars from which Mahan illustrated the influence which sea power had exercised in the world, international law, or "the Law of Nations," was in process of being moulded. "The influence of sea power on history and on law is strikingly emphasised during this period [1648–1765]. . . . In sea warfare especially rules of international law which were to receive more definite shape in later days, were being formed, and in the process the influence of British policy and British prize courts was very powerful. Though some British practices called forth strong neutral protests the foundations were being laid of those rules regarding enemy property and neutral rights which were developed and applied by great judges during the wars of the Napoleonic era."[2]

The right of blockade, of declaring contraband those materials and goods deemed to assist the enemy in his resistance, and of seizing enemy goods in transit, were the three pillars constituting "Maritime Rights." It was by means of these rights that a maritime Power exercised its pressure upon an opponent. These rights were, on many occasions, contested by other states, but not always with consistency: for the interest of a nation swayed towards favour or disfavour of a practice according to whether it was powerful or weak at sea, in alliance with or in opposition to a maritime Power, a belligerent or a neutral. Again, colonial trade, closed in peace to foreign powers, would be

[2] Dr. A. Pearce Higgins, *The Cambridge History of the British Empire*, vol. I, chap. XIX, pp. 530 *et seq.*

opened to those powers, as neutrals, in war; a practice giving rise to the enunciation of such appropriate doctrines as the "Rule of War of 1756" and "continuous voyage;" doctrines so solidly based upon the objective principle that they became the basis of sea policy of the two greatest maritime struggles of the nineteenth and twentieth centuries—the American War of Secession of 1861 and the War of 1914.

Among the rights to which British ministers attached an importance was that of capturing the goods of an enemy. The doctrine enunciated was that the property of an enemy might legitimately be taken in war but that of a friend must be respected, provided he observed his neutrality. Hence, the goods of an enemy on board the ship of a friend might be taken; the goods of a friend on board the ship of an enemy might not be taken. These doctrines were not favourably received by other Powers, who, generally speaking, took exception to a practice which might be used against themselves by the Power which commanded the sea. The effects of the war against commerce in the later stages of the Napoleonic War, when conducted by Decrees and Orders-in-Council, had been felt by all nations; and at the end of that war even those who owed their ultimate freedom to the efforts of Britain wished to prevent a repetition of the experience of the effects of economic measures from which, in other conditions, they might be sufferers. The counter policy advocated was that of "free ships, free goods," put forward originally by the Northern Powers in 1780. It was then a new doctrine. Benjamin Franklin wrote of it: "All the neutral States of Europe seem at present disposed *to change what had before been deemed the law of nations*, to wit, that an enemy's property may be taken wherever found, and to establish the rule that free ships make free goods."[3] It was then rigidly opposed by Great Britain, in spite of a practically unanimous support on the Continent, though it must be said there had been marked inconsistency in its observance according to whether a Power was or was not an ally of Britain and derived advantage from her support.

The differences in practice remained until the Congress of Paris which sat to negotiate the Peace at the end of the Russian War of 1854-5. The French plenipotentiary then proposed the abolition of privateering, which, by mutual consent, had not been employed by Britain or France during that war; the immunity of enemy goods under the neutral flag; the immunity of neutral goods, except contraband, under the enemy flag; and the rule that a blockade, to be binding, should be effective. Lord Clarendon, who on the part of England negotiated the Declaration, while recognising that the immunity of enemy goods weakened British sea power in its offensive functions, justified in public his action on the score that this loss would be amply set off by the security resulting from the abolition of privateering, particularly by the United States: but it would appear that he had another reason of at least equal and possibly greater weight. He believed that Britain would never again be able to exercise the ancient rights. Writing to Palmerston in 1856 he observed: "It is quite clear that

[3] Miss V. M. Creighton in "The Pre-war Theory of Neutrality," *British Year Book of International Law*, 1928.

we can never again re-establish our ancient doctrine re-
specting neutrals and that we must in any future war ad-
here to the exception to a rule which we admitted at the
beginning of the present war,[4] under pain of having all man-
kind against us. I am, therefore, for making a merit of
necessity and volunteering, as a benevolent act of the Congress, to proclaim as permanent the principle upon which
we have lately acted, adding to it a Resolution against privateering. . . . [The United States] sent a circular to all
Maritime Powers asking their assent to the neutral flag
covering the goods. Most of these Powers consulted us as
to the answer they should give, and we suggested that they
should not agree unless the United States at the same time
gave up the system of privateers."[5]

The United States, however, refused to abandon privateering. They put forward a counter proposal to abolish all
capture at sea, including contraband: and the suggestion
was even made to abolish also commercial blockade: proposals which, if they had been adopted, would seriously
have affected the Federal States in the War of the Secession. These proposals could not be accepted by a Sea
Power whose influence was measured by her ability to
exercise pressure at sea.

The Declaration of Paris, in its final form, established
the four rules referred to earlier. It was then widely felt
that British sea power had been disarmed. Lord Salisbury,
speaking in 1871, observed that before the Declaration the

---

[4] The war with Russia, 1854–5.
[5] Clarendon to Palmerston, April 6th, 1856. Quoted by Sir William Malkin
in the *British Year Book of International Law*, 1927, p. 26.

British fleet had been "a powerful instrument in hampering and ultimately in subduing Napoleon;" for we had the power to declare a general blockade and to search neutral ships for enemy goods. "In your reckless Utopianism," he continued, "you have flung these two weapons away, and your fleet can only blockade the particular port to which it is sent or bombard any fortress which may happen to be on the coast. I believe that since the Declaration of Paris the fleet, valuable as it is for preventing an invasion of these shores, is almost valueless for any other purpose."[6]

Lord Salisbury's statement indicates the feelings which Lord Clarendon's act provoked in the country. Later events were to show that in spite of the blunting of the weapon caused by the "free ships free goods" doctrine—a blunting which cannot be questioned—sea power and diplomacy still possessed resources, as yet untapped, in the use of the Law of Contraband. As to blockade, the comparison made with the past was not strictly correct. There is a very clear distinction to be observed between "the declaration of a general blockade" and that retaliatory act of the Orders-in-Council which declared all ports from which British trade was excluded by the Berlin Decree to be "subject to the same restrictions as if they were actually blockaded in the most strict and rigorous manner." In the blockade declared on May 16th, 1806, only that part of the coast of Europe between the Elbe and Brest was announced to be under blockade, but even in that part the act of blockade was only rigorously applied to that limited portion of the coast between the Elbe and the Seine. When the first

[6] *Hansard*, March 6th, 1871, p. 1364.

Orders-in-Council were repealed in April, 1809, and a new set substituted, a blockade of limited extent including the coasts of France, Holland, part of Germany and the north of Italy was ordered. This was followed, however, by more Orders-in-Council which admitted of so many exceptions that breach of blockade became common, and, according to Brougham, while Britain protested the necessity of isolating France in order to force her into compliance with the Law of Nations, she encouraged a clandestine traffic of her own and allowed "all neutrals who will submit to certain indignities and to conditions favourable to ourselves, as ample a trade with blockaded France as they ever before enjoyed."[7]

How far, then, it is proper to ask, was sea power hampered in the War of 1914–18 by the clause in the Declaration of Paris that blockades to be binding must be effective?—the meaning of which is that a force, strong enough to enforce obedience, and sufficiently distributed to make it risky to attempt to break through it, must command the approaches to the port or stretch of coast declared to be under blockade. Plainly no such declaration would have been of any value in the Baltic. Shipping from Norway, Sweden and Denmark could have snapped its fingers at any such a declaration. The important supplies of iron ore from the northern Swedish iron fields would not have been stopped nor the food supplies from Denmark. Outside the Baltic, would a declaration similar to that of the Orders-in-Council that the ports from the Elbe to the Ems were "subject to the same restrictions as if they were actually block-

[7] *Edinburgh Review*, February, 1812, p. 290.

aded" have made any sensible difference to the course of the war? Dutch vessels could have passed by inshore routes, in their own territorial waters, as they did; while the mine fields, laid with the purely military object of hampering the submarines, constituted a barrier to mercantile shipping more effective even than the blockading squadron of the Federals did to the shipping attempting to enter and leave the ports of the Confederacy of 1861–65.

But if sea power was less affected by the Declaration of Paris than many believed that it would be, it was not for the reasons given by Lord Clarendon. He supposed that British acceptance of the "free ships free goods" doctrine would so satisfy American opinion as to obtain from them the concession of the abolition of privateering. It did not do so, as we have seen. But even if it had done so, it could not have removed the particular danger which lay in privateering—a widespread attack by comparatively weak vessels upon commerce. Privateering is merely a method of attacking commerce by private men-of-war. The abolition of that method does not abolish the attack itself: for a state at war can without difficulty, as states have done on many occasions, convert the private ship into a man-of-war by the simple method of purchase and by giving commissions to her officers. The commerce "raiders" of the later stage of the recent war—*Möwe, Wolf, Seeadler, Leopard, Greif*— and some of the earlier ones—*Kaiser Wilhelm der Grosse, Prinz Adalbert, Cap Trafalgar* and others—were such vessels. Armed merchant vessels, when employed in commerce attack, are merely privateer writ large, though the excesses of which privateers were often guilty are obviated. Nor did the abolition of privateering remove the particular danger of a widespread attack on commerce in vessels of another form—the submarines.

There was more substance in Lord Clarendon's other reason for accepting a change in British doctrine—that if Britain should attempt to put her old practices in force she would have the whole world against her. Whether that estimate of what would have occurred is correct can only be a matter of judgment based on such experience as the war of 1914–18 affords concerning the effects of restrictions imposed upon neutrals. Restrictions, in every sense as severe as the capture of enemy goods in neutral ships, were eventually and necessarily imposed upon the commerce of neutrals. Modern instruments of war and their munitions require for their production a range of raw material hitherto unthought of, and this rendered it necessary greatly to extend the lists of contraband. Many neutral Powers—certainly not without protest—accepted the restrictions thereby imposed upon profitable branches of their trade; which were not less burdensome than those resulting from the old British doctrine of enemy goods being liable to seizure in neutral vessels: while the rationing of neutral states, begun in the later part of 1915 by means of agreements with private bodies in Switzerland, Denmark and Holland, but only fully adopted after the entry of the United States, was a measure more far-reaching than any adopted by British Governments in the past. It is permissible, therefore, to doubt whether Lord Clarendon did not overestimate the dangers of neutral opposition. It might arise. It had arisen before, when "Armed Neutralities"—a singular confusion of terms—had been created, whose object it was to compel one belligerent—and one only—to desist from interrupting the supply of warlike material by neutrals: in other words, a deliberate overriding of the Law of Contraband which civilised states had, in all ages, admitted. Britain had then adjusted her policy temporarily to the practical conditions of the situation.

But neutrals had accepted grave inconveniences created by the Orders-in-Council of the Napoleonic Wars. There is probably no single answer to the question of why many Powers did not combine, on that occasion, to resist the British action, but it seems permissible to consider that one reason was that the neutral nations adversely affected had less sympathy with the ultimate aims of Napoleon than with those of Britain. No one will pretend that sympathy plays a marked part when the interests of a people are concerned. The statesman has the responsibility for doing that which, in his view, is ultimately most to the advantage of the people whom he represents. Nevertheless, it is hardly possible to doubt that where there is a general spirit of sympathy with the aims of one belligerent, a belief that its cause has a greater measure of justice or of eventual advantage to themselves than that of its opponent, that sentiment possesses some weight. In the American Civil War, whatever may have been the sympathies of some sections of the British community and of a few statesmen with the South, the fact that the North was fighting the cause of abolition, especially after Lincoln's Emancipation Proclamation of September, 1862, meant that there was a popular feeling in favour of the North strong enough to make people accept the suffering which was caused by a blockade whose effectiveness, though it could be justified, could also be questioned. In the Napoleonic Wars the nations of the Continent, under the heel of Napoleon, resented the action at sea less than the grinding of that heel.[8]

Finally, it is important to recognise that sea power possesses the strength which it demonstrated in the Napoleonic Wars and the recent war only when it is allied to land power. Single-handed sea power can do little against any great Power. It was not a national economic blockade, or any such a simulacrum of blockade as the Orders-in-Council or the measures developed during the last war for depriving the enemy of the economic benefits of sea communication, that British ministers used in those disputes which arose between Britain and individual enemies. Those disputes most commonly arose concerning some oversea interest, either terrestrial or economic. In such circumstances, a Sea Power makes use of the command, which its superiority at sea confers, to send superior military force to the oversea theatre concerned. So, when a quarrel arose with Spain in 1739 concerning the treatment of merchantmen in the Spanish-American colonial waters, an expedition was sent there: when differences arose between France and England concerning the limits of their respective colonies in America, an army was sent to Canada: when the Government in Westminster provoked opposition in the northern colonies, an army was sent to the

[8] Cf. Memoirs of the Duc de Vicence for Napoleon's view that the European Powers should be prepared to suffer some privations for the general good of Europe which would result from Napoleonic victory.

colonies. When, finally, Britain found herself, single-handed, facing Napoleon in 1803, she could not eject Napoleon from the territories, Holland and Switzerland, whose occupation was the prime cause of the breach of the Peace of Amiens; but she did not attempt the plainly impossible task of reducing France by blockade. She was fully engaged in her own defence, and such offensive action as could be undertaken was in the form of small operations in the distant seas, and no questions of extreme Maritime Rights arose.

Nor is this form of action peculiar to Britain. It is that taken by every power which finds itself superior at sea. When the United States wished to replace the Spanish rule in Cuba, an army was sent to that island. When Japan wished to prevent a Russian occupation of Korea, she sent an army to eject the Russians. And when Italy desired to acquire Libya, she similarly did not use her superiority at sea to blockade Turkey into submission, but sent an army to take possession of the African territory.

When, on the other hand, the Maritime Power has been allied in a common cause with land powers, as Britain was in all but one of the great wars of the eighteenth century, and in the War of 1914, economic pressure becomes a far more powerful instrument. The financial needs and demands of the nations increase vastly. Trade with those countries which are enemy either diminishes or ceases, the necessity for oversea trade increases to fill the gap; and, in modern war, the needs for all kinds of materials, products of countries overseas only, become very great. The measures taken by the Sea Power are necessarily favourably viewed by her allies, who in general have shown themselves more inclined to press the Sea Power to take harder action than to oppose its use in its strongest form. Thus it is not the "whole world" of Lord Clarendon's phrase that in such circumstances is brought into opposition to her action, but such nations only as have remained neutral. While the requirements of strict neutrality or of the interests of their citizens will properly oblige them to question and resist action that is not justified by their reading of international law, human nature does not confine its attention entirely to the questions of profit and loss, weighty as those elements are in the scales of decision. Sympathy may mitigate the asperities of the formal diplomatic attitude. Thus one may distinguish a difference in the tone of some of the notes issued simultaneously to Britain and to Germany concerning their respective alleged breaches of international law in the recent war, a difference which it may be not wholly wrong to attribute in some part to a general belief that there was a greater measure of justice in the cause of the Allies than in that of their opponents.

In brief, the fundamental fact which it would seem Lord Clarendon left out of consideration is that Maritime Powers only require to use those measures which constitute "Maritime Rights" in their fullness when the principal object of their national strategy is to reduce, or help to reduce, an enemy by economic pressure: and that they only employ that measure, and can only employ that measure, when they are acting in a common cause with military allies. The possession of a power does not, as our own experience has shown on more than one occasion, mean that it will always be used, for the conditions of a struggle may not necessitate its use. But a right abrogated cannot easily be re-assumed.

After the Declaration of Paris had been concluded, the subject of the immunity of private property at sea was again brought forward. The continental Powers and the United States favoured this new doctrine, but, though there was a strong body in support of it in England, the proposal was rejected. The arguments in favour of abolition partook of two characters—the moral and the advantageous. On moral grounds it was urged *inter alia* that war takes place between Governments and not between private citizens: that private property in war on land was immune from injury and should so be at sea. It was therefore morally wrong that private property at sea should be touched. On the grounds of advantage, it was urged that the increased and ever-increasing dependency of England upon foreign supplies and upon her own export trade made it highly advantageous to her that her shipping should not be interrupted in war; that its defence, under modern conditions, was far more difficult than it had been in the past. The depredations of the *Alabama, Tallahassee* and other commerce destroyers of the American Civil War made a deep impression upon many minds, and the proposal received further impulse from that school of political thought which considered that Britain should cut herself free from all continental affairs and stand neutral in any continental quarrels. Sea power, in such a situation, could have no great international significance, except in the restricted and secondary sense of defence. If it were possible for the country to be indifferent and oblivious to all that happened in Europe, to the rise and fall of other nations, to the occupation of such territories or strategical positions as the Low Countries, the Straits of Gibraltar and the Dardanelles, or the Suez Canal, it would follow that she had no need to maintain the power to employ measures the value of which is only fully experienced when she ranges herself with other Powers in defence of some common cause. Thus, the merits of the proposal, in its political aspect, depended upon whether the assumption that Britain could isolate herself from continental disputes was correct. From that assumption it followed that the interests of Britain were primarily those of a neutral; and that therefore any doctrines which strengthened the power of sea forces to interrupt neutral trade were disadvantageous to her. The "good European" was as absent from this view as the lessons of past statesmanship.

In the strategical sense, while the call and the claims of defence bulked large, the fact that wars can very rarely be conducted to a successful end by wearing out an enemy by an impregnable defence received only little attention. To some extent, though not wholly, this followed from the supposition that detachment from European affairs was a practicable policy. It followed also from the fact that, in a "single-handed" war, the capture of what is called "private property" at sea, considered as a means of exerting pressure, would never prove decisive against a continental Power. It could wound but could not kill such states: but it could be decisive against Britain herself. In this, an important consideration was left out of account—the deterent action of capture. Mr. Oppenheim[9] had the sanction of historical experience in this respect when he remarked: "The argument that it is unjust that private citizens should suffer through having their property seized has no weight in face of the probability that fear of annihilation of its merchant fleet in case of war may well deter a state intending to go to war from doing so." The fact that states have been deterred, in some cases wholly and in others partly, by this consideration is not lightly to be put aside. It is unfortunately true that it did not deter the Central Powers in 1914, but the expectations of a rapid victory overshadowed the comparatively small injury which the temporary retirement from the sea of the merchant fleet would cause: and, for a longer war, it was confidently anticipated, and not without cause, that the restrictions imposed by the Declaration of London upon the use of sea power in respect of blockade and of a rigidly modified contraband list, through the working of which all the supplies needed in war could be obtained through neutral harbours, would render sea power an innocuous instrument.

The proposal to immunise "private property" embodied a further strategical misconception. It failed to take cognisance of the unity of all the different forms of action against sea communications in war. Blockade, the stoppage of contraband supplies, the arrest of shipping carrying enemy goods are parts of a common strategical whole whose object is isolation of the enemy. The ultimate object of the action requires to be kept in view, and that is to "disarm" the opponent, to reduce his powers of fighting

[9] *International Law*, vol. ii, p. 253 (3rd edn. 1921).

and his will to do so. Every hole that successive Conferences have broken through the wall which sea power has been able to build against a state has contributed to prolong war and to increase human suffering.

Nor is it to be forgotten that, however advantageous to Britain it may appear to some of those who urge the abolition of capture of "private property" while retaining the unquestioned rights of blockade and the arrest of contraband, this can hardly be accepted by other nations as a valid reason. One essentially naïve reason put forward on one occasion for immunising the shipping on the outer seas was that thereby it would not be necessary to scatter fighting ships about the world; and hence it would be possible to effect a greater concentration of British strength in the decisive area in Home Waters. As one of the great objects of the opponents of Britain was to prevent such a concentration, which would render invasion of Britain impossible, strengthen the British power of blockade, and increase the rigour of the control of contraband, it was not a suggestion likely to appeal to a possible opponent, to whom commerce attack is predominantly a weapon of strategical use for the diversion of stronger forces.

To return to the proposal. British ministers, and public feeling generally, opposed it. "It cannot be denied," says Mr. Oppenheim, "that the constant agitation since the middle of the eighteenth century, for the abolition of the rule that private enemy vessels may be captured, might, during the second half of the nineteenth century, have met with success but for the decided opposition of Great Britain." With great justice the same learned writer adds, however, that it was not Britain's attitude alone which eventually stood in the way of abolition. "After the growth of navies among Continental Powers, these Powers learned to appreciate the value of the rule in war, and the outcry against the capture of merchantmen became less loud." At the second Hague Conference France, Russia, Japan and Spain, together with some minor Powers, voted against the abolition: and though much of the movement in its favour finds its origin in the United States, it would be highly incorrect to assume, as it so often is assumed, by protagonists of this solution of the problem of security, that the views of a nation possessing one of the most considerable navies in the world remain the same as they were when it possessed little or no navy. As Admiral W. L. Rodgers U. S. N. has written: "The duty, the function of our Navy, is to deny the enemy the use of the sea both for military and civil traffic, and to keep it open for our own use for the supply of our armies as well as for that of the general public. . . . Commerce warfare has always been the final objective of naval efforts, and will still be so."[10] The views of Admiral Mahan, expressed even before his country had become a great Sea Power, were no less clearly opposed, on the broadest of strategical grounds as well as those of humanity, to the abolition.

The assumption, therefore, that Great Britain is the sole opponent of the rule and that she has only to propose the abolition for it to be welcomed by and accepted by all the Great Powers, is one that finds little support in stubborn realities.

[10] *American Year Book*, 1930, p. 286.

The Russo-Japanese War brought the matter to the front. British traders and merchants complained of acts done to their trade by the belligerents and of the uncertainty of the laws of capture. The second Hague Conference (1907) proposed the formation of an International Prize Court, but as some code of law to be administered would be needed if such a Court were to act, a Conference was called, which sat in London in 1909, which drew up the Declaration of London.

One event of outstanding importance had taken place since the Declaration of Paris had imposed the limitations of "free ships free goods" upon the action of sea power. The American Civil War had shown the far-reaching effects of economic pressure in war. The Northern blockade of the Southern coasts had been a decisive element in that struggle. So far from any restrictions upon sea power arising out of that war, a very considerable extension of some of the existing rules had been found necessary if sea power was to effect its purpose. It is not necessary to go into the details of the extensions of existing measures which the Northern Government found to be essential in order to achieve their end. "American courts," as Mr. Bryan observed in 1915, "have established various rules bearing on those matters (*e.g.* continuous voyage, etc.). The rule of continuous voyage has not only been asserted by American tribunals but extended by them."

The Declaration of London (1909) was an attempt to clear up many vexed questions. The British Government of the day viewed the problem of the treatment of commerce in war with the eye of a neutral rather than that of a belligerent, and, as a belligerent, with an eye to defence rather than to offence. Maintaining the right of capture at sea, it proposed to abolish the contraband doctrine, or, if it should not prove possible to obtain agreement for this drastic step, to limit contraband to articles strictly and specifically of a warlike nature. The proposal to abolish contraband was rejected by the other Powers, but lists were prepared of articles which might be declared absolute contraband: lists which the subsequent experience of war proved to be wholly inadequate in the conditions of modern war. In matters connected with blockade and continuous voyage the framers of the Declaration did not draw their conclusions from the experience of the great Napoleonic Wars or that of the Northerners in their stoppage of the contraband traffic and the breaches of blockade in the Civil War, but from more recent wars in which the aim of the superior Sea Powers was in no case of an economic character, but was concerned, almost entirely, with the command of lines of military passage. The result was that false conclusions were drawn, and the Declaration rendered it possible for supplies to pass to the enemy through neutral countries without hindrance. That this contributed to the length of the war, to an increase of loss of life during the war, and to the subsequent ruin of Europe and the present situation of the world, is hardly open to question. Eventually, when America entered the war, sea power was able to exert its pressure; but this was not until the conquests of the Central Powers had placed the supplies of the occupied territories in their hands and enabled them to continue to hold out against the effects of their isolation from the markets of the world.

CHAPTER IV

THE CHANGES IN SEA POWER

THE object which sea power has to fulfil does not change, but very great and very costly changes have taken place in the instruments with which sea power is exercised since the introduction of the ironclad ship.

THE BATTLESHIP

For some time after the French had produced their armoured batteries at Kinburn in the Russian War of 1854–5 the naval authorities, particularly in Britain and France, were engaged in thinking and experimenting on the problem of the design of the ironclad ship. The American Civil War of 1861–5 introduced fresh problems of design, and for sixteen years following that war the British naval estimates were almost stationary at figures between nine and eleven million pounds: in fact, in 1881 they were a few thousand pounds less than in 1867.[1] France, whose shipbuilding was suspended during the War of 1870–1, resumed construction a few years later, and, during the period of 1883 to 1887, while the British estimates continued to stand at from nine to eleven millions, those of France stood, with little variation, at about seven millions.

The year 1886 is one of particular interest. It was at this time that a considerable anxiety as to British strength at

[1] In 1867, £10,976,253: in 1881, £10,945,919. *Brassey's Naval Annual*, pp. 419 *et seq.*

sea was being felt. The country had passed through a foreign crisis in 1885, when the "Penjdeh incident" brought about strained relations between Russia and Britain. "An extraordinary activity prevails in the Russian Admiralty, which shows itself in the construction not only of armoured vessels, but also of modern cruisers. This is explained by the attitude of England."[2] In France, at the same time, naval thought was greatly perturbed by the potentialities of the torpedo in the future. "After the competition of the gun and the armour plate we shall have that between the torpedo-boat and the armour clad—a struggle which will bring about a new and costly change in naval warfare." So the French Commission on the Naval Estimates of 1886 prophesied: and although the view that the torpedo flotilla would cause the disappearance of the ironclad proved incorrect, later years have substantiated the forecast that a "new and costly change" would take place in naval warfare. This 80-ton torpedo-boat might cost something like £15,000. To deal with her the "destroyer," a larger and a more expensive vessel of about 220 tons, was introduced. This 220-ton vessel, costing some £30,000, has since grown into one of 1500–1800 tons, and even larger, costing some ten times as much as the original craft. And, when the invention of the submarine brought into being a formidable and costly type of torpedo-boat, this in turn—as the war was to prove—made it necessary vastly to increase the number of flotillas. Since the war, the torpedo-boat has taken wings. Whether experience will be repeated and a winged destroyer will be evolved remains to be seen, but

[2] *Brassey's Naval Annual*, 1886, p. 502.

one of the combined effects of the flotilla of surface, submarine and flying torpedo-boats is to cause an insistence upon the need for great size in the capital ships in order to sustain the injuries which the torpedo and the bomb can inflict.

While increase in numbers was mainly responsible for this general increase in all the navies, increase in size played its part. There was no small amount of doubt concerning the wisdom of increasing the tonnage of the "ironclad" ship, as the vessel now known as a "battleship" was generally called during the 'eighties and early 'nineties of the last century. Until the ships of the Naval Defence Act (1889) were designed, it had been generally accepted that a "battleship" should not exceed 10,000 tons. Lord Northbrook's administration in 1881 had expressed the intention of not exceeding this displacement, and the aggregate tonnage of thirty-two first-class British battleships in 1891 was 354,950 tons: which, as it included eight ships of 14,000 tons, represented an average tonnage of about 10,000 tons. The fourteen battleships of France aggregated 151,682 tons, and six of Russia 57,617 tons. In the same year the proposed new battleships for the United States navy were designed to be of 10,000 tons, in which a great coal endurance was to be provided.

To this general acceptance of the sufficiency of 10,000 tons for the battleship there was one exception, Italy. She had adopted a policy of building larger ships, vessels of over 13,000 tons. This, however, was not for any intrinsic reason of want of gun power, speed, endurance, or power of taking punishment in ships of a smaller size, but for purely relative reasons. The Italian administration was not able to afford to build as many ships as Italy's principal rival, France: but they considered they could achieve their desired purposes by building a fleet composed of larger, faster and more powerful ships than that of France but in fewer numbers.

In both France and England there was a strong resistance to the new policy of increase of size. Admiral Vallon, of the French navy, remarked at this time: "On admet généralement aujourd'hui, en Angleterre comme en France, que le cuirassé le plus fort ne doit pas dépasser 12,000 tonnes et le croiseur protégé 8000 tonnes. *Ce sont là des limites extrêmes que beaucoup de marins voient avec regret.*" In England, Captain Eardley-Wilmot, criticising the tendency to increase size, remarked that "if we should raise the displacement to 20,000 tons we might increase protection by armour" but that we did not do it because the hull would still not resist the ram or the underwater explosions of gun-cotton. "There is no reason," he remarked, "why a good supply of coal, high speed and a powerful armament should not be obtained with a displacement of 10,000 tons." It was in fact generally recognised that it was useless to strive to produce an impregnable ship. Captain Fitzgerald, pointed out that "there is no absolute safety possible, nor anything approaching it, in any design of warship." Fighting at sea, both he and Admiral Bourgeois of the French navy agreed, was largely a question of chances. The lucky blow might disable the greatest ship that it would be possible to build. Naval opinion in the United States appears to have been in agreement. The

Naval Department at Washington considered in 1891 that "the warship of our day has become far too complicated for the people who may be called upon to work her," and as remarked earlier, recommended a limit of 10,000 tons for the first-class battleship of that date.

Nevertheless, sizes continued to increase. By the year 1894 a definite change in the policy followed by the earlier Boards of Admiralty had established itself. In the competition which was in progress, in which each nation was taking part whether dependent on the sea or not, and the world was moving in what Lord Brassey described as "a vicious circle from which escape appears difficult," the method adopted of maintaining the strength at sea upon which British security rested was to increase dimensions and build ships larger and more powerful than those of other countries—the "bigger and better" policy. Other Powers followed reluctantly. While British ships had risen by 50 per cent. from the 10,000-ton standard to the 14,900-ton *Majestics*, foreign Powers still kept their dimensions at between 10,000 and 12,000 tons. But they could not be left behind indefinitely. The United States, which in 1891 had adopted 10,000 tons as a displacement sufficient for the security of the country, increased in 1895 the size to 11,500 tons.[3] But the importance of mobility, and the fact that mobility depends upon being able to choose freely the harbours a fleet may require to use as bases in war, did not escape attention: the Report of the Secretary of the Navy of 1898 pointed out that it was "essential to the success of defensive naval campaigns that we shall be able to use for

---

[3] *Kearsarge* and *Kentucky*.

our fighting ships those harbours which Nature has provided. Although possessing bases [in the Gulf of Mexico] the fact that there is not depth of water for fighting ships to enter them will render them of but slight benefit to us." Artificial deepening was not the true solution but decreasing the draught of ships of war to enable them to use the harbours. Though the reference was made "defensive naval campaigns," it is plain that the policy outlined of fitting the ship to use the harbour is equally true of a campaign of an offensive character—if indeed, it be possible to make that distinction between one campaign and another.

Thus the battle between the gun and the armour plate was fought out by processes of continual increasing dimensions in the size of the ships, until the size of the ship rose from the 10,000 tons, which had been universally recognised as being sufficient for the purposes for which a battleship exists, to no less than 28,000 tons.[4] The 12-inch gun, which had been considered adequate for many years as the principal armament of the battleship, grew into, first, a 13.5-inch gun[5] and later into a 15-inch gun.[6]

In view of the fact that one of the principal reasons for which the naval authorities of some of the principal Powers consider the great size of battleships of to-day to be essential is that lesser ships would be unable to survive the explosions of bombs and torpedoes, it is necessary to remark that the growth of the ship from 10,000 tons of the 'nineties to the 28,000 tons of the war period was in no way due

[4] *Agincourt* and *Canada* (1914).
[5] *Orion* class.
[6] *Queen Elizabeth* class.

to the torpedo or the bomb. It took place solely as the re-sult of the desire for a ship at once more powerful than, and impregnable to the artillery of, an opponent. But in the same way as the battle between the gun and armour had led to those increases in gun calibre referred to earlier, so the increase in the size of the ship stimulated the growth of the torpedo. Originally a weapon of 16, and later of 14, inches in diameter, it grew to be of 21 inches in diameter, since the former small weapons were ineffective, or too little effective, against the larger ships which were pro-duced in the competition for size.

Thus, that which it is necessary to recognise clearly is that the growth from the practically universally accepted size of about 10,000 tons to that of the ships of the period of the war was not rendered necessary by any develop-ments in the weapons—the bomb or the torpedo. If, at the time of the great controversies on the size of the ship in 1888 and onwards, some statesmen had had the foresight to see that increase could result only in competition, and that competition could never end so long as any Power made it a matter of policy to possess larger ships than others; and had done that which was done in 1921 and brought about an agreement to limit the size of all "capi-tal" ships to that existing tonnage, there is no reason to suppose that any Power would have been placed at a dis-advantage. The size of the gun would have automatically adjusted itself to the size of the ship. The necessity for tor-pedoes of such a size as those produced in response to the increased defensive qualities of the ship would probably not have arisen: or, if it did arise, the answer would have been found, as answers to similar problems have been found by the military men of all ages, in tactical dispositions and mobility, flexibility and facility of manoeuvre, and in weapons appropriate to meet and destroy the new danger. The alternative of mere increases in size, the provision of weighty static means of defence, is not only unscientific and costly. It is also, in the end, ineffective: for the production of a ship impregnable to all forms of attack, which is the aim of policy to-day, is unattainable.

THE CRUISER

Cruiser policy underwent similar changes in these years of development of sea power. The functions of that class of ship which goes under the title of "cruiser" are, broadly speaking, two-fold. She is the scout who obtains information, and performs such subsidiary services as her strength and speed enable her to perform for a squadron or fleet: and she is the vessel which operates on the detached services of the direct attack and defence of the lines of communication. These last services, though they are characteristic of the cruiser, are not however necessarily performed by her alone. It was a common practice in the past to stiffen the cruiser defence with some of the lesser ships of the line, and in the many considerations which affected the policy of the period to which reference is being made the smaller, or second-class, battleships were regarded as available for that duty: so, in the War of 1914–18, the older battleships, which had been rendered unfit for the main battle fleet by the introduction of the new and greatly superior types, were used on the trade routes: and we saw battle cruisers which, in reality, were battleships in which armour had been subordinated to speed, being sent to the South Pacific for the defence of the Pacific or Atlantic communications, threatened by the cruiser squadron under Admiral Von Spee.

We may, however, put aside this employment of weaker battleships. Under the existing Treaties it appears improbable that older ships will pass into obsolescence and constitute such a reserve as that which hitherto had existed. The "cruiser problem" is that of the size and the numbers of those vessels specifically called "cruisers."

Experience in the past had shown that attack upon the commercial communications of an opponent could be conducted by such small vessels as luggers, privateers of all types, and the lesser frigates. It had shown also that these, though they might not be able to overcome an escorting force, did nevertheless inflict an additional injury to commerce by the mere fact that they forced the enemy to resort to a convoy system which greatly diminished the volume and the profit of sea-borne trade. These experiences notwithstanding, those nations who designed to make a direct attack upon commerce sought a more effective procedure. This they found in the introduction of a cruiser more powerful, both in armament and protection, than the normal cruiser. A powerful cruiser came into existence for the specific purpose of harrying the trade routes. As the torpedo-boat had brought the more powerful "destroyer" into existence, so the new commerce-destroying cruiser produced a reply from England in the form of an armoured cruiser: and as it became possible that such ships could be employed in the scouting services of a fleet, and that vessels endeavouring to gain information would be frustrated and defeated by such ships, so the heavier vessels became in their turn scouting vessels and, for some time, the smaller types tended to fall out of existence. With the passage of time, and under the stimulus of competition, this armoured cruiser, originally a vessel of some 5000 or 6000 tons, grew. She became a vessel of 10,000 tons, and her size then mounted steadily until she became as large as the contemporary battleship herself.[7] Thus, we saw both cruisers and battleships of 13,000–14,000 tons in the British and the Russian navies, the difference between the "cruisers" and the "battleships" of the same size being that the available weight was used in the former to develop speed and endurance, in the latter to provide gun power and armour.

Thus, cruisers increased in size not because there was some change in the nature of sea warfare, in the functions they had to perform, or in consequence of the appearance of some new instrument which rendered greater size necessary, but solely because those who intended to make direct attack upon trade the basis of their naval strategy sought to attain their ends by producing more powerful ships than those of the Power whose trade they designed to attack. The eventual result of this policy was pure waste, for the threatened Power replied by producing ships capable of

[7] In England: *Russell*, battleship, 14,000 tons; *Drake*, cruiser, 14,100 tons. In Germany: *Grosser Kurfürst*, battleship, 10,000 tons; *Bismarck*, cruiser, 10,000 tons. In Russia: *Tsarevitch*, battleship, 12,900 tons; *Rossia*, cruiser, 13,675 tons. The tale could be continued when the battle cruiser stage began.

meeting them. The matter, however, did not end there: it had also its strategical side. Reference has been made earlier to the change in British battleship policy which occurred about the year 1894, when the old-established doctrines of keeping down the size of the ship were superseded by the new policy of "bigger and better." The same tendency affected the cruiser. A belief had arisen that the old lessons of trade protection were no longer applicable and that the great pillar of the system, convoy, was impossible. Mahan had just written:[8] "In fact, as the small proportionate loss inflicted by scattered cruisers appears to indicate the inconclusiveness of that mode of warfare, so the result of the convoy system . . . warrants the interference that, when properly systematised and applied it will have more success as a defensive measure than hunting for individual marauders—a process which even when most thoroughly planned, still resembles looking for a needle in a haystack." But this was not believed. The appearance of large Russian cruisers was held to invalidate the old lessons. The school of thought which dominated British policy at this time held that the proper way to deal with marauding vessels was to hunt them down "relentlessly," and it was in accordance with this policy of "looking for a needle in a haystack" that the first great and costly British cruisers of 14,000 tons[9] were built. The doctrine of "relentless search" held sway for the next twenty years, but the truth of Mahan's deductions was to be shown when war

---

[8] *The Influence of Sea Power on the French Revolution and Empire,* vol. II, p. 217.

[9] *Powerful* and *Terrible.*

came. "Hunting down" achieved nothing to arrest the careers of the commerce destroyers of the war—the *Emden* and the *Karlsruhe*, the *Möwe* and the *Wolf*, though it had been confidently expected that the sea would be swept clear of all commerce destroyers within a fortnight or three weeks of the outbreak of war—a forecast entirely without any justification in experience.

The matter did not end with a "building slip competition" (to use an expression of Admiral Sir Cyprian Bridge) for superiority on the trade routes. When such great and powerful ships had been introduced by some Powers, others felt it incumbent on themselves to possess vessels of the same type. The cruiser had now become a vessel which, if she could not lie in the line, could nevertheless make a very appreciable contribution to the fighting force of a fleet: as the old heavy frigate of from forty to fifty guns had occasionally done, in her day.[10] So we saw the heavy armoured cruisers of about 10,000 tons of the Japanese Navy playing an important part in the battle of the Sea of Japan in 1905.

The next stage in the growth of the cruiser was the introduction of a new type, called the "battle cruiser." The arguments for the necessity of superiority in the scouting line, which had created the belief in a need for two types of cruiser, armoured and unarmoured, in a fleet, came forward once more. What use would it be to seek information if the scouts were driven off by superior force? If a commander needs information his scouting vessels must be able to force their way into touch with the main enemy body

[10] *E.g.* the Dogger Bank battle in 1781.

against opposition, and procure it. A ship larger, faster, and more powerful than the armoured cruiser was considered necessary, and the 14,000-ton armoured cruiser of 23 knots became the 17,000-ton battle cruiser of 26 knots. Speed is one of the most costly of all elements. The cost of the ship was increased not merely by the 3000 more tons of her displacement but also by the three knots added to her speed. At the same time, ignoring all the teachings of experience, the new conception of trade defence was extended. The way to defend commerce in war was held to be to sweep the seas clear of the enemy. It was idle to send small vessels, no larger than those which attacked trade, to guard the scattered groups or to patrol those areas where, by the nature of things, shipping is bound to concentrate— the landfalls, the narrow straits, the passages where effective deviations from the direct route are not possible. Let a great ship, far faster, far more powerful, go out into the sea and the marauder would soon be brought to book, or remain in harbour terrified by the threat of certain destruction. The true type of vessel for commerce defence was the battle cruiser. The "small" cruiser was said to have no place in any scheme of naval defence. Navies should consist of three types only, the battleship, superior in gun power and protection to any opponent; battle cruisers, to push in against any opposition and procure information, or sweep the trade routes clear of commerce destroyers; and torpedo-boat destroyers hunting torpedo-boats down if they put to sea alone, dominating them in battle, and enabling the superior force of artillery and the battle line, undisturbed by attacks of any kind, to crush the enemy.

It would be difficult to exaggerate the harm which the doctrine of "building bigger" in the cruiser problem has done to the world. The cruiser, let it be repeated, is a vessel with two specific functions. Ships perfectly capable of performing those functions had been built by all the Powers for sums of less than a quarter of a million. That sum has been multiplied ten-fold under the impress of one belief—that it is possible to obtain an advantage by building bigger ships than those of other Powers. For no other reason than that was the armoured commerce destroyer initiated. She did not achieve her object. A country dependent on its commerce could not be expected to take no steps to provide an answer. The answer was provided by bigger ships still, and the belief then took hold of men's minds that the aim and direct object of naval policy should be to possess units superior to those of an opponent. But as the armoured cruiser had produced the abnormalities of her own type, so the battle cruiser was not left unanswered. The prospective opponent also produced a battle cruiser. The original 17,000-ton British vessel grew to one of close upon 19,000 tons, and she in turn to one of over 26,000 tons, while the German 19,000-ton ship similarly grew, under the impulse imparted by competition, to a 22,000, a 24,000 and finally one of over 26,000 tons. The culmination of this growth was represented in the *Hood*, a "battle cruiser" of 42,000 tons.

The victory of the British battle cruisers over the German armoured cruisers at the Falkland Islands has produced an impression in the minds of some that it proves that these vessels are either necessary or advantageous. So we see it said that if cruisers were smaller it would not be possible to make a detachment, as was then made, of a couple of ships, but that a greater number would be needed, requiring a greater total number from which to supply them. Whether this reading of the Falkland Islands campaign is responsible for the construction of new and very large battle cruisers by France[11] in reply to the 10,000-ton armoured vessels of Germany cannot be said, though it seems improbable that persons so clear thinking in military matters as the French authorities would be deceived into so erroneous an interpretation of that series of events. For the facts are plain that if that situation had been handled in time, the German squadron could have been met at Coronel by either an equal or a superior number of armoured cruisers sent out from England.

THE FLOTILLA

One of the important changes which have taken place, and will continue to take place, in the constitution of fighting strength is the increased power of flotilla craft. It manifests itself both in battle and in detached operations. The fundamental difference between the flotilla craft of the old wars and those of to-day lies in the fact that the corvettes, brigs, sloops and other small vessels which formed the flotilla had no value in battle, nor had any power of hampering the movements or proceedings of the great ships, cruising either in squadrons or singly. No matter how many of these lesser vessels might have been added to a fleet, the addition would not in any way have affected its fighting

[11] *Dunkerque*, 26,600 tons.

strength. The only instance of an assumption having been made that the presence of a number of small vessels added to the strength of a fleet was that of the eccentric Commodore Johnstone who, adding up all the guns in all the ships and vessels and transports under Lord Howe, propounded the droll view that, having a greater total weight of metal, Howe was superior to his antagonist.

The issue of any armed struggle, whether on land or sea, depends upon the result of the clash between the concentrated masses. So long as the only units which could take part in the main battles were the ships of the line, it was they alone who decided the fate of the war at sea. But in the same way as the invention of gunpowder had brought into existence an arm additional to the infantry in the battle line on shore, so the invention of the torpedo brought a new arm into the battle line at sea. It was many years before the torpedo possessed more than a moral influence, though like all new inventions it was the subject of exaggerated expectations of enthusiasts. It was said that the small torpedo-boat costing a few thousand pounds could sink the great battleship costing the best part of a million. Fifty torpedo-boats or more could be built for the cost of one battleship and a massed attack by such boats would prove irresistible. The day of the great ship was proclaimed by some to have ended.

While this extreme view was not held by all who discerned potentialities in the torpedo, the possibility that it might introduce a new and important factor in battle, acting in conjunction with the great ships, was realised. Thus, Captain Harris, R.N., in 1883 asked whether it could be positively stated that ten first-class armoured vessels would be the equals of five armoured vessels combined with fifteen or sixteen protected torpedo and gun vessels. Captain Harris may have overestimated the battle value of the torpedo vessels of his day, but his anticipation that a flotilla might be a compensation for inferiority in great ships was a recognition of the new fact that the flotilla had begun to have a value in battle which it had not possessed since the days of fireships. Certain conditions however required fulfilment. The vessels must be of a sufficient sea-going capacity to keep the sea with the fleet; the weather must be fine enough to enable them to get into the position required to attack, and to carry out their attack with a probability of success in the face of the enemy's fire. Only under exceptional circumstances would these conditions be fulfilled by the small vessels of limited endurance and sea-worthiness of the day.

Until the War of 1914–18 the torpedo achieved few successes—the sinking of the *Blanco Encalada* by torpedo gun-boats in 1891 was possible only because of a total absence of precaution. In the Spanish-American War the torpedo played no effective part. The Turko-Italian War furnished no opportunity for its use. It did little in the Chino-Japanese War, though the Japanese torpedo craft were manned by skilful and most courageous men. In the Russo-Japanese War it made a sensation by the attack upon the Russian battleships, lying off Port Arthur at the outbreak of hostilities, but the result of that attack was a frank disappointment: such success as there was was due to the gross carelessness with which, at a time of strained international relations, a squadron was left at anchor in the exposed waters outside a base without taking even the most simple steps for its security. The torpedo flotilla did nothing to decide the issue of any of the sea battles. Its contribution to the consummation of the final victory at sea consisted only in the sinking of some of the older vessels already disabled.

Thus, in 1905, the flotilla consisted only in vessels, armed with inaccurate weapons of a very short range, whose endurance at sea would not allow them to keep company with a fleet for more than a short voyage or cruise, and which, unless the weather was very fair, could not develop the speed necessary either to assume a position in a battle from which they could attack, or to make the attack with any great probabilities of success. But during the years between 1905 and 1914 considerable developments took place. Torpedo craft had increased in size, sea-keeping capacity, and speed, torpedoes became larger and faster and their range had reached, and even passed, what had been accepted a few years earlier as the effective range of the gun.

Thus the battle value of the flotilla had increased. Because it was possible for the flotilla craft themselves to inflict serious injury, if they could get into a position from which their missiles could reach the enemy, they could exercise an influence in battle. Although the great ship remained the decisive element, the essential foundation upon which the structure of sea power stood, the "mass" no longer consisted solely of great ships, any more than the "mass" of an army, after the introduction of artillery, consisted solely of infantry and cavalry. This was very clearly illustrated in 1917 and 1918. The entry of America into the war had brought a reinforcement of an American squadron of battleships to the Grand Fleet. There was then an allied fleet whose strength in battleships was more than double that of the enemy. But the German fleet had also a flotilla of some three score or so torpedo craft, and although the shipping of the Allies was being sunk at a rate which caused the gravest anxiety, and though the only vessels with which that shipping could be effectively defended were flotilla craft of the destroyer type, it was not considered that it would be safe to reduce the torpedo flotillas with the Grand Fleet in order to protect the trade. In other words, the "mass" which would decide the struggle was not composed of the great ships only, as it had been composed in the eighteenth and nineteenth centuries, but of the two arms, the great ship and the flotilla craft.

Except for an attempt to produce submarines for fleet work, for which they are unsuited, the fleet flotillas throughout the war consisted of surface craft. A proposal was made to add a flying flotilla, but the means of bringing them into action did not exist and it was not practicable to retain a large number of aircraft in constant readiness for a remotely prospective battle. Aircraft were too badly wanted elsewhere for it to be possible to demobilise several score of them permanently.

Since the war the strides which flying has made have to be taken into consideration. Aircraft can carry heavier weapons and discharge them with greater accuracy: they are faster and have a greater range of action. But unless they are carried in great and vulnerable carriers they cannot accompany a fleet, and it may be doubted whether carriers represent the best fighting return for the money they cost. Thus it is open to question whether the same sum which has been spent on building, maintaining and altering the great carriers of those nations who have indulged in this form of vessel would not have provided a more serviceable return in war in the shape of surface flotilla craft, capable of performing a great variety of duties.[12]

Circumstances may arise in which the operations of fleets take place in waters which can be reached by flying craft from the coasts of one or both combatants. In such a case it can hardly be doubted that this new arm of the flotilla would play a part in battle. It is necessary, however, not to make the same overestimation of the flying torpedo craft as has been made in earlier times of the surface types. Easy as it appears on paper to visualise the sky darkened by aeroplanes on the day of battle, there are many practical points to be brought into consideration. Naval battles rarely, if ever, arise as the result of a series of manœuvres leading up to them. Except when both fleets desire to fight, which is uncommon, a meeting has more often come about by chance than by design, and there can be no certainty that the meeting will take place within the range of the shore-based flotilla, or that weather will allow it to join or even to find the fleets in time.

But time overcomes many difficulties and the appear-

[12] Four British carriers appear to have cost £21 millions and have possibly cost more. The same sum would have provided some three score or more useful surface vessels.

ance of flying flotillas on the scene of battle is to be expected in those waters where fleets may be operating within the effective range of the air flotilla.

The flotilla of to-day, composed of its three types, also possesses greater power than hitherto in detached operations. The modern "destroyer" is a vessel of great speed, good gun power and respectable endurance. She has reached the size, and far outreached the power, of the lesser cruisers of some years ago. Concentrated forces of these vessels constitute formidable bodies. They are not, as their little predecessors the torpedo-boats were, confined to operations within a few hours' distance of their bases. Their striking range is far greater and they possess speed which, except in very unfavourable circumstances of weather, or in a few special instances of exceptionally swift large vessels, would enable them to escape from superior force. If trade has to move in convoys, any convoy passing within striking distance of a port where such flotillas lie must be prepared not only for attack by submarines but also for surface attacks in force. The small escorts which were sufficient, in the days of the War of 1914–18, to meet the submarine attack would be insufficient to give protection against concentrated surface forces. In the "danger zone" of those ports the escorts would have to obey the old and natural rule of being strong enough to meet whatever forces might issue from them. In the days when the sailing convoys had to pass through the danger area of an enemy base where enemy ships of the line lay there were two ways in which security was provided. Either a strong force was kept close off the port, and, thus masking the enemy fleet, covered the convoy at a distance; or the convoy was escorted by a force capable of meeting the enemy if he put to sea. The first of these measures is rarely likely to be practicable under modern conditions. It would require a superiority which it is improbable that any first-class Power could possess: for while it was possible to provide the necessary margin for reliefs when ships could keep the sea for six weeks, the margin needed when endurance is limited to, perhaps, six days would need to be far greater.

The alternative is, as it used to be, escort. The escorting force must be of such a strength and character as would suffice. The sallies made by the German High Sea forces against the Scandinavian convoys began with small craft, increased to cruisers, and ended, in April, 1918, with a fleet of battleships and the auxiliary craft. If we are to suppose that history is to repeat itself, as it has so often done, the same thing may recur, but with an added flotilla force of flying craft. If it be a fact, as it is said to be, that a reduction in the size of battleships below 22,000 tons or some such size is impossible because ships smaller than these are too weak to sustain the injuries which the torpedo and the bomb can inflict, then the only logical result can be that that part of the escort composed of cruisers and smaller vessels will be disabled from the air, and the convoy will be undefended against capture by the lesser surface vessels of the enemy except for such protection as would remain in the form of the supposedly immune great ships. That immunity may save themselves: but inasmuch as they could not defend a convoy against attack by a numerous flotilla their immunity fails to serve the purpose for which they exist: which is, not their own existence but the continued flow of commerce or the movements of military forces, upon which the fate of a country depends, in so far as it is dependent upon the sea.

These are not light matters: for if it be true that the only vessels which can operate with security within the range of the modern flotilla are these very great ships, then it is useless to attempt to render communications secure with smaller vessels in those areas in which flotilla craft can act. But is the theory true? Is it an indisputable fact that vessels of dimensions smaller than those which are asserted to be the minimum for invulnerability are, in reality, in the danger supposed? Is there no answer to the modern flotilla craft, surface, sub-surface and super-surface, other than great size?

This is not a matter to be disposed of by clichés, catchwords, or the repetition of stock phrases. It is a matter for serious and thoughtful examination, conducted without prejudice or the determination to prove a presupposition.

CHAPTER V

SEA POWER AND AIR POWER

THERE is a very widely held conviction that all of these discussions about the size of navies, the size of ships and the problems of international law at sea are in reality a pure waste of time. They may be interesting as matters of archaeology but have as little relation to the practical problems of to-day as the question of how the oars of a quinquereme were arranged. For sea power to-day is a thing of the past. It has had its day as a national instrument of policy. The modern instrument of all policy is air power, which has rendered sea power unnecessary, ineffective in offence, and impotent in defence.

These are three separate and distinct assertions. If they are correct, the nations may all compose their differences concerning the sizes of their navies and their ships and save many millions of their monies.

The reason why sea power is considered unnecessary is that the object in war in the future will be attained without the movement of a single ship. What, it is asked, is the ultimate object in war? It is, to overcome the will of the enemy people. Hitherto that will has been overcome either by occupation of their country or by interruption of their external lines of communication; or, more commonly, by a combination of both measures. The armies endeavour to overcome the resistance offered on land to invasion and occupation. The navies undermine the fortitude of the people by the economic pressure resulting from a destruction of its shipping business, and weaken both the civil and military resistance by preventing supplies which are capable of affording any help in the prosecution of the war from reaching the people and the army. The navies also give mobility to the armies, creating diversions, opening up new lines of attack, or depriving the enemy of territories which were sources of revenue or of material.

None of these services, according to the new doctrine, will be needed in the future. It will not be necessary to overcome opposing armies in order to enter a country or exercise pressure on the people. Attack on the people themselves can now be made directly, without any need of overcoming a defending force. Air forces will bombard the great centres of life and industry, the organisations of transport, water supply, and other internal national services, the administrative establishments and the civil population itself. It is action in this form which will decide the issue. It will decide it so quickly, that even if it were possible to create pressure on a decisive scale by sea power, that pressure would never have time to become operative. Hence, sea power is an unnecessary instrument of policy: it cannot avert disaster from the air.

Even if action in this form at sea were not unnecessary, the argument continues, it will be ineffective. However right Mahan may have been in attributing to sea power in the past such a profound influence upon all the wars in which it played a part, it cannot exercise that influence to-day. Sea power, it is said, exercises its influence primarily by the weapon of blockade. It was blockade which cut off the supplies of the land powers. Contraband, until the late war, played a minor part of cutting off supplies of purely military material. Capture at sea was secondary to blockade, lapping up such shipping and commerce as leaked through the blockade. But blockade was the great instrument which closed the enemy's ports to himself and neutral alike, isolated him from the world, and starved his people into submission.

To-day, we are told, the air has rendered blockade impracticable. Blockade requires the presence of ships of war in such positions relative to the blockaded ports, areas or coasts, as will ensure that a high proportion of ships attempting to pass in or out of those ports will be intercepted by superior force. Those positions cannot be at any great distance from the ports, and the aircraft of to-day, and still more those of to-morrow, are capable of effective action within those distances. Impossible as it already is to maintain a blockading force at sea in such positions in the face of submarines, it might be maintained, submarines notwithstanding, by ships operating from harbours secured against submarines; the lesser vessels alone, which unlike the great ships have little reason to fear submarines, performing the active work of interception. But aircraft will render even this impossible. Though the danger which they present to the smaller surface vessels of the flotilla may be no greater than that to which the lesser vessels in the past were exposed from gales, lee shores, and the "perils of the sea" in general, aircraft present a particular danger to the larger vessels upon whose support the lesser craft depend. However large the ship may be made to render her unsinkable from the bomb, she cannot be immunised from injury. The ports in which she lies, so long as they are within the range of the aircraft, cannot be so defended that she receives the same measure of protection from the air that the artillery defences give her against bombardment from the sea, and the booms, breakwaters and mines from torpedo craft. Hence blockade is no longer practicable. And not only is it impracticable for these physical reasons, but if it were attempted to impose it in some form, the nation which did so would be liable to bombardment of its cities from the air. This risk would be prohibitory.

As the virtue of a knife lies in its having a sharp edge, without which it is no more than a strip of steel, so the virtue of a navy lies in blockade. As it was blockade which had produced results hitherto, so without it sea power is nothing. And even that is not all. If these anticipations should prove wrong, sea power is still useless. The blockade can be circumvented and a nation's needs supplied through neutral ports, from whence goods will reach their destination by use of all those facilities of transport which have come into existence by road, rail, river, canal and the air.

Finally, sea power is impotent to perform those services of defence, to the needs of which specifically it owes its existence. It can no longer defend shipping against attack from the air. Those routes which are flanked by the coasts of an enemy will be constantly raided, or may even be kept permanently under surveillance and attack by aircraft from shore bases; while on oceanic routes, raiding vessels carrying aircraft will not be confined to the limits of vision from the mast-head. Their aircraft will not only be their scouts to discover enemy shipping, but also the instruments of attack: and a ship discovered will be a ship sunk.

Moreover, the defence of shipping is impossible without bases, and if those bases can be reached by aircraft, the vessels within them, fighting ships or mercantile, will be sunk by bombs or torpedoes from the air. Even also if some shipping, navigating beyond the range of aircraft, should make its voyage unscathed, that will not serve the needs of the nation if, when it reaches its destination—the great shipping ports—aircraft can attack it there, can demolish the ships alongside the wharves, the warehouses and the transport facilities of the port, and drive the workpeople who load and discharge the shipping from the docks.

No sensible person will desire to dismiss these arguments. If they are correct statements of fact they must be faced, pleasant or unpleasant as they may be, according to the views of the several nations of the world.

If it be a fact that wars in the future will be decided by direct attacks upon the civil populations; and if it be also true that the fundamental principle of the strategy of war in the air is not, as it is on land and at sea, to overcome the armed forces of the opponent, then it would follow that warfare will consist in an intensive process of cross-raiding between the opponents. There will be no "strategy of defence," but there will be a "machinery of defence" in the form of local measures, consisting principally in artillery and obstacles, supplemented, possibly—though this could only be at the cost of the offensive—by local defensive air forces. Upon the hypothesis that the decision in war in the future will depend upon which belligerent can produce the largest number of planes, and which civil population has the greater determination, it follows necessarily that all money spent in other directions, unless they should contribute towards the attainment of the principal object—the destruction of life and property—would be wasted.

How does the assumption that this is the only form which war will take stand the test of experience? There have been several wars during the last two generations. If we suppose that aircraft had existed when the disputes arose which brought about those wars, would they have been fought in the manner prescribed for the future?

A crisis arose between England and Russia in 1885 concerning an incident at Penjdeh. If air forces had then existed and if war had come, is it to be supposed that Russian aircraft would have bombed London, flying a minimum of 2400 miles to get there and back, with loads of bombs on board? And if not, what other civil objectives would the aircraft have had for this form of warfare? Would the Chino-Japanese War have been decided in this manner? And if so, what would have been the objectives?

When the United States wished to expel the Spanish troops and Spanish rule from Cuba, this would not have been effected by aircraft bombing Havana from Key West, short as the distance is—a hundred miles. Aircraft in Cuba if effective, would undoubtedly have added to the difficulties of taking an army across and landing it: that, however, is a different matter. What would have occurred would have been a struggle for the command of the line of passage between Key West and the point of disembarkation. The ultimate object of sea power is control of lines of communications, and sea power in its various forms of large surface vessels, lesser surface vessels, and a flotilla of surface, submarine and air torpedo-boats would have struggled for that mastery. In the old schemes of defence of England, a main force was kept watching the main force of the enemy, with inshore squadrons keeping observation upon his movements, while upon the English coast there was a flotilla of small vessels whose specific function was to fall upon the transports and capture or disable them. The flying torpedo-boats and gun-boats of to-day are a part of the modern flotilla, associated in the duty of defence with the surface and submarine craft. Sea power is still the defence, and the issue of that struggle between Spain and the United States would not have been decided by the bombing of Havana, or Madrid, or New York, but upon the campaign at sea between Cuba and Key West.

In the war between Japan and Russia the object of Japan was to expel Russia from Korea. The final object of Russia was the occupation and possession of Korea; the expulsion of the Japanese would not suffice to ensure the peaceful and undisturbed occupation. Japan must be invaded. It will not be imagined that Japan could have attained her end by bombing some Russian cities and bringing pressure upon the will of the Russian people. It may be thought that the invasion of Japan by Russia would take the form of invasion by air, or the bombing of the Japanese cities from Vladivostok; but it is over 700 miles from Vladivostok to Tokyo, and another 700 back, and it may be questioned whether this would have been the most effective use of these craft when a Japanese army was crossing the sea into Korea.

Italy's wish to acquire Libya could never have been fulfilled by this supposititious new form of warfare. There was one instrument, and one only, by means of which the occupation of that territory could have been accomplished—an army. No one assuredly imagines that an attempt to force Turkey to cede that territory would have been made by sending aircraft over 800 miles to bomb Constantinople; and, if it be assumed that an advanced base in the Egean Sea could have been taken as a stepping-stone, that base, on the other hypothesis of the impossibility of defence against the air, would have been rendered untenable by Turkish aircraft, operating over a shorter distance and therefore with greater efficiency.

Are such wars as these and others of the same type which have occurred in our lifetime to be considered as things of the past? Are we to assume that some change has taken place in the world which relegates what have been called "private" wars to the list of forgotten things, never to recur? If not, we are not entitled to assume that the sole form which warfare in the future will take will be the direct attack upon the "morale" of the enemy people. The operations at sea will be modified by those new instruments of sea power, the flying elements of the flotillas. What has happened as the result of the discovery of flight is not that air power has displaced sea power, but that an important new instrument of sea power has come into being which will modify the conduct of the operations at sea as the steamship in her time, and the surface and submarine torpedo-boats in theirs, modified it.

The second indictment of sea power is that it is ineffective in modern conditions because blockade is no longer practicable. The assumption underlying that indictment is that sea power was effective in the wars of the past merely through the employment of blockade against a nation.

This has already been referred to.[1] It has been shown that the blockades in past wars, up to the time of Orders-in-Council of 1807 and 1809, were military blockades: not commercial blockades aiming at the starvation of a country, but military operations designed wholly for the purpose of meeting the enemy and fighting him if he should put to sea, whatever might be his object in leaving port. Thus the blockade of Brest by Cornwallis was not an operation aiming at the isolation of the French people from the outer world: it was an operation whose object was to bring the Brest fleet to action if it sailed. It was a measure of protection to the kingdom, the colonies and the trade, because it disabled the fighting force which alone could injure, or be the means of injuring, them. The economic pressure which sea power exercised was the result of enemy shipping being unable to sail for want of protection, and of the rule that if enemy goods were carried by neutrals, those goods were liable to seizure and condemnation. That right was surrendered, as we have seen, in 1856, by the acceptance of the new doctrine that the flag covered the goods. Notwithstanding that doctrine, sea power exercised a vast and preponderant influence upon the War of 1914–18, in which, with a few insignificant exceptions, no blockade was declared. It is therefore wholly incorrect to aver that sea power has been deprived of the capacity to exercise pressure for the reason that air power has deprived it of its

[1] *Vide ante, pp. 91–2.*

ability to employ its ancient method of blockading the enemy nation.

Though we speak of the "blockade" of Germany in the late war, we have to recollect that the word is not being used in its legalistic sense. The actual measures adopted consisted in the interception of contraband goods. Contraband was given its true meaning of "goods capable of giving any help to the enemy's prosecution of the war," and the control over shipping was exercised by squadrons operating at a distance from the enemy, and in regions in which effective counter-attack upon them by air was impossible. It is not beyond the bounds of possibility that a time may come when it will be practicable for aircraft, carrying effective loads of the ammunition they use, to fly from the shores of the North Sea to the northward of the Orkneys, to cruise there in the thick weather till they find an enemy, and to return to their own ports; and that such craft may be produced in numbers sufficient to break down the control by sinking many of the vessels employed. But that time has not yet come; nor is it to be assumed that if and when such developments should take place, the vessels employed upon the service of control will possess no means of defending themselves.

At the risk of repetition, it cannot be too strongly impressed that the use to which sea power has been put by England has been entirely different when she was engaged in a single-handed war and when she was one of a coalition of Powers. In the former, she did not seek to attain her ends by economic pressure, except in the first war with the Dutch Republic and, in an intermittent fashion, in the

Elizabethan war with Spain. The matters which have brought her into single conflict with a foreign Power have been concerned either with some interest overseas—such as the security of her shipping trading in the West Indies in 1739—or the possession of some disputed territory. What she did on such occasions was to send military force to dispossess the enemy or occupy the territory. Any economic stricture which arose from the disposition of her fleets was secondary. Her rulers knew well that it was beyond her power to force compliance upon a great continental Power by isolating it from the sea, even if such a thing were practicable.

The situation when Great Britain was an ally in a coalition of continental states was wholly different. The object then was not the defence of some patch of ground, some offshoot of trade. It was the preservation of the Balance of Power, and its attainment lay in bringing such pressure upon the enemy state, by all the means available, that he would have to desist from his attempts to render himself supreme in Europe. That which sea power then had to do was to lend what assistance it could to the armies of its allies, to strengthen to the utmost their powers, and to weaken the powers of resistance of the enemy. The large armies which a European war brought into the field could only be maintained at a great cost, and the cost could only be met if the revenues were sufficient. To stop his country's shipping was to deprive the enemy of some of the revenue he needed for the maintenance of a great army. Thus while economic pressure was of primary importance in a war of coalitions, it was only secondary in a duel.

There is, however, another aspect of the influence of the air. Although economic pressure may only be of the first order of importance in a war of coalitions, and although blockade may not have been the great measure employed by the maritime Powers to produce that pressure, there is still the military blockade to be considered, and the influence which the flying flotillas will have upon that operation.

The ultimate object of a military blockade is to disable some body of the enemy forces: it may be a fleet, a squadron, a flotilla, or merely individual vessels. That which it aims at achieving is to prevent that particular force from interfering with the movements at sea, or conducting any independent operation. It consists in the stationing of a force sufficiently near to the enemy to ensure his interception if he puts to sea, of sufficient strength to fight him with advantage if he is intercepted. The fleets off Brest or Toulon, cruising at sea, performed the same duties as the Japanese fleet lying at the Elliott Islands, the British fleet at Scapa Flow, or the allied fleet at Taranto. In each case the object was the same, though the manner in which it was attained was different.

In the Russo-Japanese War the Japanese navy had to protect the transports of an army coming from Japan into Korea. The danger to which those transports were exposed was two-fold. The main Russian fleet might come to sea and sink them; or individual Russian cruisers might attack them in detail. The second of these dangers was guarded against by detachments with or near the transports; and the whole movement was "covered" by the Japanese fleet at the Elliott Islands. In the war in the North Sea, the

British fleet had to protect the troop transports on their way to France from the United Kingdom, from the Dominions, and from the countries of the other allies over sea, and the trade transports conducting the commerce. Detachments gave security against individual enemy cruisers, surface and submarine, and these detachments were covered against attack from the powerful squadrons in the Bight Ports by the main body which lay at Scapa Flow. In the Mediterranean, the detachments were protected against attacks by single vessels by means of escorts, and the whole movement of the shipping, which carried troops, supplies and trade through the Mediterranean, was covered from attack by superior force by means of a concentrated allied fleet lying in the ports in the Southern Adriatic.

One condition is essential if this form of "blockade" is to be effective. Whether the blockading force be cruising close at hand as it was at Brest, cruising at a distance as it was under Nelson off Toulon, lying in port about a hundred miles distant at the Elliott Islands, or over five hundred in the Orkneys, it must be so placed that it can ensure so far as, humanly speaking, it is possible to ensure anything in war, that it can intercept the enemy before he can strike any intended blow or reach any desired spot: or, as a possible alternative, often difficult to achieve in practice, that the threat of interception before the enemy can regain one of his ports shall be so great that he will not venture to make an attempt. The question therefore is, whether sea power is still able to play this part—to cover the passage of its armies and the sailing of its trade.

It had been recognised before the late war that blockade,

in the old form of a fleet of great vessels cruising off the base of an enemy fleet, had been affected by the appearance of the torpedo flotilla. Even if a close watch were practicable by day, it would not be possible at night; and, when the submarine appeared, it became impossible for great ships to maintain a continuous station in waters where submarines could operate. The "flotilla" had thus made it impossible to confine a force of great ships in port by cruising at sea. But it was still practicable to take station in a harbour, with steam ready at short notice, provided a harbour was available which fulfilled the needs of accommodation and proximity, and that information of any movement of the enemy could be obtained in time. Both in the Russo-Japanese War and in the War of 1914-18 these harbours were to be found; and it proved possible to obtain sufficient warning of forthcoming movements, in the one case by the added activity observed in the mine-sweeping vessels, indicating an intention to put to sea, in the other by interception of wireless communications.

The question to which those concerned with the solution of the problems of sea power have to find the answer is, would it be practicable now that the air has to be reckoned with for a fleet to lie in a harbour, if a harbour could be found near enough to enable it to fulfil these conditions? If the harbour is near enough for the fleet to interpose itself, in time, between the enemy and his objective, will this, or will it not, bring the fleet within the effective range of the flying flotilla of the enemy? And if it does, could a fleet be maintained in that base? This does not mean could a body of "battleships" lie there, suffering no injury sufficient to disable some or all of them, as the Russian battleships were disabled by the Japanese howitzers at Port Arthur. It means more, for a fleet consists of battleships, cruisers, the flotilla of lesser craft, and also a number of supply vessels, or storehouses and magazines which provide the needs of the fleet.

Dogmatic assertions either of the power of the air flotilla in attack or of the strength of the defensive are equally dangerous. The torpedo-boat was at one time expected to render the great ship obsolete. The difficulties of navigation in the approaches to the Firth of Forth and to Scapa Flow were believed to be a sufficient protection against the submarine. Man is so ingenious an animal that he finds a way of providing an antidote to most inventions. The accuracy of fire with the bomb and the torpedo have increased, and, simultaneously, the means of resisting the attack have improved. Finality is far distant. Moreover, if it should be true that a fleet cannot lie in a harbour within the effective range of an air flotilla of an enemy, that rule applies to both fleets: and the fleet whose object it is to attack certain communications will also in many—though not all—geographical situations lie within reach of the air flotilla of its opponent, and, being equally subject to disablement or destruction, will be in no condition to attack those communications. Yet nothing is less probable, if experience be any guide, than that attacks on vessels in harbour and their establishments afloat and ashore will be so successful as to sink or drive away all the fighting vessels, and that the dispute for the use of the sea communications will rest wholly with those portions of the navies which navigate in the air.

However secure the bases may be made for the fighting

fleets and mercantile vessels by means of obstructions in the air, artillery and the use of local air flotillas, the ships have need also of being reasonably safe at sea. The Conference which sat in London agreed that it is contrary to humanity that merchant ships should be sunk by submarines, and that the rules which govern surface vessels apply with equal weight to submarines: that is to say, that the act of sinking a merchant ship by means of a torpedo was condemned. It is curious that the same rules should not have been applied to the air flotilla, for there is no intrinsic difference between sinking a vessel with a torpedo fired from an underwater craft, and sinking her with a torpedo or a bomb from a craft which navigates above the surface. Presumably, the conduct of aircraft was imagined to be a matter of "air warfare" with which the Conference had nothing to do: if so, it illustrates how unfortunate it is to approach questions of this kind in the subjective manner. If aircraft had been recognised to be what they are, flying torpedo-boats and gun-boats, units of sea power, this illogical discrimination could not have been made.

But the fact remains that those methods of sea warfare which were so roundly condemned when employed by the German submarine torpedo-boats, to-day meet with the approval of all nations when they are employed by the flying torpedo-boats; and, unless this inconsistency is removed, as plainly it should be, it is to be anticipated that war in the future will be marked by the same methods. If so, will those methods be successful? Defence proved to be possible against the submarine, though at one time it was believed to be impossible. Will it prove possible or impossible against aircraft?

Here again nothing can be worse than exaggeration or underestimation—exaggeration of the powers of aircraft to establish a sufficiently complete and permanent patrol of the waters used for shipping, or of their powers of sinking ships: or underestimation of what they can do, of the various counter-measures which a nation whose shipping is thus attacked can take, or of what may be the result upon neutral Powers if the acts of the submarine are reproduced in the air.

The routes on which aircraft may be expected to possess their greatest capacity for attack are certain narrow seas— the Mediterranean, the Channel and the Baltic: and those seas are the highways of the shipping of all nations. Identification of a vessel is thus a necessity, for no one can imagine that neutral Powers would for a moment accept any declaration of a "war zone" in such waters. The difficulty of establishing identity is however to some extent removed by the evidence which is furnished by the fact of vessels sailing in convoys: and it is to be expected that, in such waters, convoys would be necessary for security against surface and submarine attacks; though whether this would be practicable is not by any means certain.

It is freely to be admitted that the defence of a convoy against an attack from the air presents great difficulties: but because that is so, it does not follow that a route is thereby rendered impassable. Although the sea looks very small on a map, and although the area of water that can be observed from a height appears very large, it is very far from being easy to maintain such a service, acting at considerable distances from their bases, carrying a sufficient quantity of ammunition to sink or disable shipping, in waters even so narrow as any of these. No one will pretend that no injury can be done, that no shipping would be sunk by aircraft. The whole question is whether it will be impossible to keep the losses within bounds that can be borne.

If, however, it should be resolutely declared that what is not tolerable in a submarine is not tolerable in any other form of vessel: that weakness or technical inability to fulfil certain conditions does not release an instrument from obligations which bind other instruments; then it would follow that this form of attack was illegal. Illegality, it may be said, does not matter: each nation may have its own view on that question; and though one may elect to consider an act illegal, that decision has no binding effect upon another who thinks otherwise, and to whom the particular practice appears advantageous. But illegality is not so easily disposed of. It is a maxim that illegal acts justify retaliation. Those who consider attack in this form upon the noncombatant merchant ship to be illegal are at complete liberty to warn those who take the other view that they hold themselves entirely free to adopt whatever measures of retaliation they may choose. If the civilian in the ship is to be shot or drowned; if instead of legal condemnation by a Prize Court, summary execution is to be the practice; and if direct protection against these abnormal practices should prove, in the nature of things, to be impossible, the people threatened with this form of sea-hooliganism may find itself constrained to use measures equally detestable and more far-reaching. The bombardment of the civilian on the sea may be answered by the bombardment of the civilian in coastal towns and cities. Where it would end, it is impossible to say. What is called "civilisation" had produced, until the War of 1914–18, certain agreements to limit the acts of war. It was recognised that indiscriminate conduct was, in the end, disadvantageous: that it caused suffering while doing nothing towards attaining the final object of war, which is Peace. The removal of those restraints upon certain forms of warfare profited no one in the recent war, and, from the profound hatreds which were created, has been one of the principal obstacles in the resumption of peace.

It may however not be necessary to proceed to retaliatory acts. It may be remarked that few of those who predict the wholesale destruction of shipping by this means are seamen, or persons with any acquaintance with maritime affairs, and that their conception of the control of shipping by means of aircraft has no foundation in nautical knowledge. It is not to be imagined that finality has been reached in the defensive. What, however, is certain is that if the inconsistency which condemns one act when committed from twenty feet below the surface but condones it when committed from two thousand above the surface is persisted in, we must expect an increase in our armaments whose extent cannot be predicted. For we shall see a race between the instruments of defence and of attack similar to those which took place between guns and armour, between the torpedo-boat in her various forms (of which the flying torpedo-boat is the latest) and her antidotes. The competition between guns and armour, as we have seen, increased the size of the "battleship" from some 8,000 or 10,000 tons to 35,000, and her cost from three-quarters of a million to seven millions and more. The competition in the flotillas has increased the size of the flotilla craft from some 120 tons to as much as 2500, and her cost from fifteen thousand to as much as three hundred thousand pounds. If the doctrine of frightfulness at sea which appears to be regarded with so much favour by some people is to be pursued, we must be prepared for developments to take the same course; and no one need delude himself with the consolation that this is in substitution for, or cheaper than, the present instruments. It will be a definite addition: of that there is no doubt. All the nations of the world will pour out their money in years of peace to gain the supposed advantages or to protect themselves from the injuries of their own inventions and, in the end, none will be one whit less insecure than it was before.

But to return to the indictment which was under discussion. That indictment was that air power had rendered sea power ineffective for the purposes of the defence of shipping at sea. The answer is four-fold. First, that "air power" is a misnomer, aircraft being themselves instruments of sea power; weapons employed at sea for the purpose of disputing the control of the sea which is the object of sea power. Second, that the effort needed to establish control of those flotilla craft, even in comparatively narrow waters, is far greater than the amateurs of commerce attack in this manner imagine. Third, that the means of defence are in a constant state of development; and finally, that the measures of retaliation, vile as they are, are practicable.

In truth, there is far less danger to shipping from the air

than from surface vessels. In those same areas in which an air flotilla can operate, surface flotillas can operate with far greater effect; and they can do so not merely in accordance with custom and humanity, but in all weathers and for a full twenty-four hours of the day. It is not as an instrument, operating by itself, dropping bombs upon merchant vessels, that the aircraft are factors in sea warfare. Their influence is measured by a more military standard, as units of the sea forces. It depends upon the extent to which their endurance will enable them to co-operate with the other units of those forces in operations directed against that which protects the shipping—the sea power of the enemy. There is no new lesson in this. It is no more than a repetition of a very old and very well-established doctrine—that the fighting forces of the enemy are the primary objective.

CHAPTER VI

QUANTITATIVE NAVAL STRENGTH

WHILE the nations of the world have added to their burdens, without increasing their security, by a competitive process of building ships larger than those of their rivals and by endeavours to produce "battleships" which shall be immune from injury, a great quantitative increase has also taken place. New navies have sprung into existence, and navies which were comparatively small have become great. For what reasons have these quantitative accretions of naval power been made?

It would not be possible exhaustively to survey the naval policies of the principal maritime Powers and the programmes which have resulted from those policies. It may, however, be possible to make some analysis of these matters. Naval armaments spring from some cause. Navies resemble all the other instruments which man produces in that they are the expression of some particular need: they are intended to fulfil some object. What then were the needs and objects which appear to have dictated these quantitative increases in naval power?

The preceding sketch of the growth in size of the "iron-clad" or battleship, and of the cruiser, shows that no single nation was responsible for the increases in qualitative power. Broadly speaking, it was the greatest maritime Power, whose security was founded upon the strength of her massed forces, who took the lead in increasing the size of the battleship: and it was the Powers in the scale just below, who, unable to dispute the general command at sea by battle, naturally turned their attention to the lines of communication as the objective of their attack and took the lead in the construction of larger cruisers. Curiously enough, both these policies were diametrically opposed to the interests of the nations. As the British administrations before the end of the 'eighties of the last century had realised, the interest of Britain was from every point of view— strategical, tactical and financial—to keep the ships of the massed body small. It was not for the nation which was superior to increase size. A nation with less resources, which neither needed nor could afford to devote so much of its revenues to its sea forces, might well seek to substitute individual size for numbers. For any given sum of money more actual power, measured in terms of weight of broadside and protection, can be concentrated in one hull than in two or more. One ship of 20,000 tons can contain a heavier artillery, better defended, than two ships of 10,000 tons, and will cost less. Hence there is a definite inducement for the weaker to redress her weakness by building larger ships. So Italy, when unable to afford so many ships as France, built larger ships; and so both France and Spain in the old wars built some of their ships of the line larger than those of Great Britain. The success of such a policy would plainly depend upon two things: first, whether the resulting instrument, the fleet, of which the ships are units, would be more efficient for its purpose; and, second, if that should be so, whether the greater Power would not be obliged to furnish himself with like vessels, and so cancel out any advantages: so that eventually no advantage would be gained.

But if there might have seemed to be some justification for a weaker power to endeavour in this way to mitigate its weakness, there would be none whatever for the stronger Power. Whereas it was not inevitable that the stronger Power should answer the weaker by imitating his policy and building large ships in reply—for Great Britain had not to any marked extent so answered either France or Spain in the past, or been disturbed by the Italian constructions of nearly 14,000 tons in the 'eighties—it was almost inevitable that, if the stronger Power added to her numerical superiority the superiority of individual size, the weaker Powers would be obliged to make increases in the size of their own ships. Every addition of a larger and more powerful class of ship to the fleet lops off, or relegates to the ranks of the obsolete, the older vessels, and so diminishes the "capital" accumulated over a long period of years: and to the nation whose security, above that of all others, depends upon her navy it becomes financially more difficult to maintain the superiority upon which in turn that security rests.

On the other hand, those nations whose inferiority in the mass would prevent them from disputing the command, and seeking victory over the enemy mass, not unnaturally turned their eyes to the lines of communications, the vital element in the life of the purely maritime Power, as their objective. Their mass would contain the enemy mass, their detachments would attack the communications. What policy as regards the size of the cruiser, the vessel employed on the detached service, did this suggest? Should the cruiser be made more powerful than those of the enemy? At a first glance it might seem that the most advantageous policy for a strategy of sporadic warfare would be to send out upon the trade routes powerful "autonomous" vessels, which would fall upon the detachments, composed of weaker vessels, employed in the defence of the communications. Yet the record of experience gave no support to such a conclusion. It was not the squadrons of larger vessels, or the individually larger "cruisers," which inflicted the principal injuries, both direct and indirect, on British commerce in the old wars, but the host of smaller craft, ubiquitously employed. Nevertheless, it is plain that there are many circumstances and conditions in which the possession of vessels individually more powerful than those of the enemy would be an advantage. But inasmuch as that is a fact, the effect would be that the threatened Power, realising it no less clearly than his opponent, would take the precaution to guard himself against the injury: which he might do either by providing himself with greater numbers of lesser vessels, or with vessels as strong as, or stronger than, those which threatened his security. The eventual result must in fact be that the advantage of size would be temporary only. Size would be answered by size, and if the advantage was then to be retained, still more size must follow: and with more size, fewer numbers, less ubiquity, less mobility, more disinclination to separate from the main body such powerful ships as the cruisers would then become. In the long run, in fact, a mere increase in cost results without procuring those very advantages for which the increase was designed. So the policy of the large commerce-destroying cruiser was as little advantageous to those who initiated it, as the policy of bigger battleships was to its founders.

This is by no means to say that there may not be advantages. If war should come before the prospective opponent should have had time to provide himself with the antidote, either in numbers or size, there would certainly be an advantage. But, fortunately, there may be long rivalry without war, and by the time that the expected war comes the threat may have been met. In the meantime the war on the building slips will have cost both the competing nations vast sums of money: and not them only, but also other nations, onlookers who cannot afford to be left behind and must themselves build similar vessels, and may also themselves add their own quota to the competition.

The growth of navies has not only been qualitative. The quantitative growth of some nations has been no less striking during the half-century. For what purpose, to meet precisely what national needs, to guard against what dangers to the nations' lives, have some nations thought it necessary to furnish themselves with navies so much greater, either actually or relatively, than those with which they were provided a half-century earlier? Were they then insecure? or had some new developments taken place which increased the risks to which they were formerly exposed from invasion or interruption of their sea communications? Had, in fact, sea power during those years become a new and essential element in their national security?

The increase did not begin in any marked manner until about 1882: thus, from 1866 until 1882 the British estimates remained at just under £11 millions and in 1882 were even a few thousand pounds less. In 1886 the estimates of the principal Powers were as follows (in millions): Great Britain £13½, France £7½, Germany £2½, Austria £1½, Italy £3¼, United States £3¼ and Russia £4. The Russian activity of 1886, already referred to, was an indication of a desire for greater strength at sea. A twenty-year plan was put forward in that year which should increase her fleet in the Baltic by eleven first-class ironclads—ships, that is to say, of 10,000 tons—and some of the second class of 7000 tons, and to add eight more first-class ironclads to the fleet in the Black Sea. In France, at the same time, increases were taking place in the cruiser and flotilla forces. These increases could not fail to excite apprehensions in England and in 1888 a committee of three Admirals expressed their decided opinion that no time should be lost in placing the British navy upon a Two Power standard. A Naval Defence Act followed in 1889 which was to add seventy ships to the navy.

As Great Britain was making this increase because of the increases abroad, so the next strongest Power was, it would appear, doing the same in consequence of the rise of lesser Powers. France was watching the navies of Italy and Germany, both of which were adding to their strength. "It may well be affirmed," wrote Monsieur Weyl, "that if we do not take care the Triple Alliance will be able in a few years' time to put in line a more powerful fleet than our own. As England wishes to be in a position to resist a coalition of any two powers, ought not we in the same way to make it our aim to be on a level with the two continental powers whose maritime ambition is now so plainly brought to light? The one hopes, in the near future, to be able to make a good figure in the North Sea, the other has already taken a position in the Mediterranean which it behooves us to take account of."[1]

Thus, the rise of the Italian navy, and its effect on the Triple Alliance, was causing apprehensions in France. But Italy in her turn had become alarmed. The French occupation of Tunis had come as a shock to her, who had looked upon that province as a future colony for the outlet of her surplus population; and this had been one cause of her seeking security in the Triple Alliance.

So a chain of political events was inexorably forcing these quantitative increases. Germany making a beginning to figure as a Sea Power; Italy, seeing her development threatened, joining the Triple Alliance; France, seeing herself insecure between her neighbours in the north and the south, building to meet that threat; Russia, definitely setting herself to make a marked increase in her fleet; and England, whose relations with France and Russia were clouded, resuscitating that traditional policy of a Two Power standard with which, in earlier times, she had furnished herself against her prospective enemies, the two Bourbon Powers.

The Dual Alliance between France and Russia was formed in 1891, but this did not check the growths of those fleets, for the navies of the Triple Alliance were growing.

[1] *The Naval Annual*, 1890, p. 509.

Corresponding increases resulted, perforce, in the fleet of
Great Britain. So, by the end of the nineteenth century the
costs of the greater fleets had reached the following figures
(in millions): Great Britain £27½, France £12½, Germany
£7½, Italy £4½, Russia £9 and the United States £10.

There, then, were the beginnings of that race in naval
armaments which, to some, it seems so easy to condemn as
a militaristic delusion of armaments for their own sake.
In no case were those armaments anything except the instruments of policy. Navies, as has been earlier remarked,
may be expressions either of a policy of which the object is
security for existing interests, or of a policy of which the
object is expansion. Admitting to the full that the two land
Powers, Russia and Germany, had military interests at
sea, the first in the Baltic and the Black Seas, the second in
the Baltic and the North Seas, and that naval force was
needed by both in those respective waters, it is not possible
to say that either country depended upon the sea for its
security against any Power with which it might come into
conflict. By the land, and by the land alone, could either be
subjected to decisive pressure. By no possibility whatever
could any Sea Power, however strong, compel compliance
upon either of those great military states, to whom, even
if the sea were closed, supplies could be furnished by land.
Yet it was those two land Powers who originated the principal quantitative increases.

Since the beginning of the twentieth century the growth
had been most marked in three great nations—the United
States, Germany and Japan.

Fifty years ago the navy of the United States cost two

and a half millions (£). To-day it costs her about twenty-five times as much. That increase, like those of other Powers, owes much to the growth in the size of the ship, to the developments in engineering, to the invention of the torpedo, to the rise in costs and to the submarine; but in the same period the growth in the cost of the navy of Great Britain is only fourfold[2]—from some thirteen and a half millions to fifty-six. There is therefore a large balance of a purely quantitative nature to be accounted for. For what reasons did this quantitative increase become necessary for the security of the state? Was the nation in danger? Have new responsibilities fallen to it demanding increases, or have new threats to its security arisen?

The "Maritime Powers" of the world, as I have shown, have always been those which, by the individual efforts of their citizens, have incurred responsibilities and developed interests over sea. As traders they have built themselves merchant fleets which carried their goods, or the goods of others, more economically or more safely—in other words at a greater mutual benefit—than those of other nations: or as colonists have settled in oversea territories and there created new centres of population. For the security of this commerce and those colonies they have needed fighting forces. So, too, if the only line of approach to their territory has been the sea, fighting forces at sea were the best security against invasion, the alternative—a possible one—being to furnish themselves with land forces in strength sufficient to meet those of any probable invader: a burden

[2] I use the word "only" in comparative sense, not in the sense of its being unimportant or trivial.

which would be unnecessary if the enemy could be prevented from crossing the sea.

It would appear from the Report of the Secretary of the Navy in 1876 that the need of a navy to the United States at that time was due to two things. The coasts must be secure against invasion, the harbours from bombardment, and the coastal trade from injury or serious interruption. The Secretary expressed the opinion that these objects could be attained by a navy composed of a monitor force, a torpedo flotilla, and vessels designed specifically as rams; in brief, in a local force which could effectively meet any attack from the sea from any other Power. "With such a force, with no colonies to defend, I think we may well dispense, for the present at least, with the heavy and unwieldy ironclads of European nations, and also with the monster cannon necessary to penetrate them. Any vessel which can safely cross the seas to enter our harbours, or to lie upon our shores, will be found vulnerable to cannon of moderate weight and calibre, while the heaviest armour will not protect a ship from the attacks of torpedoes managed by brave and well-instructed officers." Although we may to-day consider that the value of the torpedo was overestimated, we need to recollect that this was the view of a navy which had more recent experience of war than any other. In the Secretary's opinion—and it is to be presumed, the view to which he gave expression was that of the sea officers—this would provide for the security of the country: which is the ultimate object of a navy. But as war can rarely be conducted by measures of passive defence only, some provision was necessary for striking power. For that purpose "fast unarmoured cruising ships" which would be "on equal terms" with the enemy's similar ships were considered necessary for the attack upon the enemy's commerce. Vessels of about 3500 tons displacement were thought adequate for this purpose. "Equal terms," it is to be observed, not terms of material superiority, were then deemed sufficient.

Thus, of the three elements in sea power—a fighting navy, colonies and shipping—the United States possessed the first only, and her sea power, though not that of the wider kind possessed by a nation which is called "a Sea Power," would give security to her interests. The country and its interests would be safe from attack. The oceanic shipping at that time needed no defence, for the country was not dependent upon it. The merchant navy had dwindled into a very small proportion, for although before the Civil War it had been able to compete successfully with the merchant fleets of other countries on its own merits and without public assistance, it had since lost its position as a national asset. This was not due to the losses it suffered from the Confederate cruisers, which had not exceeded five per cent., but to "the burdens of taxation which the war had imposed on all the industries of the country, but which operated with peculiar hardness on the shipping interest ... thereby subjected to the unrestricted competition of foreign rivals." It was this, together with other economic causes—according to some authorities the high costs arising out of a policy of high protection—which had ruined it; and the sea-borne commerce of the United States was now more economically carried by the merchant ships of other nations. As there were also no American colonies in 1876 so the needs of security were then regarded as being fully met by a local mobile force consisting of what in truth was a "battle fleet" composed of numerous small but powerful vessels, which would oppose size by greater numbers, a torpedo flotilla, and rams: these last being of a type which, since it had been effectively used by Admiral Tegetthoff at the battle of Lissa, were both then and later highly esteemed by many naval officers in all countries.

The precise type of intended vessels is, however, not the main point, which is, what object did the Secretary seek to attain, and in what manner did his responsible advisers, men who had great experience in war, propose to attain it? The aim was security of coasts, harbours and the indispensable coastal shipping. The solution was a local force of small but powerful vessels of three types, and a sea-going striking force of comparatively light vessels which could go anywhere and were strong enough to deal with the similar light vessels of other Powers.

A little more than ten years later Mahan's first book appeared. Mahan had set himself to study the problems of sea power and had made some deductions which appeared to vitiate the soundness of the existing naval policy. The fundamental need he held to be a merchant navy. The necessity for a fighting navy, in the restricted sense of the word, "springs from the existence of a peaceful shipping and disappears with it, except in the case of a nation which has aggressive tendencies and keeps up a navy merely as a branch of the military establishment." But if a navy was necessary to defend an important merchant shipping, it

could do so only if there were suitable foreign stations for
its use "in those distant parts of the world to which the
armed shipping must follow the peaceful vessels of commerce": the ancient experience of all nations that naval
force can only act where the means of its maintenance—
bases—exist. Such colonies or bases the United States did
not possess. "Having therefore no foreign establishments
either colonial or military, the ships of war of the United
States will be like land birds unable to fly far from their
own shores."[3] How far then, he asked, did the existing conditions of the United States involve serious danger? She
had no oceanic shipping to defend, for all her needs were
furnished by the shipping services of other nations. She
had no colonies to defend. And, being without any possessions over sea from which a fighting navy could give any
protection to shipping, she would not be able to defend it
if, in time, it should revive. Further, her whole national
policy had of recent years been directed systematically towards "internal development, great production, with the
accompanying aim of self-sufficingness, rendering the
United States independent of external supplies": or to
what to-day we should call "economic nationalism." Such
foreign trade as there must be, even in the most self-sufficient state, would be safeguarded by the new rule agreed
upon in 1856, that "the flag covered the goods." Thus her
cargoes, carried in neutral ships, would be moved in complete security in war, except when they consisted of contraband goods or when they were on their way to blockaded
ports: and "paper blockades" could, with safety, be dis-
counted in the future.

[3] *The Influence of Sea Power upon History*, pp. 81–3.

This being the position, what need, Mahan asked, has the United States of sea power? "Her commerce is even now carried by others: why should her people desire that which, if possessed, must be defended at great cost?" His answer was that the need lay in security against blockade of the principal ports, and that security of the ports demanded the existence of a mercantile navy. Even though the neutral ship might move in security carrying the cargoes, she could not enter a blockaded port. Those local squadrons of small vessels of the "monitor" type and torpedo craft could not prevent blockade. Blockade did not require the presence of a strong force, close in shore, where the small battleships, the rams and the torpedo craft could tackle it on equal or better terms. With a force of light seagoing vessels working inshore for the purpose of observation of individual vessels, a fleet could, from that commanding position to seaward, effectively close the port. The blockade of a whole coast, like that conducted during the Civil War, was not necessary to bring economic ruin to the country. He observed with truth a fact that is often lost sight of to-day, when the length of a coast line is made the criterion of naval strength, that the flow of commerce depended upon freedom of entry and departure at the few great routes of sea-borne commerce. It was these few ports that were of importance. If these centres were closed, trade would dry up into insignificant and wholly insufficient quantities. The neutral would not risk breaking blockade except as a blockade runner: and though undoubtedly blockade runners would get through, a nation could not be supported by such precarious and petty transport. Certainly the people would not starve. But they would suffer most grievously from the cessation of commerce—the loss of money, the dislocation of business, the delay of industry, the unemployment—which must inevitably accompany such a situation. Nor was this all. A nation at war needed war material, and, at that time, he doubted whether the United States was capable of producing what it needed. Hence, he wrote, "the enemy must be kept not only out of our ports, but far away from our coasts." The coastal navy of the Secretary's outline in 1876 could not do this. Sea-going ships were needed.

There, then, we reach the reason why, in Mahan's opinion, a merchant navy was necessary. He doubted whether a sea-going navy, on the necessary scale, could be maintained without being "rooted in" a merchant navy. It was needed to furnish the personnel of the fighting fleet which itself was needed to prevent the ports of the country being closed by blockade. Whether a merchant navy should be built up by subsidies or by individual effort he did not attempt to say: that was a question for economists.

The justice of this outline of purely strategical requirements and the criticism of the inadequacy of the "local navy" are too obvious to need any comment. Bigger ships were certainly needed. Whether, however, the reason for his doubts—and they were doubts, rather than positive opinions—as to the possibility that a sea-going navy of such a strength as the security of the country demanded could be built up and maintained in a healthy condition without a merchant navy, were well founded, may be questioned. He argued from the example of the navy of Louis XIV, whose withering away he attributed to the fact of its having no root in a healthy merchant marine. The reason for that withering may, however, be more properly attributed to the higher policy of the king, who, seeking to found the prosperity and glory of France in conquests on land, diverted her wealth and her enterprise from colonies and trade into armies and war. The destinies of the country were placed in the hands of the military profession instead of in those of its enterprising merchants and adventurers. If King Louis's eyes had been turned seaward instead of landward, and if continental conquests had not drained his pockets and brought into birth great coalitions to oppose him, the merchant fleet would have grown, colonies would have been founded and kept, and a fighting navy would have arisen, not because it was "rooted" in a mercantile navy but because it would have been necessary for the protection of the oversea interests in colonies and shipping which the genius of his people, untrammelled by Government or Court, would have created.

Moreover, other nations have produced fighting navies without the existence of mercantile fleets. Neither Turkey nor Japan possessed that "root" for their navies: and a great navy, fully competent to safeguard the ports of the United States from blockade, had already come into being before 1914 without a great ocean-going merchant navy.

In 1912 it was no longer argued that the need for a merchant navy arose from the necessity firmly to establish that sea-going fleet which was needed to preserve the harbours of the United States from blockade and its coastal commerce from interruption. A new conception, composed in part of national dignity and in part of finance, had then arisen. The quantity of American goods carried in foreign bottoms was esteemed to be "humiliating to pride and patriotism and impoverishing to the national pocket."[4] Leaving the great imponderable of sentiment aside, it may be left to economists to determine the question of impoverishment, and to say whether the taxpayer profits more by having his goods delivered to him by the cheapest form of transport or by having to provide subsidies to keep alive a service of transport which could not survive without them.

When, in his later years, Mahan made his exhaustive study of the War of 1812 he recalled another reason for a navy, to which attention had been drawn by the Secretary of the Navy in 1891. A neutral state which possessed no means of taking action was liable to find its interests at sea injured by belligerents' actions. "Our situation as a commercial neutral between these mighty contestants [in a European war] to some of whom our exports of beef and pork and grain and cotton will be a necessity, while to others they will become a main object of attack, is one for which we must make an adequate provision before-hand."[5] Mahan, referring to this aspect of the problem of sea power, related how, in 1794, when such a risk existed, Gouverneur Morris had urged the provision of a navy of twelve or twenty ships of the line, with a due proportion of frigates, to avert such a possibility. Great Britain had then over one hundred ships of the line in commission. "I am tolerably certain," wrote Morris, "that while the United

---

[4] In value 91¼ per cent. of external trade was carried by foreign ships in 1910. *Statistical abstract of the United States*, 1911.

[5] *Report of the Secretary of the Navy*, 1891.

States pursue a just and liberal conduct with twenty sail of the line at sea no nation on earth will dare to insult them." Mahan remarked that while Morris certainly did not imagine twenty ships to be equal to a hundred, he estimated accurately the deterrent force of such a body prepared to act upon an enemy's communications or interests at a great distance from the strategic centre of operations. "A valuable lesson of the War of 1812 is just this, that a comparatively small force, a few frigates and sloops, placed as the United States navy then was, can exercise an influence utterly disproportionate to its own strength." A parallel to this is to be observed in the small British army, which, though it furnished a bare 40,000 men in the Peninsular War, exercised an influence wholly out of proportion to that number; and a very little consideration will show how true that picture is.

In 1886—ten years after the Secretary's report to which reference had been made—the armoured fleet of the United States still consisted of coast defence vessels, larger than those of ten years earlier but still not greater than 6000 tons. The majority were vessels of about 4000 tons. The contemporary battleships in Europe were of from 8000 to 10,000 tons.

In 1890 the need for sea-going ships was recognised. The fleet of coastal vessels, even in larger numbers and even if capable of meeting foreign ironclads in battle, were not able to go where they would be needed. The report of the Secretary of the Navy in 1889 outlined the new policy. "As our purpose is defence not conquest, our navy should be as small as possible, but we should not be left at the

mercy of states having less than one tenth of our population and one thirtieth of our wealth. . . . To meet the attack of ironclads, ironclads are indispensable. *We must have
the force to raise blockades.*" The beginning was therefore
made of a modern fleet of ironclads of 10,000 tons. From
1892 onwards the fleet grew. Fleets in Europe were growing and their growth could not be neglected. And, as those
nations were increasing the size of their ships, so must
those of the United States. But it is essential to note that
this increase in size was not because the battleships of
10,000 tons were too small, *quâ* battleships, but because
they were not powerful enough to meet the larger battleships of other nations. Nor was the increase related in any
way to the distance which ships had to travel from their
bases. The purpose, in fact, of the fleet, the function for
which it existed, was not altered. The security of the ports,
security against blockade, security of the trade were the
objects, and the proper objects, of American sea power.
There was a lack of bases, but these were in process of being acquired round the coasts. The Spanish-American War
gave America oversea bases in the Caribbean and the
Philippines, thereby extending the reach of her sea power
from the coasts into more distant waters. Trade was increasing, and with the facilities which bases abroad provided for the fleet it was practicable to afford a more extended defence: and it was now worth while to possess
cruiser forces, hitherto little needed for security because,
for want of facilities in those more distant seas, they could
not act.

The Great War brought a new element into the problem

of the United States sea power. The questions of blockade, of contraband, and of continuous voyage had been left in an unsatisfactory state by the Declaration of London, and it was not long after hostilities began that the Entente Powers began to suffer from the flow of contraband goods which, pouring into the enemy country by way of neutral entrepôts, furnished him with his means of existence: the same trouble, though not in precisely the same form, as that with which the Northern States had been faced in the Civil War. Into the vexed questions which arose out of the series of British Orders-in-Council from 1914 onwards it is neither necessary nor possible to go. It is enough to say that differences of opinion occurred as to whether the legitimate rights of the neutral Power were being violated. Happily, there existed precedents in the Prize Court decisions of the United States, and the extensions made in the doctrines of continuous voyage, which afforded justification for many of the disputed measures. But the fact that traders were unable to reap to the full the rich profits of the abnormal trade which, in the nature of things, arose, caused a strong wave of sentiment to pass through the country, particularly among folk who had no knowledge of history and sea law, and aroused a feeling that the rights of the neutral could only be safeguarded by a navy far stronger than that which existed. In February, 1916, President Wilson pronounced that the United States required what he described as "incomparably the most adequate navy in the world." The expression is one that it is difficult to interpret, for a navy is either adequate or inadequate according to whether it can fulfil the functions it exists to fulfil. In response, a great programme of construction was adopted in the following August, including ten battleships and six battle cruisers, and although on the entry into the war in the following February this was suspended, it was resumed after the war. In 1920 the object of naval policy was announced to be "the creation of a navy equal to the most powerful maintained by any nation in the world." The difference between this and the requirements of Mahan is obvious.

The question to which this necessarily gives rise is that of adequacy. The strength of the navies of the maritime nations has been determined throughout the ages by the needs of security against the two forms of injury to which a nation is exposed by sea. A navy which can guard the nation against invasion by sea and preserve those sea communications, military and economic, which are essential for its national existence, is adequate. The reasoning of Mahan for a stronger navy than that existing at the time of his writing lay in the fact that that navy was inadequate to avert the danger against which the United States must be secured—the danger of having her major ports blockaded. As the exercise of blockade demands a great superiority of strength, even in the most favourable conditions of the possession of effective bases in the region of the ports or coasts to be blockaded, so it follows that equality is not a condition essential to the prevention of blockade: and it can hardly be a matter of doubt, in the light of long experience, that a very high degree of superiority would be needed for the conduct of a blockade of ports so remote as

those on the seaboard of the United States, from the naval
bases of any maritime Power in the world.

Invasion of territories of such great expanse, with so
large a population, possessing such manufacturing ability
and resources, would be impracticable. The mere matter of
the tonnage needed to transport such an army as would be
needed, even if it were possible to defend it on passage,
would be beyond the resources of the shipping of any
Power, either military or maritime. But it is not to be
imagined that these elementary facts have not been recognised, or that it was for the purposes of the defence of the
country against either of these afflictions that a navy equal
to that of the strongest naval Power was considered necessary. What was felt was that no less a navy than one equal
to that of a belligerent who might abuse the nation's rights
and interests could procure respect for them.

So far as the use of armed force is concerned, this is an
assumption which cannot be maintained. The occasions on
which the legitimate rights of a neutral are liable to suffer
occur when the control of the sea is in dispute between the
navies of belligerents. It is incorrect to suppose that intervention in defence of a nation's rights is impossible except
with a navy equal to that of the stronger.[6] It is sufficient if
the scale should be turned and superiority changed into
inferiority. It needs but little consideration of the late war
to realise how even a comparatively small naval force
would have turned the scales in favour of the Central
Powers and rendered the submarine and cruiser campaigns

[6] *Vide ante*, p. 169, and Mahan's reference to the War of 1812.

of the Central Powers not merely successful but decisive. Tirpitz himself said: "One single ally at sea would have sufficed in the Great War to enable us to fight with the most favourable prospects for the freedom of the seas." [7]

Neither is it correct to assume that armed force is the sole weapon which, in modern conditions, a neutral has at its disposal. The withholding of essential supplies or serv- ices, or the breaking of trading relations, are most power- ful means of coercion; for a nation at war requires a vast supply of raw materials which are not produced within its own borders. No greater mistake could be made than to imagine that the lesser European Powers were impotent because they possessed no naval forces. For all their supe- riority at sea the Entente Powers could not compel the Scandinavian Powers or the Dutch to cease their traffic with the Central Powers. Hardly any greater blow could have been inflicted upon the armies and navies of the En- tente than the withholding of the supplies of liquid fuel without which the movements of their fleets, their land transport, their tanks and their aeroplanes would have been crippled, if not wholly arrested. When shortage of shipping rendered it necessary to draw food from the nearer sources of production in order to economise ton- nage, the United States was an important source of sugar, bacon, cheese, butter, cereals, as she was of many mate- rials of military equipment—hides, leather and munitions. It needs no more than a slight exercise of the imagination, or an examination of how the problems of supply were solved, to realise that powers of compulsion fully as effec-

[7] *My Memoirs*, vol. I, p. 92.

tive as, and in the end less costly than, those of armed force lay in the hands of those neutral states who could deny those indispensable supplies to the Allies. The failure, in an earlier war, of Jefferson's embargo affords no precedent, for conditions were wholly different when the country was not a source of indispensable supplies.

Nevertheless it was for the purpose of the maintenance of the right to conduct trading operations which, by devious routes and processes, finally reached and aided the Central Powers to continue their resistance, that the doctrine of the necessity of naval equality was propounded.

The establishment of the League of Nations did nothing to mitigate the costly burden. At the time at which it was anticipated that the United States would be a Member of the League, the needs of equality with the strongest Power were reasserted. "The League of Nations must be strong enough to restrain, if necessary, its strongest member. No international navy made up of ships of heterogeneous types whose discipline would differ in language and command, could hope to cope with the British fleet. There must exist in such an international force a single unit which, with the assistance of the forces of the League, would be able to enforce the mandates of the League against any Power. The United States has satisfied its aims and may be relied upon to support loyally the League of Nations. . . . "[8] This argument President Wilson considered "logical and reasonable," in forgetfulness, possibly, of various occasions in the world's history when the navies

[8] "Memorandum prepared by the Naval Advisers in Paris," *New York World*, March 21st, 1919.

of more nations than one have combined effectively, both strategically and tactically, against a single navy. Failures there have been: but the failures have arisen from divergencies of political aim and from errors in the political direction of strategy; not from differences in discipline, in language or in command.

Apart, however, from the fact that effective combination is practicable, there remains the highly important fact that if such a combination of nations were to be formed against a great maritime Power, the economic effects of the total cessation of all commerce—the complete economic boycott which would result—would be decisive: for the fact of being a maritime nation implies a dependence upon, and necessity for, oversea commerce.

The United States decided, however, not to join the League. Two reasons were then asserted for the need for naval strength equal to that of the strongest Power. The ocean-going traffic in 1926, foreign and coastline, of the United States was valued at $14,000 millions, or approximately as much as that of the British Empire, which was calculated at $15,000 millions. If Great Britain had her "food-lines" at sea, without the use of which she would starve, the United States had hers. "Although our actual food-lines are land-lines they are long and must be served by proper and uninterrupted means of transportation ... manganese is essential for the manufacture of steel. We have a wholly inadequate supply of manganese ore, and such as there is is of comparatively poor quality. If we cannot make steel, or our ability to make steel is seriously curtailed, our whole railroad transportation would become so crippled in a short time as to be unable to keep up with the necessities of transportation. Our whole motor transportation system depends on an adequate supply of rubber. All our rubber comes to us from over seas."[9] Among other necessities mentioned were tin, tungsten, nickel, coffee and sugar.

Besides the foreign trade there is a coastwise service which performs indispensable services for the distribution of goods, in particular oil, lumber and coal, and its protection demands a number of cruisers. The calculation of this number was made in the same manner as British calculations of cruiser numbers had been made before the Treaty of London: that is to say, by the number of points at which cruising vessels would be needed to be stationed—the "focal points" of the coastal routes, and the number of convoys which would be required to be kept in operation to maintain the distributive service.[10] The cruiser forces needed for the service of the main fleet had to be added to this, and therefrom the total cruiser force needed could be estimated. This very correct method of calculation is applicable to the cruiser strengths of all nations, Great Britain included. In place, however, of this correct solution of the quantitative problems of cruiser strength, a standard of relative strength in cruisers was adopted. There can be very few people who entertain any fear that the United States could be invaded. Mr. Hoover, it is true, expressed the desire in 1928 that the navy and the army should be of

[9] Statement of Admiral Hilary Jones, U. S. N., on Trade Routes.
[10] Statement of Admiral C. Hughes, U. S. N., *Congressional Report*, No. 834, of March 3rd, 1928.

such a strength as to have complete defence against "even the fear" of invasion,[11] but one also who had given more thought to naval problems, Mr. Roosevelt, had dismissed the possibility in 1919, even if there were no navy: and since then the development of aerial flotillas has rendered security doubly secure.

Thus we reach what would appear to be the object of American sea power—the preservation of vital external sea communications. This demands a "battle fleet" strong enough to ensure against blockade and therefore, *per se*, strong enough to prevent any bombardments except those of a runaway character such as those made on the English coast in 1914 and 1915, against which no naval force can ensure immunity: and a cruiser force sufficient to provide the escorts of the necessary convoys and defence of the focal points. The principle to which the calculated strength gives recognition is one that has always hitherto been familiar to British statesmen and seamen, namely, that the number of cruisers needed is neither proportional to the number of battleships nor to the cruiser forces of other nations. Admiral Hughes explained this to Congress, and it was upon precisely such a calculation as that put before Congress by Admiral Hughes that the strength of the cruiser forces of Britain had always been determined. Mr. Balfour expressed it at Washington in the first of the many Conferences.

Three fundamental errors have informed more recent discussions of what is called the "cruiser" problem. One is the idea that the cruiser strengths are relative. A second,

[11] Speech at Elizabethton, Tennessee, October, 1928.

that cruisers must be of the dimensions of those of to-day. A third, that great size can take the place of oversea bases. It may further be observed that vessels employed at focal points would be operating at those great distances from a base which are supposed to necessitate great size. The "cruiser problem" caused a most unfortunate friction. That friction need never have occurred if the old well-known principle mentioned by Admiral Hughes had been adhered to: that the number of cruisers depends upon the number of positions in which they are required, and is not relative directly to the number of those of other nations; and if wholly incorrect ideas as to the need of size, whether for overcoming merchantmen or for making long ocean passages, had not taken hold of men's minds.

There is, however, another important element in the problem of American sea power. For at least forty years American opinion has been particularly sensitive to all that happens in the East Asian Seas. After the Russian War, Japan outlined a naval programme which would eventually give her a fleet of sixteen battleships, but this was not actually adopted until 1920, though increases were made between 1914 and 1916. How far the adoption of the full Japanese programme was the result of the declaration of the American policy to create "a navy equal to the most powerful maintained by any other nation in the world" cannot be said with any certitude, for that programme antedated the American declaration. But there would seem to be little doubt that the Japanese programme caused anxiety in America, for its fulfilment, in the then strength of the American fleet, would place American interests in

China and the Philippine Islands at the mercy of Japan. There would, however, appear to be a possibility that the decision to grant independence to the Philippines may cause a reconsideration of the question of whether the very great size of the ship, which has been so strongly insisted upon in consequence of the long distance which American fleets have to cross, may still be considered necessary: and, on the other side, Japan may well be expected to consider whether her security is not assured with the quantitative proportions established at Washington, in view of the great advantages which her geographical situation confers upon her. The sea power of neither nation would be adversely affected by a general reduction in size, and the benefits of this measure would extend to Europe.

Some eighty years ago Bastiat remarked upon the difference between the bad and the good economist. The former, he remarked, took account of the visible effects of measures: the latter brought also into his consideration that which it is necessary to foresee. Among the things which have to be foreseen is the future of European navies. One of the great problems of the day is that of what goes by the name of German equality of status: in other words, the claim that a nation shall not permanently be forbidden to possess weapons of the same kind as other nations. Whether that equality is conceded, or taken at some future time, will it be to the advantage of the world as a whole if, when it comes, a new element of discord is thrown into the European arena by the construction of a new fleet of ships of the greatest size? Inevitably France must feel herself obliged to possess similar ships, and in numbers sufficient to render herself secure. In turn Italy must do the same; and once more this must react upon Great Britain, and, in its turn, upon America and Japan. Much, therefore, hangs upon the decisions which will be made on this qualitative question: for it, in its turn, will produce most far-reaching consequences upon the quantitative problem. Reference will be made later to one of the effects in relation to the problem of the sea power of France.

Turning to Germany, what were the national necessities which made it essential, in the eyes of her statesmen, for her to create not merely a naval force, but a navy on the scale of that which she developed in the years between 1894 and 1914? A navy, as Mahan had remarked, may be the expression either of the defensive idea of protecting some existing interests at sea, or of the expansionist idea of extending either interest, territory or power. If a nation has a great oversea trade, and depends for its existence upon that trade, it needs a large measure of naval force. If that trade sails in many seas, protection by naval force can be given only if there are natural harbours, capable of defence, for the use of the ships in all those seas. Finally, if a nation has expanded into colonies, naval force is needed to maintain the communications with those colonies. Small scattered communities necessarily depend for their security upon the roads, which unite them to each other or to a central community, being safe for the passage of reinforcements or the movements of their merchandise.

At the time when the first stirrings of a desire for an expansion of her existing naval strength made themselves felt in Germany, she had neither colonies nor oversea commerce. The German—or to be more correct, the Prussian—navy in its earliest stages was, for all practical purposes, a branch of the army, administered by a small department of the War Ministry. The services which it existed to perform were those of coastal defence, which were necessarily closely related to military operations. The people of Central Europe had for long formed a powerful state, and their power had rested in their strength on land. The Empire of the Hapsburgs had not merely existed through many struggles without sea power: it had been one of the Great Powers of the world. It was secure, and such changes as had taken place in its constitutional divisions had been, almost without exception, due to internal influences and in no case had been caused or affected by weakness at sea. The old "empire" had, in fact, experienced no need, at any time, of sea power for its security, beyond such local forces as particular local needs demanded.

The creation of the new Empire of 1870–1 brought with it a new outlook. General Von Stosch, the head of the naval department from 1871 to 1883, had more ambitious conceptions than those of mere security. According to Admiral Von Tirpitz he "started from the idea of developing Germany's maritime interests and strengthening and protecting 'Germanism' and German labour throughout the world."[12] Under his successor, Count Von Caprivi, the navy was developed with a view to the existing political situation with Russia and France combined as probable enemies, and "a gradual advance was made from mere coastal defence to the demand for a High Sea Fleet." But

[12]Von Tirpitz, *My Memoirs*, vol. 1, p. 14.

still there was no question of creating sea power beyond what would be required for the military operations of a war on two fronts.

Under Tirpitz, the idea of German sea power took the shape which led eventually to the vast development, the results of which were so profoundly to affect the course of the world in the twenty years between 1894 and 1914. Germany's trade and shipping had developed with great strides, and, in the eyes of the rulers of Germany, a navy to protect it had become a "political" necessity. The navy, Tirpitz remarks, "never seemed to me to be an end in itself but always *a function of those maritime interests*. Without sea power Germany's position in the world resembled a mollusc without a shell. The flag had to follow trade."[13] Sea power was regarded no less as a necessary part of Germany's political equipment. "Only the fleet which represented alliance-value to other Great Powers, in other words a competent battle fleet, could put into the hands of our diplomats the tool which, if used to good purpose, could supplement our power on land." Power on land in fact, adequate as it had always proved to safeguard the interests and maintain the security of the Germanic peoples, was not sufficient for the new policy of acquisition and expansion.

Sea power was therefore deemed necessary for the political strength which it would confer on the country, for the military strength in an European war against the Dual Alliance, and for the protection of trade. But sea power, in its full sense, was not to be obtained without oversea pos-

[13] *Ibid.* vol. I, pp. 58–9.

sessions. Bismarck, it would appear, had recognised this as early as 1865 when he said to the Danish minister that Prussia could never become a great maritime Power without colonies, and that though German statesmen coveted Holland, it was less for its own sake than for its colonies.[14] Moreover, trade could not be protected without bases. "It was a matter of the highest interest for us to have not only Denmark in our hands but also Holland and her colonies if it was for nothing more than the urgent need of coaling stations."[15] Thus the political aim included the absorption of Denmark and the Low Countries and their colonies. With the positions oversea thus acquired, and with a navy, German sea power would, added to her great land power, give her a commanding influence in the world.

It was realised that the annexation of the smaller Powers could not be effected without a great war, and must await favourable occasion for its fulfilment. But when, at a later date, opportunity offered itself for acquiring a naval base in China, Tsing Tao was obtained.

In accordance with this far-reaching political aim, an Act for the enlargement of the fleet, which provided a Seven Years' programme of construction, was passed in 1898, and this was followed two years later by one yet more extensive. The "security of Germany's economical development and more especially of its foreign trade throughout the world" was described as a "vital question." A naval war, even of one year's duration, would annihilate Germany's sea trade and bring about calamitous condi-

[14] Lord Morley, *Life of Gladstone*, vol. II, p. 320.
[15] Von Bülow, *Memoirs*, vol. II, chap. VII: Von Schoen to Von Bülow.

tions both economically and socially. "The object of the navy in a war against a superior naval Power, was to render blockade difficult." But it was realised that the protection of shipping throughout the world would not be practicable. "Under the existing circumstances, in order to protect Germany's sea trade and colonies there is one means only, namely Germany must have a fleet of such strength that, even for the mightiest Naval Power a war with her would involve such risks as would jeopardise her own supremacy." Thus the security of the colonies and the trade was to lie not in the direct protection of the lines of communication but in the threat which a concentrated fleet would offer.

Deterrents, as has been remarked earlier, are not to be disregarded as factors in the preservation of peace: but some grave misinterpretation both of the policy of Great Britain and the psychology of its people informed the view that such a threat would influence the conduct of a country which, for two hundred years, had been peculiarly sensitive to the danger to which it would be exposed if the Continent came under the domination of a single Power. No greater mistake could have been made than that of imagining that, however great the risk to which England would be exposed at sea if she should become involved in a continental struggle, she would be deterred from action by that risk: for by sitting aside she would be exposed to the far greater risk of the total loss of her security when Europe should be under the hegemony of one Power.

What then was the character of the aim of German sea power? It was the expression of a national policy of expansion, not the outcome of the need for the security of Germany's existing territories and interests. The naval Department, by which from Stosch to Tirpitz the increase in the fleet was fostered, was taking upon itself a part in the framing of national policy. The fleet was the instrument of that policy. Was the function of the fleet the security of the coasts of Germany, its commerce and its lightly populated colonies? The reply is given by Tirpitz, its great begetter. "It was in my view our fleet's mission *to react fruitfully upon the narrow horizon of many Germans at home by means of its experiences abroad.* In conjunction with Germans abroad, who were to be bound more closely to the home country, the fleet was to deepen the understanding for our national existence, which in consequence of the increasing population and industry was no longer confined between the Rhine and the Vistula but had to sink its roots more and more in activities overseas."

The question of whether expansion was a national necessity, whether for economic or other reasons, is one for others than seamen to discuss. The fundamental essence of the problem of German sea power is the object for which that sea power was created. Was it the security of the existing Germany, or was it the building up of a greater Germany?—an object which, admittedly, may be claimed as coming within the meaning of the word "security": security for the future of the German race. That "greater Germany" could only be obtained at the expense of other nations, and the strength of the navy was based upon the needs of the situation which this policy of expansion would create. It exceeded the strength necessary for the security of the existing Germany: and, if the growth of the fleet gave rise to apprehensions abroad, that is the inevitable result of producing armaments which appear to other nations to exceed the existing needs of national security against the two dangers to which nations are exposed from the sea—invasion and isolation. Invasion by sea was an impossibility: but isolation? The answer lies in the fact that with her merchant fleet laid up in her own and neutral harbours, with her direct communications by sea interrupted, she was able to sustain the resulting siege for four and a quarter years against a maritime coalition which rose from three nations in August, 1914, to five in February, 1917. It is incorrect to speak of the indispensability of sea power to a nation so little dependent upon it as this prodigious power of resistance demonstrated Germany to be.

Japanese sea power, in its initial expression, arose from the necessity for security. The unrelenting expansion of Russia into Eastern Asia threatened Japan. She saw the prospect of Korea becoming a Russian province. As England for over two centuries had consistently regarded the occupation of the Low Countries by a powerful naval and military state as a threat to her own security, so in a similar way Japan regarded the occupation of Korea by Russia. As Antwerp would be a pistol pointed at the heart of England, so the southern Korean harbours, separated from Japan by no more than the width of the Korean Straits, would be a similar constant danger to Japan. She must render herself secure against the twin menaces of invasion and interruption of some of her most important lines of external communication. Whether she proposed to oppose the advance by military action, or to acquiesce in the establishment of a Russian Korea, a navy capable of meeting the navy of Russia was essential to her security. Hence a new navy arose in the East under the threat of danger from the expansionist policy of a military neighbour. When, as the result of the successful struggle with Russia, Korea passed into the hands of Japan, that danger was removed: but it remained necessary that she should be sure of communications across the sea with her new oversea province. Trade developed and military responsibilities for the preservation of order were incurred.

The strength of the naval forces needed for the security of those communications in the waters in which they lay is not to be measured merely by the strength of those other Powers. An important element is geographical position and military strength. In the geographical position of Japan, separated from other maritime Powers by some of the widest stretches of ocean in the world, a physical blockade of the country would be impossible even if her naval force were a fraction of that of any of them. Blockade is impossible without a great superiority.[16] Invasion in the face of the great and efficient army is an impossibility. There cannot be any question that Japan would be secure against those two principal injuries with a massed strength of far less than that of any possible opponent. Cruiser strength, on the other hand, is not a question of proportion except in that part which performs the auxiliary services for the

---

[16] The "Three Admirals Report" of 1888 expressed the view that, with a base close at hand, the minimum superiority needed for a blockade of an enemy was four to three.

massed fleet. It is dependent, as has been said earlier, upon the number of positions in which defence is needed and in which defence is practicable owing to the possession of bases. The solution of the "cruiser problem" of Japan should not lie in establishing some higher, or lower, proportion of cruisers, but, as in the case of other nations, in reducing the size of the cruiser to those dimensions which had always been recognised as sufficient in the past, and in leaving each country to decide the number she needs. The re-adoption of the old principle of making the instrument adequate to its purpose would serve the interests of both economy and of good feeling.

The sea power of France has always had a strictly objective purpose. There was a time, when the introduction of the ironclad ship rendered the existing wooden ships obsolete, when it appeared to British eyes that France, starting from a new beginning, intended to take the opportunity to furnish herself with a navy equal to that of England. Certainly there were fears in England that this was the object of Napoleon III and British ministers were convinced that the Emperor aimed at conquest and aggrandisement. Louis Napoleon sought to dispel this deeply-rooted apprehension. He complained to Lord Malmesbury in 1861 that the suspicions were unfounded. "Let each build what he considers the right number. You ought to have twice as many as I, as they are your principal protection."[17] The basis of French naval requirements was well stated in November, 1860, by Admiral Jurien de la Gravière, a most distinguished officer and writer, who, writing to a friend in

[17] Baxter, *Introduction of the Ironclad Ship*, pp. 321–2.

the British navy, pointed out that France and England
had no reasons for war and would be wise enough to live in
peace, but "the great subject of disagreement is the increase which each nation is making in her navy. *You* wish
to be incontestably masters at sea, and to fear neither us
nor any maritime coalition. We do not object to this pre-
tension up to a certain point. We should not wish, however, that your security should be such, that you should
imagine yourselves able to treat us in any way you like." [18]

The justice of this wish is undeniable. The difficulty lay
in translating it in quantitative terms of strength. For the
fleet which appeared necessary for Great Britain purely for
the purposes of security against the two perils of invasion
and destruction of her vital commerce—of which the former at that time loomed most threateningly—appeared to
French eyes to be sufficient to enable Britain to dictate her
will to France by the destruction of her trade or the capture of her oversea possessions. In other words, the fear
was that British security would spell French insecurity.
Since the time when this was written two things have happened which should be of use to indicate the way out of the
apparent dilemma. The history of some of the wars of the
past has been written more exhaustively, the economic
effects of sea action have been studied, the extent to which
it has exercised an influence has been more fully analysed.
We know better how far Britain, when she was strong
enough at sea to defend her trade and territories, was able
to "treat France in any way she liked." What we can
plainly see now is that, even with a navy twice the strength

[18] *Ibid.* p. 149.

of that of France, a navy whose powers had not been blunted by the Declaration of Paris of 1856, and still further shackled by the Declaration of London, England never considered that she could take liberties, and still less adopt a dictatorial tone, in her dealings with her great neighbour. British statesmen were never under the delusion that it lay in the power of Britain to produce a measure of pressure by any of the means which sea power conferred, which could prove decisive. And they were no less well aware that, however strong the navy might be, war could not be indulged in without heavy losses to her own commerce. What occurred in every single-handed struggle between the two countries—and it is worth noting how few "duels" between England and France there have been in the last two centuries—was that, while French trade was stopped, English trade sailed but was injured. England's superiority at sea enabled her to inflict greater damage to French sea-borne commerce than she herself suffered. The reason French trade could not sail was not that French harbours were placed under blockade, but because French fighting forces were kept under observation by superior forces and could not give protection to their shipping, which, unprotected, had perforce to remain in harbour. British trade suffered from the twin effects of the direct losses from capture by squadrons, single ships and privateers, and of the indirect losses resulting from the convoy system which was rendered necessary by that cruising warfare. No greater mistake could be made than to suppose that the Britain of the eighteenth century deemed herself so safe at sea that she could flout France.

British statesmen remembered only too well the injury which the corsairs had inflicted on British commerce in the wars of Louis XIV lightly to expose that commerce to a similar rough handling. Burke, in 1769, recalled the fears that had always arisen. "At the beginning of that war,[19] *as in the commencement of every war*, traders were struck with a sort of panic. Many went out of the freighting business. But by degrees, as the war went on the danger came to be better appreciated." Commerce revived when the navy had given evidence of its power and it became possible to conduct trade safely in large fleets under regular convoy. But there was no light-hearted confidence, no assumption that Britain, however great her superiority at sea, could treat France in any way she liked. For she could not expect to escape serious damage to her own all-important interests at sea.

This experience was repeated in the War of 1914–18. It was fully recognised that, while it would be possible to cause German shipping to lie up, the stoppage of that shipping, injurious though it would be, could never be a decisive blow to that great country with its prodigious resources and its power to draw uninterrupted supplies from its neighbours. When war became imminent the same anxiety that had been felt in earlier days, according to Burke, was again expressed in the City of London. Nonintervention was urged, and shipping companies proposed to order their vessels to the nearest neutral port and to remain in harbour, in consequence of the fear of capture. In fact, notwithstanding her superiority at sea, a superiority

[19] *I.e.*, the Seven Years' War, of 1756–63.

which proved sufficient for her security, British ministers never imagined that this gave them power to treat Germany in any way they liked. They had to take account of Britain's vulnerability. Admiral Jurien de la Gravière's friendly letter was in fact based upon the assumption that British security could be attained only at the cost of French insecurity. That assumption would only have been correct if both nations had been equally dependent upon the sea for their national existence. Both must suffer if they fought, but while loss of the use of the sea to one means inconvenience—serious inconvenience indeed—it does not mean surrender. To the other it means unconditional surrender.

The almost universal spread of a desire for sea power, with a consequent growth of navies throughout the world, has been largely the result of the words "the influence of sea power." Sea power has indeed exercised influence, but sufficient consideration has not been given to the conditions in which it has been able to do so. It has its limitations, and it is in a clearer recognition of these limitations of sea power, standing by itself, that the solution of many of the difficulties of the quantitative problem of naval armaments is to be found. The influence which sea power can exercise arises from the economic pressure which it can bring to bear, and that pressure only becomes effective on those occasions in which the Sea Power is allied to Land Powers, when some or all land frontiers are closed, and when great armies cause great expenditure which can be supported only by commerce. These occasions arise only when the world is confronted with a would-be dictator who seeks to establish a hegemony in some part of the world.

To return to the situation in the time of Napoleon III. The question of establishing a fixed relative strength between the navies of England and France was considered. A proposal was actually made at that time by the Secretary of the Admiralty, Lord Clarence Paget, for limiting the French and British navies in such a way as to assure the British superiority, the need for which Napoleon had admitted and Admiral Jurien de la Gravière accepted, and to effect large economies for both nations. It was rejected by Palmerston, for the reasons that British naval force must be regulated by that of other Powers as well as that of France, that if such an agreement were made there would have to be "a perpetual inquisitorial watch kept up by each Power over the dockyards and navy of the other, in order to see that the agreement was not broken through, and this would lead to frequent bickerings, besides being intolerable to national self-respect."[20] To-day, looking backwards with the knowledge that comes after the event, we may be inclined to agree with Admiral Sir Charles Napier—himself an officer who cherished no delusions as to the need for British superiority at sea—who wondered that the British Government had not then come to an understanding with Napoleon III to limit naval competition.

During the War of 1870–1 French shipbuilding was partially suspended. When construction was resumed, the broad principle governing the French policy regarding her

[20] Baxter, *op. cit.* p. 323.

sea power was to obtain security for her coasts and ports, and to possess power to strike effectively against the sea-borne trade. Security was to be attained by an ironclad fleet and a torpedo flotilla, though there was an influential school of thought which was convinced that the developments in the torpedo and in torpedo-craft had rung the knell of the great ship. Although this conclusion was never formally accepted it affected the constitution of the fleet, and led to that considerable expansion in the French flotillas which resulted in the production of the British antidote in the successive forms of torpedo hunters, gunboats, and finally the "destroyer." As a French writer of the day observed, a new and costly element in sea warfare had come into existence, though those quantitative effects which we can observe to-day could not then be foreseen.

To conduct an offensive against enemy trade, on the oceanic routes, the qualities considered necessary in the vessels employed were, as has been indicated earlier, superior speed, power and endurance: in other words, the ships should be more powerful than those normally employed in defence, with speed sufficient to enable them to evade superior strength, and endurance which would render them capable of making the extended voyages which commerce destroying would demand. In accordance with this theory of trade attack by a few very powerful ships, operating without support, ranging over wide expanses, the "armoured cruiser" came into existence, a vessel of over 6000 tons,[21] completely outclassing the contemporary unarmoured British vessels of from 2800 to 3400 tons then de-

[21] *Dupuy-de-Lôme*, 6297 tons.

signed for the defence of the trade routes. The effect was
that Great Britain proceeded to produce cruisers of over
7000 tons. Before long, the French unarmoured cruiser
reached 8000 tons[22] and the armoured cruiser over 11,000.[23]
Although all the qualities of endurance and speed could,
according to the Committee on the French estimates of
1888, be obtained on a displacement of about 4000 tons,
under the influence of the desire for individual material
superiority this size was more than tripled.

It is, however, the quantitative aspect of policy that
concerns us at this point. Competition dictated the size
of the cruiser. What dictated the size of the navy? Was
France, in those years of what is called "the race in armaments," aiming at security or expansion? The answer
seems to admit of no doubt—security. The provision of a
means of offence is by no means incompatible with the aim
of security. She required to be secure against blockade, to
preserve communication with her colonies. A high proportion of her trade moved by sea,[24] and, if she could not expect to maintain this in a war with Great Britain, it was
not Great Britain alone that she had to consider among
her possible adversaries. But neither in the ships of the line
of battle nor in the oceanic cruising vessels has there been
any marked quantitative increase. Such increase, however,
there has been in the flotilla. The exploits of the German
submarines in the war showed the power of this new type

[22] *Château Renault*, 8018 tons.
[23] *Jeanne d'Arc*, 11,270 tons.
[24] In 1883, *Imports*: by land, 34 per cent., by sea, 65 per cent.; *Exports*: by
land, 31 per cent., by sea, 68 per cent. *The Naval Annual*, 1887.

of craft, and what great expenditure of effort was necessary on the part of the Entente Powers to preserve the lines of sea communications which were vital to their success. So a great submarine flotilla has been brought into existence, and, together with it, a very considerable surface flotilla, comprising vessels whose dimensions exceed those which three of the signatories of the Washington Conference agreed to take as a limit. This increase in the flotilla is thus both quantitative and qualitative, and it is accompanied by a great rise in actual, or strategic, power owing to the greater capacities of endurance and speed of the vessels of which it is composed. The questions to which it gives rise are—would the security of France be imperilled without these numerous flotillas? Would she be exposed to danger of invasion by sea, to the interruption of the military line of communication between France in Europe and France in Africa without such numerous forces? Or would she be exposed to the danger of a vital interruption in her sea-borne commerce? These are questions upon which much must depend. The increase in the power of the modern flotilla is one of the most significant elements in the problem of sea power in the future, and some may well be thinking that in narrow seas and waters the flotilla is the fleet of the future.

In asking the preceding questions one must, however, try to understand another point of view which has been expressed by a most able and fair-minded French flag officer, Admiral Castex.[25] The flotilla is the instrument of

[25] *Théories Stratégiques*, vol. IV, pp. 118 *et seq.*; also in the *Journal of the Royal United Service Institution*, 1933.

that minor offensive against sea communications which, though it may not be decisive, may make an important contribution to a decision by forcing dispersion upon a superior opponent—an element in the *guerre-de-course* to which Admiral Jurien de la Gravière had drawn attention nearly a century ago. And it has another aspect. Though material results may not be great, moral effects will be appreciable. Honour will be preserved and courage revived, and, in future, prestige and respect acquired whose results may be of considerable importance. Here we find ourselves in the realm of the imponderables which neither statesman nor strategist can afford to disregard or to treat lightly. The more sympathetically these are considered, the less difficult will it be to arrive at conclusions on the purely concrete lines of strategical policy.

The great quantitative increase in the French flotillas has, however, another aspect. The Washington Conference had determined that the size of the "capital" ship should be 35,000 tons, and that the tonnage which France should possess was to be 175,000 tons. This would give her five capital ships only. That number was, in the opinion of the French authorities, insufficient for the security of her communications with her oversea possessions, for which no less than ten were considered necessary. Inasmuch, however, as the British quota of capital ships had been fixed at fifteen, this could not possibly be acceptable to Great Britain, whose position would be insecure with such proportional strength. The dilemma which was produced was therefore either that Great Britain must increase her quota to at least twenty of these great and costly vessels, or

France must have a number insufficient for her needs, and be exposed to all the disadvantages which arise from "too many eggs in one basket": for the disablement or loss of one ship would reduce her force by one-fifth. No one need be surprised either at the refusal of France to be furnished with a battle fleet so constituted, so inflexible, and so liable to find itself reduced by the accidents inseparable from warfare at sea, or at the refusal of Britain to agree to propositions which would place her at the mercy of France, or to face the prospect of the greater burden of adding five more of these costly vessels to her fleet. Nor is it a matter of wonder that, finding herself denied the possibility of possessing an effective battle fleet, such as she had always possessed in the past, France should turn her eyes definitely to the flotilla as her means of security.

Yet the problem was not insoluble. In the opinion of the writer the true solution lay in a return to a smaller type of ship. It has been shown, beyond the possibilities of doubt, that the size which ships had reached had not been due to the intrinsic needs of warfare but to the extrinsic effects of competition: and the more recent proposals of the British for a reduction of over one-third in the size corroborates this. If, instead of fixing so high and so unnecessary a figure on the capital ship, a far lower figure had been adopted, there would have been no reason why quantitative proportions acceptable to both Britain and France in their battle fleets should not have been arranged, with a considerable reduction in the burden of all naval armaments: and, at the same time France, in possession of a battle fleet suitable to her needs, would possibly and even probably not have felt it necessary to make those great extensions in her flotilla which she has made in compensation for her lack of a battle fleet.

Turning to Italy, we find a navy of comparatively recent date. It had its great predecessors in the navies of Venice, Genoa, Tuscany, Naples and Sardinia, and the maritime tradition goes back to Rome, but the Italian navy of to-day only came into being after the unification of the country in the second half of the nineteenth century. The young United Italy was quick to recognise its need at sea. Its coasts were exposed to injury, its merchant shipping to attack, and an invader by land would derive a great advantage if he could use the sea for his army's communications. The many struggles of the eighteenth century had shown how important a factor the command of the sea routes had been at the heads of the Gulf of Lyons and of the Adriatic. The sea could not be the main line of invasion, for the forces which would be needed for conquest would greatly exceed what would be transported by sea if the landing had to be made in enemy territory or territory in enemy possession; but the use of the coastal routes for the conveyance of the stores and supplies would confer a great advantage upon an invading force: the advantage, for example, to which Wellington said he owed so much in the Peninsular War, and which was denied by the British fleet to those French, Spanish and Austrian armies who desired to move across the head either of the Gulf of Lyons or of the Adriatic. The security of those routes then depended upon the enemy's main fleet being confined to port by superior force, and his transports being prevented from moving by the lesser cruising vessels and the flotilla. To-day, that flotilla acts also in the air, and an effective air flo-tilla can play much of the part which was played by the surface flotillas in the past. But it is not only the coastal routes, moving within the range of air flotillas, that might be of importance. Forces in a main theatre may be weak-ened if an enemy is able to create diversions elsewhere, and the command of the sea has often afforded the means of so doing.

The Italian Delegation to the Conference in London in 1930 outlined in general terms the view taken as to Italy's needs, and the reason for them. "Italy's geographical situ-ation is peculiarly unfavourable. She has not the advan-tage of an ocean frontier: she is dependent for her very existence on supplies three-quarters of which are conveyed from overseas along vulnerable trade routes dominated at short distance by naval bases of various Powers. More-over, Italy possesses no extra-Mediterranean naval bases, a fact which renders the task of protecting her merchant shipping on the high seas particularly arduous."

These assertions are indisputable. Italy is very far from being self-supporting. She lacks many of the most impor-tant raw materials of industry: she does not produce all the food her population needs. These must reach her by sea, either directly through her own ports or, as they reached Germany, indirectly through the ports of neutral neigh-bours: but, if those neighbours should themselves be the enemies, that route would be closed.

As we have seen, there are three methods by which sup-plies coming by sea can be prevented by sea power from reaching a country—blockade, capture at sea, and the application of the doctrine of contraband. To what extent does it appear that Italy needs sea power to secure herself against isolation brought about by any of those measures?

It has already been observed that blockade, in the extended sense of a complete closing of all the ports through which a country's foreign commerce passes, demands a superiority at sea, even under the most favourable geographical conditions of the possession of bases in close proximity to the regions or places it is intended to blockade. Close proximity to the objective in Italy's situation implies also close proximity to air flotillas. The intending blockader would require to be able to maintain cruising forces in the area of approach superior to any with which Italy might at any moment make a sally, not merely from the blockaded port but from other ports in other regions: as Cornwallis, when blockading Brest, had to be secured against his fleet finding the squadrons from Rochefort, Cadiz and Toulon falling upon his back. The only form of cruising vessel which can be kept cruising under the conditions of to-day is the vessel of the flotilla type—the vessel small enough to feel no fears of the submarine and little fears of air craft; for immunity from injury from torpedo, bomb and mine will never be produced by increase in the size of ships. This blockading flotilla force, like all blockading forces that ever have existed, can only be maintained in position in sufficient strength, by a number of vessels greatly exceeding the forces at the disposal of the blockaded.

The task of a blockader, even of one only of the groups

of the Italian ports, would demand a very great superiority. It is not too much to say that it would not be practicable unless or until two things should have been successfully accomplished. A marked superiority must have been acquired over the surface flotilla in the immediate vicinity; and those forces composed of greater vessels and, possibly, of flotilla craft in addition, which could fall upon a blockading flotilla from other ports not within the effective range of air flotillas, must be put out of action: as the superior British forces, for instance, fell upon the scattered German light forces in the Heligoland Bight, or the *Goeben* upon the *Raglan*.

Long experience of sea warfare has shown the difficulty of forcing action upon an enemy. If it suits him to maintain a watching attitude from behind his defences, there he will remain, ready to seize any favourable opportunity which may occur or be created, unless the national situation is rendered intolerable: but the dilemma which arises is that the situation can very rarely be rendered intolerable. We do indeed occasionally hear it lightly said that blockade, by imposing great hardships upon a people, is a means of forcing an inferior fleet to sea to fight in order to relieve an intolerable situation. This theory has the appearance of plausibility, but it has no sound strategical basis and it is contradicted by the evidence of experience. Theoretically it is false because a blockade cannot be established without a great superiority, and, therefore, the fact of establishing a blockade implies that the enemy either is initially, or has been rendered, too weak to fight. In other words, that he is convinced that battle can only spell defeat. The idea that, in desperation, the fleet would be ordered to sea, to relieve by battle the sufferings of the country, is vain: for if such an inferiority exists the only result of putting to sea must be defeat, and defeat could only accentuate the sufferings. The fleet itself might risk immolation at sea by a superior force if the only alternative were its own destruction or starvation in harbour— the alternative which Nelson thought might arise if provisions could be prevented from reaching the combined fleet in Cadiz. It might then attempt to escape starvation, in the hope, not of breaking down the blockade by a victory, but that some at least of the ships' companies would save their lives. Practical experience confirms theory. In no case in all the many wars at sea in which an enemy has been forced to keep under the shelter of the defences of his ports has a blockade forced him to sea to fight. Neither Spain, Holland, France or Germany, suffer though they did from pressure at sea, sent their fleets to sea to fight the superior forces which were the cause of that pressure.[26]

Thus, to subject Italy to blockade, in the sense of a closing of all its ports by blockading forces, so stationed as to conform to those obligations which international law imposes, would require a very great superiority on the part of an enemy: from which it follows that something less than equality is adequate to avert national isolation by sea by this measure. So long as ports are not under a de-

---

[26] The occasions on which Torrington was ordered to sea to fight a superior French fleet, and Tourville to fight a superior Anglo-Dutch fleet, do not furnish exceptions to this experience: nor are they encouraging examples of ordering an inferior force to sea to engage one known to be superior.

clared blockade they are open to neutral commerce provided the commerce is not of a contraband nature.

Thus, there is no doubt that any danger of a national blockade, within the true meaning of that word in international law, could only be imposed upon Italy by a Power possessing a very great superiority both of force and of position: or, in other words, that something less than equality is sufficient to avert the danger of isolation by this measure. So long as ports are not under blockade neutral bottoms can enter and leave, but under an essential qualification: they must not carry contraband goods.

Contraband, as we saw in the War of 1914–18, has acquired a meaning more extensive than that which, under simpler conditions, sufficed. The goods to which the word "contraband" has been applied are those which assist an enemy to offer resistance. In the past, when nations were more self-supporting than they are to-day, when industry was not so fundamental an element in national life, and when its raw materials were less varied, it was sufficient to confine the scope of contraband to certain specified goods of a military nature: to weapons, to articles of military transport (*e.g.*, waggons, horse-harness, etc.) or the few raw materials which were needed for the manufacture of explosives. To-day, those conditions are different, and the unwisdom of attempting to establish a settled, precise, and permanent list of articles and materials which shall be free or deemed contraband was shown in an unmistakable manner in that war. Italy would need much from foreign sources. It would, therefore, not be sufficient for her security that she should be merely immune from blockade.

She would need no less such forces as would prevent an opponent at sea from establishing such a system of surveillance over the lines of approach as would enable him effectively to intercept, visit and search all neutrals who might be employed in her traffic. Any system of interception demands a widely dispersed force: and that force can only act in security under the protection of a mass. The "Tenth Cruiser Squadron" which performed those duties to the northward of Scotland for four years was able so to act only because it was sheltered behind the protecting arm of the Grand Fleet. So, as it always has been, must that "mass," which is called the "battle fleet," be the deciding element: and Italy's security against isolation must rest upon the possession of a battle fleet capable at the very least of disputing the command. With these considerations in mind no difficulty will be found in understanding the reason why Italy has asserted her need of a battle fleet equal to that of the strongest continental Power. In the memorandum she presented in 1930, referred to earlier, she stated: "Italy is prepared *a priori* to accept as the limit of her armaments any figure, no matter how low, provided it be not exceeded by any other continental European Power."

The problem of cruiser strength raises other questions. In so far as cruisers are units of a battle fleet, there is an equal need for cruisers in each of two opposing fleets. But in what was referred to as "the task of protecting Italy's merchant shipping on the high seas" there is one thing which is demonstrated by a wealth of experience. Even if Italy should possess those "extra-Mediterranean bases," to the lack of which the memorandum referred, the defence of her merchant shipping could not be assured unless she should also possess a considerable cruiser superiority. The numbers of cruising vessels which were needed to give protection against the various scattered German detachments —Von Spee's squadron; the *Emden*, *Karlsruhe* and others —are within the recollection of everybody. Equality in cruiser armaments would not serve the desired purpose of protecting merchant shipping on the high seas.

In actual fact, there is every reason for removing the quantitative question of the cruiser from this part of the discussion, for by no conceivable compromise could parity of security be obtained by agreement. Sporadic warfare will not, in any case, be the decisive element in war. The decision will be with the armies and with the massed naval forces of all arms—the battle fleet.

All the attempts artificially to regulate quantitative cruiser strengths can have no other result than dissatisfaction or insecurity. The case of Italy confirms the opinion that the true solution of the cruiser problem is to keep the size of the ship down to the lowest possible limits compatible with the attainment of certain definite strategical aims; and the experience of the War of 1914–18 showed that these aims were attainable by cruisers whose dimensions were a bare half of those which were adopted at Washington.

CHAPTER VII

THE SUBMARINE

IT IS natural that the attitudes which the several Powers have taken regarding the submarine should have been governed by considerations of the advantages and disadvantages which would accrue to each from its abolition or retention. Those attempts to arrive at a decision on the basis of its "offensive" or "defensive" character resulted in nothing more than special pleading. Those nations which desired its abolition argued that the submarine was a purely offensive weapon, possessing little or no commensurate value in defence, while those who wished to retain it argued that it was essential for their defence and that, since its use had been restricted by the Treaty of London, and it was no longer possible to use it in the manner in which it proved so destructive an instrument in the War of 1914–18, it could not be counted as an offensive weapon.

Simple as the words "offensive" and "defensive" are, their application is a matter of peculiar difficulty, whether it is concerned with instruments, with operations or with policy, for while the object to be attained may be of a purely defensive character, offensive measures may be the most effective means of its attainment. When England was threatened with invasion by the army of Philip II, Drake's offensive action of attacking the enemy fleet in its harbours was the most sure form of defence. When she was threat-

ened again with invasion from France, the offensive measure of the challenge to the French fleet, in Brest and elsewhere, was the foundation of the country's defence. When
the route to India was threatened by the use of the Cape
either as a French base or as a source of supply for another
French base, Mauritius, defence against this danger took
the form of offensive action in the capture and occupation
of the Cape of Good Hope; and one of the predominent
features of the wars at sea has always been offensive action
by the Sea Power against the bases of an enemy, one object
of action being the defence of trade. "When one navy is
overwhelmingly preponderant, . . . when the enemy con-
fines himself to commerce destroying by crowds of small
privateers, then the true military policy is to stamp out the
nests where they swarm."[1] "Stamping out the nests" is a
defensive operation, and whether the vessels employed are
battleships, as they were in the West Indies, or blockships
as they were at Zeebrugge, their character is not affected:
they do not become offensive in character because they
are employed in an offensive operation the aim of which is
defence.

It is not without interest to observe that the discussion
on "offensive character" was confined to three types of
vessel: the battleship, the aircraft carrier and the submarine. The characters of the cruiser and the destroyer were,
by implication, assumed to be defensive. Yet, as any one
acquainted with the history of war at sea is aware, the
lesser types of vessel were used on precisely the same oper-

[1] Mahan, *The Influence of Sea Power on the French Revolution and Empire*,
vol. II, p. 252.

ation—trade destruction—as the submarine. If she is deemed offensive because she possesses power to attack trade, so too must the light cruiser which ranges the trade routes, and the destroyer which sallies out in force from bases on their flanks, be considered offensive. It is, in fact, impossible to discriminate between the instruments used. If the submarine attacked trade, her accessory in that action was the battleship which, by containing the enemy battle fleet, forced it to withhold from the defence of trade the numerous destroyers which were needed simultaneously for the fleet and the trade routes.

In so far as any test of defensive character is possible, it may be found in a quantitative form. If a navy as a whole, or certain categories of its units, appears larger or more numerous than the needs of defence seem to require, the interpretation which will be placed upon it will be that its object will be not defence, but offence. It was that which caused Admiral Jurien de la Gravière to make his protest concerning the strength of the British navy.[2] It was that also which on the English side of the Channel raised the fears of the country when it saw a great French iron clad fleet in course of construction, combined with the development of a powerful base. It was that again which created anxiety when Germany proceeded to build a fleet, the strength of which appeared entirely disproportionate to the needs of her security. So it is with the submarine. A flotilla whose strength appears to be entirely unrelated to any scheme of defence will necessarily cause the Powers to associate it with an offensive intention. It was that con-

[2] *Vide* p. 190.

sideration which caused Mr. Balfour at Washington to ask, "How then shall we think of this encouragement to submarines?"

At the opening of the Washington Conference, Great Britain proposed the abolition of submarines. It was natural that she should do so. They were instruments from which she had suffered greatly and they had proved of very little value to her. All the other Powers were then in favour of their retention, and in consequence no agreement was reached. The "Root Resolutions," which limited their action but were gravely ambiguous in form, were accepted, but as they were not ratified by France they became null. At the London Conference the United States altered its attitude. "The argument," said Mr. Stimson, "that the submarine is a purely defensive weapon seems to us difficult to reconcile with the offensive use which has been made of it at great distances from its home ports. . . . There is a very weighty argument in the fact that the construction and maintenance of submarines impose upon all navies higher levels in those classes of ships which are used against submarines." The Delegation was consequently in favour of the abolition of the submarine.

Italy was in favour in principle of abolition, if abolition would contribute to further reductions in other armaments, and was prepared to abolish submarines provided other Powers would agree to a drastic reduction in the size of capital ships; but unfortunately both Great Britain and the United States were opposed to this course.

Japan opposed the abolition. "With this comparatively inexpensive vessel she can contrive to look after her extensive waterways and vulnerable points. Japan desires to retain submarines solely for this purpose." She was prepared to "outlaw the illegitimate use of this legitimate and defensive agency of war."

France was definitely opposed to abolition. She argued that the submarine is a ship of war like others: that she is a defensive weapon, indispensable to some naval Powers: and that the use of the submarine should be, and can be, regulated as is the use of other ships of war. She claimed that the lesser and smaller Powers had a right to possess navies corresponding to their requirements and their means of national defence. But while she declined to accept the abolition, she expressed herself willing to subscribe to an international agreement regulating their use.

The final result of the London Conference was the acceptance, as established rules of international law, of an article (Part IV, Article 22 of the Treaty of London) that:

"In their action with regard to merchant ships submarines must conform to the rules of international law to which surface vessels are subject.

"In particular, except in the case of persistent refusal to stop on being summoned, or of active resistance to visit or search, a warship, whether surface vessel or submarine, may not sink or render incapable of navigation a merchant vessel without having first placed passengers, crew and ship's papers in a place of safety. For this purpose the ship's boats are not regarded as a place of safety unless the safety of the passengers and crew is assured, in the existing sea and weather conditions, by the proximity of land or the presence of another vessel which is in a position to take them on board."

It would be a mistake to suppose that these provisions have deprived the submarine of its capacity to attack merchant ships. If trade has to sail in convoys, as in narrow seas where routes are flanked by hostile bases it would, in all probability, be obliged to do, it is possible to argue that attack by torpedo fire would be admissible. It can be said that convoy is a military formation and that therefore it is permissible to attack the ships without the processes of visit and search. The doctrine is, however, a dangerous one. International law makes no exception to vessels under convoy. The surface ship is not relieved of the necessity of bringing a vessel to by the fact of the vessel being under escort. A stronger reason may be found in the fact that vessels taking part in a military operation carrying troops or the stores of an army will also be proceeding under escort, and that when great military stakes are at issue the lines of communication can justifiably be attacked; and that it is impossible to distinguish a military from a commercial convoy. Further, it is not difficult to visualise conditions of attack by combined forces of surface and submarine craft, in which it could be claimed that the surface craft have by implication summoned the merchant vessels to stop and that they, having refused to do so, are guilty of a persistent refusal to stop and so render themselves liable to be sunk; while the presence of other vessels provides the security for the people on board.

Submarines are moreover armed with medium artillery and have great radius of action. They are, in fact, cruisers, and are capable of acting against merchant ships in accordance with all the formalities which govern the conduct of surface vessels. Their artillery enables them to summon a ship, to overcome her resistance, and to take possession.

It has been ably argued that the submarine enables a weaker Power to strike back at one which is stronger in surface vessels; and that though this may not produce a decision, it will have valuable results in prolonging the resistance, and, by conducting a vigorous minor counter offensive, divert force from the major operations upon which the decision depends; and that even if the material effects should be neither great nor decisive, the moral effects will be appreciable in preserving honour, reviving courage, and commanding respect. These results may readily be conceded, provided the warfare is not disfigured by such atrocities as those which deprived the navy of Germany of the respect which its skill, courage and resource had earned for it in other operations of the war at sea.

The question whether it is desirable or necessary to retain the submarine does not depend upon whether it is predominantly offensive or defensive in character, nor upon whether advantages may accrue, in particular circumstances, to some one or other Power. Undeniably there are conditions in which its work may be defensive. Acting in combination with the artillery of a fortress it may render a bombardment more difficult, by forcing a bombarding squadron to keep under way. It is a deterrent to blockade. And it may with perfect legitimacy be advanced that diversions of force by means of counter offensives are frequently measures of a defensive character. The question is rather whether, taking that long view of the whole problem of sea power which it is our duty to take, the existence of the submarine does, in actual fact, contribute to security, or contribute to it to a degree commensurate with the very great additions which it causes to the expenditure. Of what nations can it be said that they are more secure since the submarine has been added to the navies of the world?

Let us recall the ultimate object of sea power. The Sea Powers of the world became Sea Powers in consequence of a need for security against those two injuries to which the peoples composing them were exposed—invasion and the destruction of their means of livelihood which depended upon the sea. How far is the submarine an essential unit of naval force for the safeguarding of any great nation against either of these forms of injury?

An invasion by sea of a great modern military state may be dismissed as impracticable, even if there were no opposition at sea. The number of men which can be transported would never be sufficient to conduct an invasion in the face of the opposition of the military forces of any modern Power. The expedition to the Dardanelles, where a force of under 100,000 men was carried over sea and landed, does not invalidate this, for that number, landed in the territory of any modern state, would quickly be overwhelmed by the masses which such a state has at its disposal. The Allies had not the Turkish army to meet, for the bulk of that army was elsewhere in the Caucasus. They had only to meet a portion of it, actually inferior in number to their own expeditionary force. The expedition had no opposition to meet at sea, and it was able to acquire a secure base in which to assemble and from which to make its final move to the landing-places.

There are, however, invasions on the lower scales either of diversionary operations, or with the object of the capture of an outlying possession or base: such, for instance, as those in which the Japanese army of some 24,000 men captured Tsing Tao, the South African Forces conquered German South-West Africa, or the Germans, with about 23,000 men, captured Oesel. The last of these was conducted in spite of the submarines in the Baltic; in the two others submarines would undoubtedly have added to the difficulties of the operations, and hence, in all probability, would have prolonged them. Even if capture is not finally averted, a prolongation of a defence is always advantageous, for men and material are withheld from other theatres and operations where their services are needed. But at the most this is an insufficient reason for the retention of an instrument which causes so vast an addition to the burden of armaments, not only by its own cost, but also in the cost of all the counter-measures to whose existence it gives rise and of which the very numerous surface flotillas are the most prominent.

As an instrument for the local defence of such outlying positions as may become the objects of attack the submarine has an undoubted utility. But the flying torpedo-boat and gun-boat have come into existence, and the security for such places as the submarine is able to furnish may now be furnished by these new forms of flotilla craft. Submarines hampered the Dardanelles operations. An efficient air flotilla, capable of attacking the military zone

when it made its landing and during the course of its operations, and also of bombarding the men of war and the
transports in their base at Mudros, could hardly have
failed to have been a more effective form of defence. As
the submarine replaced the surface torpedo-boat, so
it appears that the flying torpedo-boat has every prospect
of doing all that the submarine would do in that respect,
and even more, and at a lesser expenditure.

Another form which invasion, or attack upon outlying
possessions, may take is that of bombardment from the
sea. Bombardments are of two kinds: prolonged and
systematic bombardments aiming at the destruction of
the facilities of a base—its dockyards, its storage of fuel
and other supplies—and those spectacular but ineffective
raiding bombardments which were made during the course
of the late war on Hartlepool, Scarborough, Philippeville,
the Isle of Thanet, Madras and various places on the Italian coasts on the Adriatic.

The submarine is an added security against a systematic
bombardment. It is an auxiliary to local artillery. It forces
the bombarding force to keep on the move and so lessens
the accuracy of its fire. It may be open to question whether
its influence in this respect is greater than that of an air
flotilla. On that question there is, in all probability, a difference of opinion which is only capable of being finally
resolved by experience. Even, however, if there should appear to be a balance of advantage in favour of the submarine, such a balance has to be weighed against the
eventual cost which the expenditure upon submarines and
the flotillas and other counter-measures involve. And, in

the end, the main defence against bombardment lies in the artillery. The old principle still holds good that a gun on shore is worth a broadside afloat. New inventions have done nothing to mitigate the superiority of the shore battery over the ship.

In the case of the "runaway" bombardments, the submarine is of very little use. The characteristic of such operations is their unexpectedness, and the only instrument which can come into action with sufficient rapidity to deal with them is the gun. Neither submarine nor aircraft could have been of any effective use in any of these attacks. The only way in which either could have prevented the injury caused by those bombardments would have been to maintain, in a constant state of readiness, at every place where there was a possibility of such a bombardment, a force of submarines actually cruising or an air flotilla ready to take the air. Not only would neither have been able to come into action so rapidly as an artillery defence, or to do anything if the attack were made at night, as it was at Madras, but the waste of strength involved in the demobilisation of so great a number of mobile units would be contrary to every principle of the employment of force, and would provide the greatest possible encouragement to an enemy to employ this method of diversionary attack.

In short, the submarine, powerful instrument as she may be, is not necessary for the purpose of providing direct security against invasion in any of its various forms. She constitutes an undoubted threat to an army on its voyage. She forces the intending invader to allocate a very considerable force of small vessels to the escorting force. She obliges him to possess a base which can be rendered secure against submarine attack, and to take all the extensive measures which such defence demands—nets, booms and mines; and forces upon him the consequent necessity of providing himself with the net-laying, boom-constructional and mining apparatus. Simultaneous and co-ordinated attacks by submarines upon shipping in other parts will add further to the difficulties of the invasion, by obliging the enemy—though only if he is dependent upon the unbroken flow of trade—to provide the smaller vessels needed for its defence: if there is insufficient force both to defend a vital trade and to protect the expedition, the expedition will be impracticable. The British Admirality, it may be recollected, demanded the withdrawal of the expedition to the Eastern Mediterranean, as the needs of small craft for the security of their communications made so great a demand upon the numbers available that it was considered impossible to give defence to the trade if the expedition was persisted in.

All of these may properly be counted to the advantage of the submarine. But if the security desired can be no less effectively obtained by air flotillas, which can also attack the enemy from their shore bases on the line of passage, and, even if that be not possible, can attack the expedition at the point of arrival not only while it is at sea but also within its advanced base, until effective defences are created, then the end—security—will have been attained without recourse to all the far-reaching expenditure, both in war and in peace, which the maintenance of the submarine forces will have entailed.

Effective as the submarine may be in attack upon mercantile shipping, she is of negligible use in its direct defence. A convoy cannot be defended by submarines, and
though submarines might prove of service if it were desired
to patrol areas in which commerce attack by raiding vessels was considered possible, they are far less efficient instruments for that purpose than surface vessels.

Yet it was for these specific purposes that Japan claimed
the need for submarines. Her memorandum of February
11th, 1930, quoted earlier, asserted that with "this comparatively inexpensive" vessel she could "continue to look
after her extensive waterways and vulnerable points," and
that she desired to retain submarines solely for this purpose. This view of the submarine's utility is not borne out
by experience. The contribution which submarines were
able to make to the even more extensive waterways of the
Allies in the late war was negligible. They scouted in the
Heligoland Bight, and this may be properly counted as a
contribution; but they gave no notice of the sailing of the
forces which bombarded the English coast, of that battle-
cruiser squadron which was intercepted at the Dogger
Bank, of the German fleet which put forth and fought at
Jutland, or of the British fleet which simultaneously sailed
to meet it, of the fleet which put to sea in August, 1916, or
of that which put to sea to attack the North Sea convoys—
or, more properly speaking, their escort—in April, 1918.
They were used on a few occasions in the very minor rôle of
decoy vessels. The War, in fact, afforded no example whatever of the utility of the submarine in defence of the waterways of trade. "Vulnerable points" is a term of wide appli-

cation. There are vulnerable points in local areas of trade, but those, as remarked earlier, are more effectively protected by surface craft, whatever may be the type of vessel, surface or submarine, which might be used to attack trade in such parts. There are vulnerable points on land— the bases of the fleet and the great cities. The problem of their defence against three of the possible forms of attack —military forces, systematic bombardment and "runaway" bombardment—has already been discussed: against the third form, aerial bombardment, the submarine can afford no protection.

Finally, the submarine is very far from being a "comparatively inexpensive" vessel. Per ton she is the most costly of all craft. It may be argued that more service per ton is obtained from submarines than from any other craft. This is extremely doubtful in view of the fact that for those particular purposes for which, solely, the retention of the submarine is desired, the submarine has shown herself of little value. It is not moreover "per ton" that the comparison should be made. It is rather whether for the same expenditure a greater general return in effective craft could not be obtained. Per ton the submarine costs approximately twice as much as a vessel of the cruiser type; and, if such exaggerated speeds as those which have come into favour in recent years were not indulged in—unnecessary as they are for vessels employed against "raiders"—the disproportion would be greater. Expense, moreover, it must be repeated, is not confined to the submarine. All of those other craft and measures to which her existence gives rise have also to be called into the account. If one country possesses submarines, all will possess them; and as the submarines of each Power are potentially offensive instruments on the routes of communication and threats to the larger ships, so each has to provide itself with small surface vessels to guard its battleships, its merchant ships, and its military transports. The antidote for the submarine has been the destroyer, and large destroyer forces are created which, except for the submarine, would be unnecessary. And as those destroyer forces themselves become, as they have become in recent years, large flotillas of vessels approximating to the size of cruisers, so they, originally created for the defence of the communications or the fleets, became, within the limits of their endurance, which are considerable, potential attackers. They form cruiser squadrons of a very effective type, and it becomes necessary for those Powers whose security depends upon sea trade or the movement of troops, to provide either a large number of destroyers or some other form of defence. To attempt to control this by the establishment of ratios is to ignore the most elementary principle of defence, and can result only in one thing—insecurity to the Powers more vulnerable at sea. The alternative is competition: a war of the purse.

Nor is it to be lost sight of that one of the reasons for which the present great size of the battleship is said to be necessary is the existence of the submarine: and that the great size increases the initial cost and the cost of maintenance, while at the same time a whole host of appliances for guarding harbours by mines and nets, and scientific detecting instruments, are called into being.

It is assuredly a misuse of words to describe as "comparatively inexpensive" a vessel which creates so vast and far-reaching an expenditure.

Japan is in no danger from invasion, for there is no country which could obtain the command of the sea necessary to transport an army to her shores, nor carry an army of the strength that would be necessary to subdue her. Nor is she in any danger of blockade, for in her geographical position, and with the surface ship strength which was willingly accorded to her at Washington, any blockade of her islands is impossible, while any attempt to prevent goods from reaching her, even if the most totalitarian interpretation were placed upon contraband, would be fruitless. She fears none of these things. She desires submarines solely for the protection of her waterways, which they cannot protect, and vulnerable points, for the defence of which they are of little value.

That, however, is not the whole case. While submarines are of little value defensively, in the hands of an enemy they are potentially offensive instruments against those very waterways whose security is desired. The only British vessels which were capable of acting against the German communications in the Baltic were submarines. The only German vessels which could inflict serious injury upon the Allied communications in the North Sea, the Channel, the Western approaches and the Mediterranean were submarines. So unless the Japanese surface fleet be swept out of existence by a victory at sea as sweeping as that of Tsushima, a contingency that may be dismissed without the smallest hesitation, submarines are the only vessels

which could operate, except in the most trivial and sporadic manner, against her communications with her mainland possessions and sources of supply. They only could
penetrate and maintain a prolonged campaign in the
waters between Japan and the mainland, and oblige her to
take defensive measures which absorb, as the experience of
the war plainly showed, a great number of lesser vessels,
drawing them away from the service of the main fleet and
from other operations. Words used by Mr. Balfour at
Washington to Italy may be recalled: "The fact that you
are going to give a general blessing to submarines . . . puts
it in the power of every state that has a freeboard at all to
make itself a formidable, aggressive enemy. You talk of
the submarine as if it were by nature something that encouraged defence and discouraged attack. It is nothing of
the kind." With the substitution of "that has a first-class
navy" for "that has a freeboard" Mr. Balfour's words
might be addressed to Japan.

The other Power which has resolutely supported the submarine is France. Her reasons, as expressed in her memorandum, have been quoted. Like Japan she is in no danger
of invasion by sea. Like her, though for different reasons,
she is immune from blockade. Mr. Balfour may again be
quoted: "France is nearly self-supporting in point of food,
and France has a great land frontier which gives her access,
directly and indirectly, to all the great markets of the
world. No maritime Power can blockade her." France has
important maritime lines of military communications, un-
assailable in the Atlantic except by submarines and aircraft. If she should be engaged in war with a continental

Power, and the transfer of troops from Africa to Metropolitan France should be essential, the security of those
lines would become of the first importance to her. The last
thing she would desire would be to be obliged to weaken
her main concentration or prejudice its powers of action,
by being under the obligation to make considerable detachments of flotilla craft from her main fleet in order to
provide for the defence of that line of communications.

Finally, among the major Powers whom France has to
consider there is Germany. Whatever may be the immediate result of the German claim for equality of status, the
eventual result is beyond a shadow of doubt: that whatever forms of fighting instruments are possessed by other
Powers will be possessed by Germany. Mr. Balfour foresaw
that this must be so. "The submarines which the French
propose to build will be no protection against the submarines of Germany." That which would be needed is a surface flotilla in two seas, and our experience has shown how
large that flotilla would need to be; and in those waters in
which aircraft can act, an air flotilla, which would be provided at the expense of the air forces employed in the campaign on land. Admittedly the submarine flotilla would be
an instrument of considerable utility in a war against England, and if that is considered the more probable contingency the policy is justifiable: but a battle fleet on the scale
elsewhere suggested[3] would appear to give a better security
at a lower cost and be of more general utility.

There is a third category of Powers which appears to support the submarine: the lesser Powers. To them the sub-

[3] *Vide* p. 263.

marine makes an appeal and we see them furnishing themselves with these "inexpensive" vessels. Yet what purpose
do they serve? If they contemplate conflicts between each
other, the submarine adds equally to strength or weakness
of each, and can contribute nothing towards the decision
between the land forces. But it is believed to possess some
influence as a safeguard against the greater Powers. The
continued independence of the "small" Powers does not,
however, depend upon their own forces. It rests upon the
fact that some great Powers would resist the absorption of
the small by other great Powers. Thus Von Bülow records[4]
that when the Kaiser expressed the view that a close alliance must be established with Denmark, Bülow in reply
pointed out that Denmark would not willingly enter into
alliance. It would have to be forced upon her, and the Government and the Court would ask for help from England
and Russia. England would at once adopt the attitude of
protector of the small nations and would defend her
against an alliance forced upon her by Germany, and it
would pave the way for an Anglo-French-Russian co-operation for the maintenance and the independence of Denmark. Similarly he remarked: "One would have to be mad
to think of a forcible annexation of Denmark, of Switzerland, of Holland, of Belgium,"[5] and again, "I had seen, in
the documents I had studied at Semmering, that the
naval authorities were thinking of a number of bases on the
potentially rich coasts of the Pacific. We should just have
to wait for the right moment and take possession of them."

[4] *Memoirs*, vol. II, chap. VIII.
[5] *Ibid*. vol. III, chap. I.

In other words, the small states from whom those bases and territories were to be filched would be left in their possession only so long as there were powerful states who would resist their annexation. No quantity of submarines would have saved any of these states in Europe or elsewhere.

Even if the security of the "small" Powers did not depend upon the great, submarine flotillas would not preserve them. So long as submarines continue to exist the greater Powers are bound to furnish themselves with large surface and possibly air flotillas for their own security: force which must greatly exceed any that the "small" Powers can possess and would neutralise any counter action which their submarine flotillas could take. The idea, expressed by some speakers, that the submarine in the hands of the "small" Powers is the reply to the "battleship" in the hands of the major Powers, because it would prevent the great ship from bombarding its ports, is coloured by two errors. The first is that in a dispute between one of the great and one of the "small" Powers the former would not attempt to bring the latter into subjection by a bombardment of its great cities. The second, that even if such barbarous methods were employed, a small force of submarines would be powerless against the strong flotilla forces which the great Power would possess, and unable to make its way through minefields if they should be laid. It is not, in fact, the great vulnerable ship which would be called into use but the lesser craft of the anti-submarine type, then umbers of which are necessarily increased by the retention of the submarine. Lesser Powers have certainly been coerced by greater within the recollection of many of us. The coercion has never taken the form of bombardment of the open cities, but of the closing of the ports to trade or the prevention of the movements of troops across the sea. The action of the Allied Powers against Turkey, which culminated in the battle of Navarino, was to prevent Turkey from moving troops into Greece. When pressure was brought upon Turkey to cede Thessaly to Greece, as provided in the Treaty of Berlin, Mr. Gladstone ordered the fleet to seize Smyrna and its Custom House in order to divert the most important customs dues from Turkey. At the time of the Armenian massacres, the intention was to coerce Turkey by seizing Smyrna, Salonika and Crete. So-called "pacific blockades" were employed at Athens and Durazzo, and what corresponded to the blockade in Crete, to prevent outbreaks; and while it may with truth be said that these blockades were conducted by battleships, it is no less a fact that any and all of them could with equal efficiency have been conducted by the lesser craft. It was not because very great ships were needed to overawe or overcome resistance, that they were employed; but because they were the instruments available and were the most convenient to use. Submarines would have prevented these blockades.

Bombardments there have unquestionably been. Pressure was exerted both at Algiers and Alexandria by bombardment. The fortresses at each place—not the towns—were the targets of battleships and bombarding vessels. It may, however, be not unreasonable to presume that the circumstances which led to either of these bombardments are most unlikely to arise among the civilised communities and those lesser states whose security is under consideration.

Thus, in conclusion, while there is no difficulty in refuting the accusation that the submarine differs from other cruisers in being of a specifically offensive character, or that she possesses no defensive qualities; or in showing that, in certain conditions, the possession of a submarine flotilla by a weaker Power will make some compensation for an inferiority in ships of the greater classes; or that the minor counter offensive is not a proper, effective and legitimate form of action; it still remains to be shown that any ultimate advantage to any particular Power results from the retention of this type of vessel. The idea that she is inexpensive is a palpable delusion. She is most costly in herself and she is the direct cause of still greater expenditure on counter-measures. She forms one of the excuses for the retention of the great size of battleships. She forces the provision of great flotillas, and she is the primary cause of the demands for more speed in those flotillas; and speed is one of the most costly of all the ingredients in the recipe for a fighting ship. Nets, booms and mines to guard harbours against her, and ships, specially built to carry and lay the nets, the booms and the mines, have to be provided. The demand for the abolition of air bombing is opposed because of its asserted efficiency against the submarine.

Yet there remains one argument. Abolishing her will not prevent her resurrection if war comes. The designs can be prepared, the torpedoes can be made, and the plant for construction can be provided in peace. We saw how submarines were increased by Germany in the War. There is nothing to prevent a repetition of that experience. Some may suggest that an international agreement might be made not to build these craft even in war. If an international agreement of such a kind is to have any binding effect whatever, there must be power behind it. The only power which can safeguard agreements is that of the neutral. There is little evidence in the experience of the past to show that the neutral is ready to step in and act as a protector of the sanctity of treaties. None did so in the years between 1914 and 1918, in the face of unmistakable breaches. Nor has anything that has occurred since the War given rise to any expectation that neutrals would act differently in the future. Lord Grey said: "One lesson from the experience of the War is that we should not bind ourselves to observe any rules of war unless those who sign them with us undertake to uphold them, by force if needs be, against an enemy who breaks them." [6] The whole spirit of intense nationalism which is characteristic of the world of to-day, and the steady opposition to any form of collective action, or the undertaking of any responsibilities, forbid the belief that any such an undertaking is practicable.

The question then is, is the danger of such construction so great as it is believed to be? The argument rests upon the assumption that the submarine would be produced in numbers sufficient to influence the situation more quickly than the counter-measures—the light vessels and the various kinds of apparatus—could be produced. But the submarine has not only to be built; her officers and crew have

[6] *Twenty-five Years*, vol. ii, p. 102.

also to be trained to its use. Training cannot begin till craft
are ready, and training is a highly important factor: the
War showed a very marked deterioration in the perform-
ances of the later German submarines, who lacked the
more highly trained personnel which began the campaign.
Whether there would be that gap in time between the production of submarine and anti-submarine deserves careful
and unbiassed examination. But there is this to remark.
The situation would not differ very greatly from that which
has been accepted by the terms of the Treaty of London,
for the "quotas" of destroyers to which the Signatory
Powers have limited themselves would be completely inadequate for protection against submarines at the outbreak of war. In a war with a country cooped up in a corner
of the North Sea and with an outlet into the Mediterranean, over 400 destroyers were found necessary to defend
the trade of the Allies: there were in addition the flotillas
of those Allies. In home waters over 270 were in use, apart
from lesser craft. To imagine that the hundred[7] or so destroyers for which the Treaty provides would be able to
give, under more exposed conditions, the degree of security
which could only be given by over three times their number would be seriously to delude ourselves; and the same
may be said of the other European maritime Powers. What
is more, the merchant navy at that time was more numerous, and therefore more capable of standing loss. The losses
which could be survived by a numerous mercantile marine,
and replaced by a prosperous shipbuilding industry, can-

---

[7] *Viz.* 150,000 tons: the limit of size of the destroyer (apart from the few
flotilla leaders) being 1500 tons.

not be stood by the organisations of today with their far lower vitality.

Thus in so far therefore as there would be danger owing to the attack being developed more quickly than the defence, it would be nothing new: for it is one to which we are already exposed and with two adverse conditions attached to it—that whereas to-day the attack could begin at once, if no submarines should exist it could not be begun until they had been built and their crews trained: and that the burden of expense is greater, since all of its machinery has to be borne in the years of peace, and, during that time, the whole tendency is for "improvements" to be made, increasing the cost both of the instruments of attack and defence. One is inclined, therefore, to ask whether that objection to abolition is as valid as it appears and whether those who object may not in reality be rejecting a gnat while swallowing a camel.

CHAPTER VIII

COLLECTIVE AND INDIVIDUAL SECURITY

THE principles which govern the size of anything which man creates for his use, from a knife to a sky-scraper, from an office staff to a water-power supply, are applicable to naval establishments. What are the relevant principles? They are that an instrument, organisation, establishment—let it be what it may—shall be of such a size and character as will enable it to fulfil the object for which it is brought into existence: being neither larger than is needed to perform its task, nor too small. The whole question depends upon the task which the tool has to perform. "The very essence of a tool is the being an in-strument for the achievement of a purpose ... the word implies not only a purpose and a purposer, but a purposer who can see in what manner purpose can be achieved and can contrive the tool which shall achieve it."[1]

If this be true—and can its truth be denied?—is it not the merest common sense, as far removed from "Utopian-ism" as anything can be, to ask that nations should state precisely the reasons for which they need navies of the size they advocate? In an earlier chapter I have illustrated the great variety of reasons which at different times have been put forward to explain why there is a national need for a navy. At the bottom of every reason the attractive talis-manic word "Security" appears; but the word itself is

[1] Samuel Butler, *Note Book*, p. 18.

given many different interpretations. All the greater naval nations assure the world that a great navy is the surest guarantee of peace; that it gives security against war, and is therefore a highly beneficent institution. Or the security aimed at is security for the nation against the dangers to which it would be exposed if it were weak at sea. It might be forced to abandon its sovereignty, its territory, its trade at the point of the bayonet of the invader or through being deprived of the necessities of life or the means of procuring them. Security may again be interpreted to mean an assurance for the future of the race. The population is growing, manufacturers are developing, and therefore territories must be acquired for the future surplus production. It is true that this may require the annexation or absorption of territories now in the possession of others, or monopoly of markets now open, but it is held to be justifiable because it is necessary for security, and a people is entitled to security. In addition to these interpretations of the word there is yet another form of security: that those who are themselves engaged in a fight shall not suffer losses in their normal commerce, or be unable to profit from the abnormal demands which arise as a result of war between others. [2]

While all of these appear to be perfectly legitimate forms of "Security," they do represent fundamentally different

[2] *E.g.* R. Hooper in the *Yale Review*, January, 1918, remarked that the fleet "was the product of the difficulties in which the United States found itself as a neutral in 1915 and 1916" in which, as the position of the United States was made intolerable, President Wilson made his historic tour in the winter of 1916 into the West, which found expression in the following August in the Naval Bill providing for the greatest fleet ever projected by any nation not at war.

interpretations of the word. Would not the problems of naval armaments be rendered more capable of solution if we all knew what interpretation each of us places upon the word? Whether Peace or Protection, safety as a belligerent or as a neutral be the object, what would seem to be needed is a methodical examination by responsible statesmen of the measures by means of which the objects of the preservation of Peace and the protection of the interests of the several nations—in so far as they are related to the sea— can be attained. The first step in the process appears to be to come to a definite conclusion as to whether Peace and Protection are to be assured by collective or individual effort. At the present moment we have advocates of both systems.

COLLECTIVE SECURITY

France has consistently, with a logic which is flawless, urged the adoption of "collectivity" and the same view has been taken by some sections of thought in other countries: but the methods by which it is suggested that collectivity of action should be put into force differ.

If the Pact of Paris has any real, any practical meaning, if it expresses the fixed determination never to make use of force in the settlement of any international dispute, only one answer to the question of "Collectivity or Individual Effort?" appears possible. The measures must be collective in the Pact itself. But there seems reason to question whether the Pact does really represent an unbending determination that peace shall be maintained and protection given to any people who may be attacked, or whether it is not rather the expression of no more than a pious wish. There is a great difference between a "will" and a "wish."

Collective action may take two forms. Either there may be a permanent organised force of all arms, in an unarmed world, to exercise what, in civil life, is the work of the police: or individual nations may each provide themselves with armed forces, engaging themselves to employ them in the common cause of action against any nation who breaks the peace. But as no force can be set in motion without a controlling authority, so collective action necessarily implies the pre-existence of machinery by means of which judgment can be pronounced, and execution ordered. Whether such machinery is within the scope of practical politics is obviously a question which statesmen only can decide.

If it should be decided that it is politically practicable to pronounce judgment, and to direct the execution of appropriate measures of coercion, the next step in the process would be to determine the means by which collective action is to be undertaken.

COLLECTIVE ACTION BY INTERNATIONAL FORCES

Collective security by means of what has been called an "international police force" would require the existence of a permanent armed force in an unarmed world, whose certainty of action, readiness to act, and irresistible power, command confidence as complete as the confidence in the internal police forces of nations. Wherever in the world the determination to preserve peace exists, there will be formed a force capable of suppressing disorder. Force is an indispensable factor. Though it may not always prevent outbreaks of violence, riot and robbery, it is a deterrent: and, if conflicts take place notwithstanding the force, it ensures that order is sooner or later restored and justice done. In India or Palestine, Syria or Algeria, Africa or America, outbreaks between factions, races or classes are always liable to occur; and, if they occur, they are quelled by organised armed force. If there is sufficient force, strongly directed and promptly used, disorder is put down quickly. If force is insufficient, much damage may be done: but the fighting between the sections of the community is stopped and, eventually, order is restored. The "Pax Britannica" or of any other kind results from the fixed determination that peace *shall* be preserved, not from a platonic affection and desire for peace. It is the result of a will, not of a pious wish. Mere expressions of the wrongfulness of fighting will never preserve peace or prevent fighting, nor will peoples be prevented from strife by any object-lessons of its cost, assertions of its futility, or assurances that nothing is ever gained by war: for history affords ample examples of nations having obtained profitable results from aggressive action against others.

If the decision of the statesmen should be, in the first place, that collective action is both desirable and practicable, and in the second that the instrument should be a police force, there would be no need for national navies in the form in which they now exist. The duties of a navy in peace are of a police or a philanthropic character. Those, for example, which are performed by the naval forces of various nations in the China seas and rivers are for the common purpose of suppressing piracy and banditry: services as international in their nature as those conducted by the Ice Patrol in the North Atlantic against the common enemy of the shipping of all nations, the iceberg. The cruising ships of all the Powers perform acts of humanity on such occasions of great natural catastrophes as earthquakes at Jamaica, Messina, Hawke's Bay, in Greece, or a hurricane at Honduras. None, however, of those occasions call for the use of ships armed with either 16- or 6-inch guns. They require organised bodies of men equipped for the purposes of maintaining order, extinguishing fire, rescue and salvage. They would be no less effectively performed by corps of disciplined men trained to police, rescue and salvage work and carried in unarmed ships.

There are also other services which navies have to perform in peace in the preservation of internal order or the protection of their nationals in the troubles which arise in the less civilised states. Civilians may have to be evacuated from a town, as British subjects were removed from Kabul by air transport and from Hodeidah by ships. Ships also are called for to assist in suppressing disorders, as British vessels were in Crete, in Palestine, in Cyprus and in Alexandria, and American vessels in Nicaragua: and presumably other nations experience the same need. But the value of men-of-war on these occasions does not rest in their armaments of heavy guns, but in the fact that they can land bodies of armed men and if necessary cover their disembarkation with light artillery: and in the further fact that, in the majority of cases, a man-of-war is the most

readily available source of armed men, in numbers comparatively small but large enough to check disorder. This
duty could be performed by any lightly armed transport
vessels manned by military forces. There was indeed, some
years ago, a British cruiser, manned by marines, in the
West Indies: a perambulating police station. Her armament was not even so large as those mounted in many
armed merchant vessels during the War, but it was adequate for the purposes of her mission. The United States
Marine forces have performed services of a similar character. The basic principle of the preservation of order in
such situations as those described is that order is best restored by "the man-on-the-ground," not by bombardment.

The provision of such vessels as these, for the services of
peace, would not be inconsistent with the establishment of
international naval forces: for their weakness would render
them wholly negligible as fighting units when opposed by
even the smallest types of ocean-going vessels constructed
specifically for fighting at sea.

It is incorrect to say that joint international naval action is an impossibility. The ships blockading Crete and
preventing the spread of the disturbances were French,
Italian, British and Russian. The fleet which destroyed
the Turks at Navarino was composed of British, French
and Russian ships. The vessels employed in the Mediterranean in the War of 1914–18 were Italian, French, American, Japanese and British. Co-operation and co-ordina-
tion are moreover easier afloat in a fleet than ashore in an
army; and yet the army which fought under Wellington at
Waterloo was successful, though it was composed of

British, Belgian, Hanoverian and Dutch troops, and was opposed by an army of one nationality. Certainly a command composed of different nationalities is weaker than one, of the same size or even smaller, of a single nation. But as, if the hypothesis of an international naval police (in conjunction with similar military and air forces) were accepted, there could be no individual navies other than such vessels employed in the preservation of internal order or the philanthropic work already referred to, this disability would not arise. The superiority in armaments would be irresistible.

Whether it would be possible for the services of peace to be performed in this manner, and for an international armed naval force to be maintained, is one thing. Whether it is politically practicable is another. But, let it be repeated, the latter is a question for statesmen only, and they may be well expected to hesitate before taking a step so far-reaching, however strong their inclinations or however convincing the logic of such a step may appear. There is indeed one consideration, in the purely naval sphere, which cannot be left out of account. Although armies may be disbanded, it has always proved possible to improvise bodies of men who can fight on land. The War of Secession in America, the South African War, and the War of 1914–18 gave ample evidence of this. Navies are less easy to improvise. The possibility that, in a really great crisis, the machinery of peace might break down, cannot be dismissed by mere repetitions of optimisim. It is impossible, looking round the world to-day, not to see that some very great differences regarding policy exist in the world, some of them so fundamental that there is reason to believe that nations would fight rather than abandon their policy. If such a breakdown should occur, a nation whose security and national life depend wholly upon freedom of movement at sea would find itself at the mercy of other Powers: for a force capable of injuring it so vitally as to compel its surrender could be put into existence, and effectively set in motion, far more rapidly than one sufficient for its defence, mainly on account of the mere numbers required. An island nation has no continental backdoor through which supplies can reach it if the sea is closed.

If collective action involving this complete surrender of sovereignty, which may leave a nation wholly exposed in the event of a breakdown of the machinery of peace, is not considered practicable, there is another form in which it may be employed. Each nation, retaining in its own possession such national forces as are sufficient and adapted to the needs of its defence, would unreservedly engage to place those forces at the disposal of the common cause in defence of any nation which should be the victim of aggression. If the system of an "international force" is a "police" solution this might be said to correspond with the "hue and cry." In principle it is a system of alliances, the terms of the alliance being that each member engages to put its forces into use against a common enemy—the aggressor—on the understanding of reciprocal service by the others.

The principal difficulty of both these forms of collective action would seem to lie in that characteristic of man upon which Montesquieu remarked that men are led continually to wish for the advantages of Society without incurring its burdens. Every one wishes for security, but none is inclined to incur the risks which appear inseparable from it. The old experience of the Amphictyonic League seems to reproduce itself. The members of that League had a sovereign jurisdiction over the cities who were parties to it, could decide their complaints and condemn to punishment the guilty city. "But their verdicts were not always put into execution when they struck at a powerful nation which could offer resistance. The position of the Amphictyonic League will but illustrate its powerlessness to become the common tribunal of Greece. Not all the Greek states were represented—neither the Ætolians, the Achaeans nor the Acarnanians had a voice in the Assembly. . . . The orders of the Amphictyons were executed only when a people found it in their interest to do so . . . when it became necessary to defend Greece against the Persians the League could do nothing. More than half the members followed the arms of Xerxes."[3] We have our Ætolians, Achaeans and Acarnanians to-day, and we find that decisions of our modern League do not prove binding upon powerful nations, and that there is a reluctance to employ force against such nations. If collective action is to be effective as a prophylactic against war and a protection which shall give confidence, a very solid guarantee of action would seem necessary. But the history of guarantees, formulated in Treaties and Alliances, furnishes melancholy reading. Lord Landsdowne remarked, in the course of the discussions of the Anglo-Japanese Alliance, that we may

[3] Daremberg and Saglio.

expect such obligations to be fulfilled only when it appears to statesmen, taking an enlightened and patriotic view, that it is to the advantage of their country to do so; and San Giuliano, excusing his country from joining the Central Powers, remarked with undoubted truth that it would be necessary "to convince the good sense of our people that the advantages to be gained would be commensurate with the dangers and sacrifices incurred." So too, though the Suez Canal Convention proclaimed the neutrality of the Canal, when that neutrality was violated by two of the signatory Powers, Signor Salandra declined to take action to guard it.[4]

Decision on this question is plainly one for statesmen. If it should be their decision that collective action is desirable and practicable, the manner in which it shall take shape, and the practicability and effectiveness of the various forms of action, have still to be determined.

The problem is to compel compliance upon a powerful individual state. What part could sea power play in collective action?

There are two means of bringing pressure upon a people. Armed forces may enter their territory, overcome opposition, and force submission by putting all such restraints upon the life of a people as superior force enables them to put; or the country may be isolated and every form of intercourse across its frontiers by land and sea prohibited. This is "blockade" in its most drastic and complete form, such as Napoleon designed against England in his Berlin

[4] I have given other instances of the same phenomenon in my *Imperial Defence and Capture at Sea.*

and Milan Decrees. The action of fighting forces in such a "blockade" is that of custom-house and revenue officers. The war—for war it would be—would be conducted at the Custom Houses and Post Offices through which no goods or correspondence to or from the offending nation would be allowed to pass, or only such goods as the combined authorities should permit by licence. No merchant vessel of the offending Power would be admitted into any harbour or furnished with any of its needs. No foreign bottoms would carry its goods.

The ostracised nation might strike back. It might invade territories of the weaker neighbours, or send out ships to do injury to the shipping of any or all of those who refused to conduct business with it. To do so would be to invite active retaliatory action, and need invite no more. The siege would continue as sieges of fortresses have continued notwithstanding sallies by the garrison.

Even the greatest nations cannot stand isolation for long. Russia, in the days of Napoleon, when international trade had not become as important as it is to-day, was seriously distressed by the circumscription of her export trade caused by the Continental System: and in the late war she was beginning to suffer from the results of isolation so early as December, 1914. Calculations made by the Committee of the Twentieth Century Fund on Economic Sanctions[5] indicate very roughly the part which foreign trade plays in the economic life of the nations. Taking the United States as the starting-point for comparison, the "intercourse index," or proportional importance of the

[5] *Boycotts and Peace*, edited by Evans Clark. Harper and Bros. 1932.

foreign trade of the great Powers, is there shown as follows: United States 1.0, Japan 1.8, Italy 2.4, Germany 2.6, France 3.7, United Kingdom 5.1; the figures for the United Kingdom being based only on foreign trade and not including the trade with the rest of the Empire, which amounts to about one-third of the whole external trade of the country. Thus there is considerable variation in the extent to which isolation would affect the several Powers, but even those which are least dependent upon their foreign trade,[6] like the United States, could not stand the economic effects of a world boycott for long.

What part would sea power play in such an economic boycott?[7] It is not uncommonly assumed that the whole duty of that part of the boycott which relates to the sea frontiers would fall upon the British navy, and that the action which it would have to take would be to conduct a blockade of the kind to which we are accustomed: ships or squadrons stationed in the approaches to the commercial ports, covered from action by the naval forces of the blockaded nation by squadrons and fleets placed in suitable positions. This picture misconceives the action. The definite act of restraint would be the general embargo. There would be no question of stopping, examining, and bringing into port for adjudication ships suspected of

[6] "It is usually estimated that only about 10 per cent. of the combined domestic and foreign trade of the United States is foreign, while the corresponding figure for Great Britain is 62 per cent." Quoted from D. M. Anderson Jr., "The World's Economic Dilemma" in *Boycotts and Peace*, p. 206 n.

[7] Boycott has been defined as "Conduct whereby two or more states combine to interfere with the economic or political freedom of another, as by cutting off trade with its territory." C. C. Hope, *Political Science Quarterly*, June, 1933.

carrying goods either directly, or indirectly, through neutral ports, to the blockaded country: since, by hypothesis, all communications would be severed at their source, no regular trade would pass, and there would be no neutral ports through which trade could filter as it did in the War of 1914–18. In fact, the act of trading would be "contraband" in the true, the proper meaning of the word. There would be no need to interfere with that part of the internal distributive system of the country, the coasting trade. Interference would be confined to the external trade. There would be no need to station ships to capture the mercantile shipping of the offending Power, as that shipping would not sail except between its own ports: since it could not go elsewhere, all ports except its own being closed to its commerce. But inasmuch as there always are some persons who will seek to make profits by conducting a forbidden trade, so the stationing of vessels to perform the duties of revenue cutters and intercept such "free-traders" would be required. This duty could not fall upon one only of the Powers, any more than it did in Crete or off Durazzo. It would be a duty in which vessels of all the navies would co-operate.

Those who condemn this form of offensive on the score of the inefficiency of blockade in the past, fail to appreciate that no such a complete blockade has ever yet been attempted in war with the single and partial exception of the blockade of the Southern States by the Federals in the War of the Secession, which was hampered by the existence of neutral entrepôts and blockade runners. In none of the great wars in which Great Britain has engaged has she attempted to conduct a complete blockade, with an economic object, of an enemy Power. The paper blockade of the Orders-in-Council of 1809 was riddled by the licence system, and trade continued to pour freely into France in many parts. Moreover, there is a wide difference between an attempt to shut off so vast a region as the whole of Europe, in an era when countries could largely supply their own wants of food and materials, and a closing of all communication, by land and sea, with a single Power, in the conditions of economic interdependence of to-day. However highly "economic nationalism" may succeed in making it possible for countries to live by taking in their own washing, they still have to depend upon others for many of their raw materials and their food.

Examination of this problem would throw some light upon the quantitative elements in the problem of sea power. If joint action is to be taken against an offender, the share which each should take should plainly be relative to his strength: as, for example, each nation which contributes to the upkeep of the Ice Patrol in the North Atlantic makes a provision proportional to the quantity of its shipping using the North Atlantic route. Thus strength would, in the first place, be dependent upon economic need, and tempered, either upward or downward, by the elements of geographical situation and the ability which oversea possessions confer in rendering protection possible: and those who, as the resultant of these, needed sea forces most, and therefore possessed the largest measures of sea power, would eventually furnish the largest contingents to the common cause.

The qualitative element is also affected. The services to be performed would not call for the use of great ships, of submarines or of aircraft carriers. Each nation would possess a fleet proportioned in number to its needs and thereby affording it a safeguard if the machinery of peace should break down. The fleets would merely be composed of vessels smaller than those of to-day, and without some of those instruments of to-day which have added to the burden, without adding to the security, of nations.

The difficulty of this solution is in fact not of a military character. It lies elsewhere, partly in the reluctance of nations to take the risk of being engaged in a war in which their interests may not be directly involved, partly in the risk of unknown committals; partly also in the risk that, when the time came, some nations would fail to fulfil their engagements, as others have done before; and partly in the loss of trade which a nation taking part in the boycott, or blockade, would itself suffer in some of its trades. On the military side, there is the doubt, already referred to, that the pressure produced by economic action is too slow acting to be effective. The long-drawn-out resistance of the Central Powers is quoted in evidence.[8] This objection fails to take account of the great quantity of supplies which were collected before economic pressure became effective, and of the fact that Italy did not declare war for a year, nor the United States for two years and a half; of the in-

[8] "Yet handicapped in these ways (*i.e.*, lack of nitrates, cotton, rubber, copper, manganese, mercury, chrome, nickel, tin, petroleum and sulphur), hemmed in on two land fronts, and subjected to the full pressure of the British sea power, Germany, with the help of her allies, stood off most of the world for four years." *Boycotts and Peace*, p. 189.

sistence of various neutrals on continuing to send supplies; of the many loopholes which it was impossible to close— while, for example, Sweden was a neutral friendly to the Central Powers; and, by no means least, of the great volume of supplies obtained from the occupied territories in Belgium, Poland and Rumania and the Ukraine. Moreover, and this is far more important, it is impossible to compare the attitude of a nation at war, and its endurance of grievous and grinding shortage while it still entertains a hope of victory, or at least of avoidance of defeat, with the attitude of one which is considering whether it will expose itself to the risk of such injury. The deterrent effects are to be taken into account; and the deterrents are of a double nature. There is that of the chaotic conditions which would be created within twenty hours of the boycott, the widespread unemployment and closing down of foreign business, the cessation of all foreign sailings of the trading fleet: and that of the extremely strong probability that military victory—a successful invasion of one of the weaker neighbours and seizing of its supplies, or the capture of some isolated and exposed position of one of the confederated Powers—would fail to relieve the pressure. That pressure would remain in force until any territory invaded had been evacuated: and any military attacks upon any one of the confederates would not only meet with the combined resistance of the whole, so far as it should be geographically possible, but also lead to retaliatory action in one of the many possible forms. So long as the boycotted Power desisted from armed action in any form it would not be attacked.

251

The late war furnishes no evidence that an economic boycott by sea and land power would fail to have a deterrent effect. Such evidence as the War affords is that there was no prior fear of isolation. A speedy victory was expected on land and while[9] that was being gained, all the needs of the country could be provided by the large stocks accumulated in advance, any further needs could be met by circumventing the action of sea power which, in the supposed interests of humanity, had been emasculated by the successive Declarations of 1856 and 1909.

The question of whether security by collective action is possible is, in fact, neither a military nor a naval one. It is purely political. It depends entirely upon whether there is will or a mere wish behind the Pact of Paris. If that Pact is no more than an expression of a love of peace, if it lacks the driving force of an irresistible and intensive desire, then we are not entitled to expect any solution of the problem of naval armaments through its existence. "The Abbé de St. Pierre," wrote Frederick the Great, "sent me an excellent treatise on the means of restoring peace to all Europe and on the manner of preserving it continually. The thing is exceedingly practicable, nor is anything except the consent of all Europe and some other such trifles wanting for its accomplishment." The sneer was justifiable and the same thing may be said to-day. Economic boycott is "exceedingly practicable" but the consent of the world is needed for its accomplishment. It does not abolish the

[9] "It will be a violent storm, but very short: I count on a war of three or at most of four months and have organised all my policy on that assumption." (Bethmann Hollweg to Von Bülow in August, 1914.)

need for navies and armies. There must be power to enforce the isolation, and the form of that power is sea power to prevent illicit communication at sea, and land power to close the doors on land.

COLLECTIVE ACTION BY CO-OPERATION

The alternative method of collective action which has been widely advocated is the formation of an international air force which shall be used to destroy the property and life of a people whose Government has given offence. It is commended highly on the score of the ability it confers to take action immediately, irresistibly and effectively; in contrast to what is assumed to be the slow and ineffective action of economic force. Yet so far as speed of coming into operation is concerned it can begin no more quickly than economic action; for neither measure, bombardment nor boycott, can be put into force until judgment has been given by some established and acknowledged body of international authority, agreement reached that action shall be taken, and orders given for the execution of the measures prescribed. Those three processes are as indispensable to bombardment as to boycott and can proceed no more quickly in one case than in the other: indeed, if we should be asked whether a decision were more likely to be given to apply force by slaughter or by depriving a people of the economic benefits of trade, the answer would seem to be that there would be more hesitation to take lives and destroy property, which cannot be restored, than to stop the movement of goods which can be resumed directly the cause of the offence is removed.

All of these essential preliminary steps to action take time, and while, in certain cases, but by no means in all, the killing and destruction can begin within a few hours of the issue of the final order for its execution, the economic measures begin no less quickly. Not a train passes the frontier, not a transaction of any kind can take place. Shipping of the offending nation cannot enter a harbour, receive supplies, or discharge goods, except under such licences as may be given in order to minimise the injury the boycotting Powers would inflict upon their own people. No goods would be laden by the offending shipping in any foreign port, and no supplies—fuel, food, water—furnished: nor would the faciiities of any port be at its disposal. The entire shipping industry of the offending nation would be paralysed and its foreign trade would cease. Certainly businesses in all the boycotting Powers would suffer, but while the injury would be distributed among them it would be concentrated on the one offender. While they would lose that percentage of their total trade with the offender, he would suffer to the extent of one hundred per cent. of his foreign trade, with such reactions upon his internal trade as result from its dependence upon external supplies and markets. The bombardments of the air force would be felt in the cities selected for bombardment. The economic blow would be felt in every city and factory throughout the country within as short a time as the bombardment. And, whereas there are Powers which lie far beyond the reach of air bombardments and could not be touched with any serious result until means had been provided to transport air forces to positions within reach, the economic arm, independent of distance, would come into being immediately. But neither life nor limb, house or factory, church, monument or museum would receive the smallest injury.

In contrast to this most far-reaching and eminently humane method of compelling compliance upon an aggressor, we are invited to organise an instrument whose effectiveness depends entirely upon its powers of destruction of life, of buildings, of means of communication and sanitation, within a state. A method which cannot reach some powerful states, and cannot be effective against others; which will destroy what it cannot give back, and will leave behind it, as a reminder, the graves and the ruins to be a no less permanent obstacle to the resumption of friendly relations: in other words, of Peace.

SECURITY BY INDIVIDUAL ACTION

If, however, this determination to ensure peace or to deal with a perturbator, by common action, is absent; or if statesmen deem it impossible to place confidence in the engagements made by others; or if they cannot, in practice, commit themselves and their successors to take action without reservations, the logical conclusion would appear to be that each nation must for its own security arm itself in its own defence, or form defensive alliances with others. Since it then has to depend upon itself only, or upon allies with whom it can negotiate agreements, its armaments must be adequate for its security, either singly or in association with others, and the meaning which it attaches to the word "security" must be reasonable. In that event the investigation of the problem of naval armaments and sea power becomes one of first defining "security" and then, in the words of Admiral Sir Cyprian Bridge, to determine what is "the smallest fleet that can do the work it is wanted to do" and what are "the smallest and least costly ships that can play their part in war."

It must be obvious that there can be no such a thing as complete security: that is, total immunity from injury. Any nation which should desire invulnerability would need a navy so immense that it could hardly fail to avoid being regarded as a danger to all other Powers. Security, in fact, is a question of degree. No great nation, it is suggested, should be at the mercy of another in consequence of that other having it in his power to inflict a vital blow so rapidly that surrender to his demands is rendered inevitable.

If the many difficulties of a political character which stand in the way of the adoption of a collective system of security at sea, either by the method of the international police or of the international Hue and Cry, are deemed insuperable, and if each must, therefore, provide, as each has hitherto done, for his own security, or for the quota which he must furnish to the alliance, the problem is to discover the smallest aggregate force in point of numbers, size and types which can perform the functions necessary for security: and to eliminate all those types which are not, fundamentally, necessary. Answers to two questions are required. What dictates the size of a navy? What dictates the size of the fighting ship?

The ultimate object of a navy is concerned with the security of communications—either the security of its own, which was the object, for instance, of the Japanese navy in the war with Russia, or the insecurity of its enemy's, which was the object of the Russian navy. Almost inevitably the strategy which results from the circumstances requires the employment of a main body, or "mass," in concentration and of detachments on the lines of communication. The analogue is to be found in land warfare. A mass is set in motion whose object it is to overcome the mass of the enemy. As it advances it leaves behind it and is dependent upon a line of communications, which is liable to become the objective of its enemy. Hence there are two separate though not independent forces, the troops in the field and the troops on the line of communications.

The size of the army in the field is dictated by the size of the opposing army. The number of troops employed in the line of communications depends upon the numbers of convoys needing defence and on the requirements of garrisons holding important positions. The one is relative, the other is, in the first place absolute, being relative not to the total number of an enemy force but to the reasonably probable number of the detachments with which an enemy may harass the posts or the convoys. At sea, the fleet corresponds to the army in the field and the cruising vessels to the troops on the lines of communications.

Hence, that which dictates the size of the navy is in two parts. The strength of the battle fleet is relative to the strength of the probable opposing fleet, and is governed partly by its numbers, partly by the geographical situations and the form which the strategy must adopt. The

cruiser strength must suffice to furnish detachments in all
the positions in which they are required, in strength sufficient to meet such attacks as it is reasonably possible to
anticipate.

THE BATTLE FLEET OR "MASS"

Obviously, since the size of the battle fleet depends upon
the size of its opponent, some standard is needed by which
to measure. All standards—the yard, the metre, the pint or
the ton—are arbitrary. In the problem of armaments, is it
possible to establish an arbitrary standard by which all
"battle fleets" shall be measured?

Admittedly there are many practical difficulties. Yet we
know that some standards have gradually developed in the
past. Competition continued until a point at which one of
the competitors felt that he could not continue to compete
and at that point the navies settled down. In the eighteenth century, France and Spain each furnished themselves with as many capital ships as their finances would
admit: in round numbers—they varied from time to time
—France might have seventy or eighty, Spain fifty or
sixty. As the political conditions appeared to make it probable that England would find herself opposed by a coalition between France and Spain, so this constituted the
standard for the strength of the British fleet; an alliance
with Holland, to come into operation in certain defined
circumstances, furnishing a margin. As it was the settled
policy of Great Britain to maintain her fleet at this Two
Power standard, so it was recognised that there was little
use in straining the national finances of France or Spain to

enter into a shipbuilding contest. The security of those countries was primarily dependent upon the strength of their land forces. Their alliance made it impossible for England to impose her will upon either of them by sea.

Standards were adopted at the Washington Conference. The United States had expressed her intention of having a fleet equal to that of the strongest Power, for reasons which have been discussed elsewhere. Japan was accorded a relative strength of sixty per cent. of these, France and Italy each a strength of one-third. For reasons to which reference has already been made this was inacceptable to France; it gave her only one-half of the number of ships of the line which, in her opinion, were necessary for the security of her communications with her oversea Empire. Germany was not represented at the Conference, for the Treaty of Versailles had fixed her strength for the time being, and she was not permitted to possess ships of the size which the Conference proposed to discuss.

The "standard" in this case was the quantitative size to which the United States was prepared to reduce its proposed battle fleet, namely fifteen ships. The numbers of battleships to be possessed by the other Powers were related to that figure. This solution was mathematical, not strategical. It took no account of the strategical needs of the lesser among the maritime states: and it took no account of the future of Germany.

If we accept the principles that lesser Powers have as much right to security as greater Powers; and that the greater Sea Powers are the greater because of their dependence on the sea, and therefore their needs are greater;

and that their needs are dictated by the strength of the lesser; then the true starting-point of the investigation is not the strength of the greater but the strength of the less great. The correct method is not to adopt an arbitrary strength for the greater and then to accord some proportions of this to the lesser, irrespective of whether that strength conforms to their needs, but to proceed in precisely the reverse fashion; fixing strength for those lesser ones which will give them, so far as it is humanly possible to do so, such strength as will meet their needs, and from that to calculate the resulting needs of those whose dependence upon the sea is greatest. This, as remarked earlier, is what has happened in practice, the size of the "battle fleets"—and it is with "battle fleets" that this part of the investigation is concerned—of the lesser Power having been determined ultimately by the purse, and that of the greater by the strength of the lesser. The standard for Great Britain was successively the fleets of the Bourbon Powers, the Dual Alliance, and Germany: the standard for Italy, until the time of the War, was the fleet of Austria: the standard for France, up to the time of the Dual Alliance, the fleets of the next two European Powers: a standard which would appear to have been recognised later as unnecessary as the sea could not play a decisive part if she became embroiled with an alliance of Germany and Italy, whose joint land forces would decide the issue, however strong France might have been at sea. The standard for Japan before the Russo-Japanese War was the Eastern squadrons of Russia.

Thus, while no generalisation can express an exact or a

full truth, it is not very far from the truth that, until the time when Germany adopted the policy of world-wide Germanism, the measuring rod of naval battle strength was the fleet of Austria. It was the strength of her fleet which dictated the five-to-four strength of the Italian fleet. It was the strength of the Italian fleet which, if it did not precisely dictate, largely influenced the strength of the fleet of France. In the North of Europe there is nothing to show what dictated the strength of Russia, as laid down in the programme of 1888 to which reference has already been made. It had the appearance of being arbitrary, though it is proper to attribute it to some strategical cause. The strength of England was dictated by the joint strength of the two next Powers, France and Russia, with each of which political relations were unsatisfactory. Thus, though these several strengths were based upon regional require-ments, they were in actuality interdependent: and until the bombshell of the German policy was thrown into the machinery, a considerable measure of stability and secu-rity had been attained.

Is it possible and is it practicable in the world to-day to proceed upon similar lines? Can we select as a starting-point the navy of one nation and build up by agreement the quantitative strengths of the other Powers as they were built up in a practical manner by the sheer course of events?

No one will be so foolish as to pretend that this is an easy matter; but it does not appear impossible to approach the problem on the lines of those principles of which we have had a practical demonstration. Is there a nation whose sea power can be taken as the measuring rod of the remainder? I suggest that Germany is such a nation and that, provided provision is made for her own security within the Baltic *vis-à-vis* her two neighbours, Russia and Poland, the quantitative battleship strength of Germany, as established by the Treaty of Versailles, would properly serve as the starting-point of general agreement. We can reach stability, as it was reached earlier, by processes of competition, but increase in the weaker must inevitably, as long as the purse holds out, result in increases in the stronger, whose strength, as we have seen, has always been determined by the weaker. But eventually, at the cost in money and in international ill-will, stability is bound to be reached: and that stability may not impossibly be one which leaves a nation, whose dependence on the sea is paramount, insecure, through inability to maintain the measure of strength by means of which alone it can protect itself.

The Treaty of Versailles assigned to Germany a strength of eight armoured ships. They would have been "battleships" if they had been as large as the great ships of other Powers, but, being too weak to "lie in the line" against the large ships with which other nations proposed to equip themselves, they were "armoured cruisers." The number, eight, had no strategical significance. Presumably it was intended to be a convenient tactical measure, giving Germany a battle squadron of two divisions of four ships each. This was the usual arrangement, both in England and Germany.

If then a beginning should be made by taking the German strength of eight ships as the datum, from which to calculate the needs of other nations on a basis of "parity of security," which is the only true form of "parity" though the word has most unfortunately acquired a mathematical connotation, we have then to consider the next Power in the scale. Which nation is most affected, most liable to injury at sea, by German sea power? To this there can be no other answer than, France. We have seen that France, at the Washington Conference, expressed the view that the battleship strength which she needed for the security of her Mediterranean communications and her Empire was ten ships of the line. The question which arises to-day is, with what strength would France consider that she would be secure at sea against Germany? There can be little or no doubt that a war between those two Powers would be decided on the land as in 1870–1 and that the sea would play an auxiliary part. The economic element could not be decisive, for neither Power, however great its preponderance at sea, could so isolate the other as to produce a decision. Military supplies, even if the sea were "commanded," would be able to reach either over its land frontiers. The experience of the War of 1914–18 demonstrates this beyond a shadow of doubt. What number then, would place France in a position to ensure that the scales were not turned against her in her military operations by action at sea?

Admittedly the answer to this question can be given only by France. Any figures, therefore, that are suggested here are to be considered as illustrative of the system rather than as opinions of the actual need. Let it then be supposed for this purpose of illustration that France should consider either a five-to-four superiority, which was the proportion which Italy deemed necessary for herself against Austria, to suffice: that is ten ships: or that no less than a fifty per cent. superiority would be required: that is, twelve ships.

Would either of these figures place Germany at the mercy of France? Bearing in mind the impossibility of effective economic action; bearing also in mind that an even greater superiority in the War of 1870–1 did not affect the course of events; and recollecting that an even far greater superiority, combined with the closing of the frontiers with Russia and Italy, was unable to produce a decision until after over four years of war, it cannot be said that even the greater of these figures would add in any degree to the offensive power of France. It would not enable a blockade of the ports of the North Sea to be put into operation. It would not be sufficient to conduct even a brief operation in the Baltic. But it would suffice to ensure that no military operations of a combined order, prejudicial to the main military campaign, could be undertaken in the Channel. For the battle value of the flotilla of to-day and to-morrow—surface, subsurface and supersurface—has also to be reckoned with.

If, for the sake of argument, we should suppose that the higher proportion was considered necessary for French security, our attention passes to the other sea in which that security is involved. What would be the reaction of Italy to this figure—twelve?

Italy has plainly asserted that her security demands a force not less than that of France. She draws about eighty-five per cent. of her imports and exports from countries outside the Mediterranean, the bulk of which reaches her from the westward. She has no alternative line of approach in another ocean. And if France regards communication with her North African Empire as essential, in order that that large proportion of her military strength which is maintained in Africa shall be able to move in security to France to reinforce the metropolitan armies, Italy may reply that it is equally in the interests of her own security that this reinforcement should be prevented. In other words, that she is no less interested than France in sea power in the Mediterranean.

The Washington Conference provided for equality in battleship strength between the two Mediterranean Powers and it would appear improbable that Italy would accept any departure from that relativity. Departure could indeed only be attained by a shipbuilding contest which would come to an end only by exhaustion of the financially weaker Power: a contest which could not take place without repercussions upon the strengths of the other principal European Powers, Germany and England, and ultimately upon Japan and the United States.

It would therefore appear that whatever strength might have been agreed upon for France, Italy would assert the right to maintain the principle of equality in battleship strength.

Passing upward another step in the maritime hierarchy, the Power which next comes into consideration is Japan. Until the Russo-Japanese War brought an end to Japan's danger from Russia, the strength of the Japanese fleet was dictated by that of Russia. What, so far as can be seen, dictates that strength to-day? Japan is insular, increasingly dependent upon her external trade to maintain a constantly growing population which does not produce food enough for its people. She has acquired possessions on the mainland of Asia with which it is indispensable that communication shall be maintained. It is beyond her powers, since she possesses no oversea bases in the main routes of commerce through the Indian Ocean and Mediterranean, and in the Atlantic and Pacific where her merchant ships ply, to afford direct defence to her shipping. But while she may suffer from the loss of that shipping, or of its services, in a war, her national needs could still be furnished by sea by neutral shipping, provided she were secure against blockade and could maintain communication with her dominions in Asia.

Blockade demands superiority of force. In the geographical position occupied by Japan that superiority would have to be considered. The figure allotted to Japan at the Washington Conference was one of sixty per cent. of the strength of the strongest Powers and, though there was a strong demand made for seventy per cent., it was a demand which it was impossible to maintain on the grounds of strategy. Insistence upon a higher proportion, a proportion plainly exceeding the requirements of security, could hardly fail to be held to imply that the interpretation of the word "security" was security for expansion, and to lead to refusal; and if insistence were then maintained, to increases by other Powers with interests in the Far East. This would end only with the power of the purse, as it has always, leaving matters as they were before but with an increased burden upon the shoulders of all the nations directly concerned; and in its turn, would lead to increases by Powers not directly concerned with the situation in the Far East but very directly concerned with the effect that such increases by others would produce upon their own security.

If then the answer of Japan should be that she required sixty per cent. of the battleship strength of the strongest Power, this could only be expressed in quantitative terms by an announcement of the figures desired by the strongest Power.

Two Powers remain—the United States and Great Britain. The policy of the United States has been plainly announced—equality with Great Britain. It would, therefore, fall to Great Britain to state what she required.

The policy which Great Britain, up to the time of the competition with Germany, had maintained, was that of the Two Power standard. That standard applied to European Powers. Although it originated in the political conditions in which it appeared that Great Britain was exposed to certain coalitions, it was a policy which, even when that possibility was not present on the political horizon, gave a stability to the general situation. It made no invidious selection of particular Powers as potential enemies. It gave her the margin of superiority which her entire dependence upon the sea demanded. The re-adoption of this policy, in the event of adoption of the figures pre-supposed for Germany, France and Italy, would result in the British requirements being twenty-four ships, which, in its turn would give Japan a force of fourteen or, preferably, fifteen ships.

This brings us to the qualitative element in the problem. No one, it may safely be asserted, desires to see such an increase in expenditure as would be represented by adding another nine ships of 35,000 tons to the fifteen already provided for, each of which costs some seven or more millions to build, and nearly half a million each annually for maintenance, with a replacement every twenty years. Nor, it must equally be supposed, does any one wish the re-armament of Germany to take the form of substituting ships of 35,000 tons for those of 10,000 tons to which she is now limited. Yet it would be blindness itself to refuse to recognise that if other Powers insist upon their battleships being of that size, Germany will require that she shall not be forbidden to possess similar instruments: perhaps not to-day, but we have to take a long view; on Bastiat's words not merely to "voir" but to "prévoir." Moreover, the essence of any scheme of proportional allocations of strength is that the comparisons are made between similar instruments. Hence it is of the highest importance that an investigation of a more profound nature than that which informed the adoption of the present great ships should be conducted.

How widely opinions differ on this matter has been shown earlier but it may be repeated. The United States takes the view that the present size of 35,000 tons is irreducible. Japan has given 28,000 tons, France is building ships of nearly 27,000 tons; Italy, though she had expressed herself prepared to go to lower figures, will not be prepared to accept a size smaller than that adopted by

France, and has recently (June, 1934) announced her intention to build ships of 35,000 tons. Great Britain has tentatively proposed a reduction to 25,000 or even 22,000 tons; and it is by no means certain that, notwithstanding what is said by constructors as to the impossibility of building a ship possessing the qualities desired of withstanding the effects of the bomb and the torpedo, that this is not reducible: for, as long experience in other forms of warfare have shown, the effect of new weapons may be counteracted by tactical methods, by more open formations, flexibility and mobility.

It is often asserted that a reduction in the tonnage of the ship would involve a greater expenditure. This is very far from being the fact. If the unit tonnage of 10,000 tons should be adopted, the total tonnage of the greater battle fleets would be 240,000 tons in place of the 525,000 of to-day: and reduction of armaments would not take the contradictory form of an increase in the armaments of Germany. Even if a higher figure of 15,000 were adopted the total tonnage—360,000 tons—would be less than three-quarters of that of the fleets of to-day. Nor can there be any doubt that the fleets themselves of all the Powers would be better instruments regarded as a whole, than those composed of a lesser number of extremely costly vessels. Every naval thinker of forty and fifty years ago was fully aware of this, and deplored the growth in the size for reasons nautical, strategical, tactical and administrative.

THE CRUISER

From the battleship we pass to the cruiser. We are considering, let it be recollected, the problem of "security by individual effort," on the assumption that though collective security is practicable in a purely naval sense, its adoption is considered impossible for political reasons.

The "cruiser" is a vessel which either works with the main body of a fleet, mainly for acquiring information but also for the many minor duties which constantly arise, or acts in detached services, of which the direct operations in defence and attack of sea lines of communication are the most prominent. The "cruiser problem," like that of the battleship, is in two parts. What dictates the number of cruisers? and what dictates their individual size?

As there are two kinds of duty, so the question of number is a two-fold one. What dictates the number of cruisers attached to a fleet? There is no generally accepted proportion or method of calculation, some considering that the number bears a definite relation to the number of ships of the line, while others connect it with the area of water which the "eyes of the fleet" have to examine.

What experience have we of the numbers with which fleets have been provided in war? Counting only "light" cruisers—that is to say "true" cruisers and not their heavy supports, which are a modern innovation arising out of the increased size which cruisers attained as the result of the policy which has been described earlier—at Tsushima Togo had twenty;[10] at Jutland Von Scheer had nine and Jellicoe twenty-three. Admiral Hughes, U. S. N., estimated

[10] Namely, sixteen cruisers proper, and four armed merchant vessels. The Russian fleet was first sighted by one of the latter. The heavy cruisers were in the line of battle.

that twenty-six was the number needed with the American battle fleet.[11]

The experience of sailing-ship warfare affords no guidance for us today. The conditions were different in every way. In general, the number of frigates which a fleet or squadron possessed was very small and was dictated, first, by the number needed for repeating signals, but eventually by the number which was available when the needs of commerce protection had been satisfied. One note runs continuously through the despatches of all the Admirals of the eighteenth century—that they never had enough for their needs. Two short extracts will illustrate what some of those needs were. The first relates to the duties as scouts. Admiral Graves, about to sail for North America in March, 1780, writes thus to the First Lord: "Your Lordship will pardon me for taking notice that there is only one frigate attached to eight sail of the line going upon foreign service. *Frigates are not inapplicably called the eyes of the squadron: they certainly are the scouts and the voice of it.* To have but one eye is certainly too little and to have but one scout deprives you of half your powers; since upon any second occasion you must either detach a capital ship, to the weakening of a small squadron, or remain in a very uninformed state." The second relates to the help which cruisers could give to disabled ships. The occasion was that critical summer of 1779, when a British fleet under Sir Charles Hardy was facing a superior combined Franco-Spanish fleet in the entrance of the Channel. The Controller, Charles Middle-

[11] Report No. 834 of March 3rd, 1928, made to the House of Representatives.

ton, then wrote thus to the First Lord: "It is very material at this time to supply Sir Charles Hardy's fleet with every frigate, sloop and cutter that can possibly be spared. In case of defeat in the Channel they may be the means of saving every disabled ship." The disabled ship of to-day no less welcomes the help which the lesser craft can give her. She too may have to be towed out of action and protected by a screen of lesser vessels against attack by torpedo-craft: as the *Lion* was after her disablement at the Dogger Bank. Finally, one may quote the expressive words of Nelson, written a few days after the battle of the Nile, which are truly a summary of what his many predecessors had said in different forms. "Was I to die at this moment, want of frigates would be found stamped on my heart. No words of mine can express what I have and am suffering from the want of them."

To attempt rigidly to formulate a "correct" establish-ment of strength for this function of the cruiser, would be impracticable, in the lights of the different opinions which are held as to what should govern it; of the approach in size which the larger vessels of the flotilla have made to the cruiser and the possibilities of their use as scouts; and of the further possibilities that aircraft can, in fine weather, act as far-reaching eyes of a fleet. The undesirability of a rigid international formula governing allocation is in-creased by the fact that it cannot be certain that all the battle forces will act in one body, accustomed though we are to-day to see a concentration of the whole force. No one can foresee the conditions under which all the several navies may have to act, and while it may appear that in almost any conceivable circumstances all the battleships of one Power would be concentrated, those of another, acting under totally different conditions, may have to operate in more places than one at a time. Great Britain, for instance, has had to maintain simultaneously large concentrations in the Channel and the Mediterranean, or in the Channel and the West Indies. In the Russian War of 1854–5 she had a fleet in the Black Sea and another in the Baltic. France has continuously had to base one fleet on Brest and another on Toulon, and Russia has necessarily had a Black Sea fleet and a Baltic fleet. The most that can be said is that account has to be taken of this necessity, and that, very roughly speaking, the "cruiser needs" of a fleet are in the neighbourhood of a score of vessels.

Passing from this element in the quantitative needs of cruisers to that of the requirements for the detached services, the broad principle hitherto has been that the number needed is governed by the services which these vessels have to perform. On very many occasions British flag officers have been called upon to indicate their requirements in cruisers, on the stations under their command. In every case the reply was made in the same form. The "focal points" where shipping came together—landfalls, narrow straits, points of departure and arrival—were summarised, and the number of vessels, including the services of relief, which were wanted to cruise in these areas, formed one portion of the requirements. The number of convoys needing protection, and the force which would have to be assigned to them, which varied according to the areas through which they had to pass, formed the other portion.

An exactly similar process of reasoning was followed in 1928 by Admiral Hughes, U. S. N., in explaining the needs of the United States. It follows so precisely the lines of the old British practice that it deserves quotation at length.

"In the event of war, the protection of our coastwise traffic would be essential to the efficient conduct of the war. . . . Our foreign commerce, particularly that from South America and in the unengaged ocean, should be assured of reasonable protection against enemy raiders. The dispositions of ships of the cruiser type would vary widely according to the special conditions obtaining at the time. The principal focal points of commerce on our eastern coast are the large shipping centres, such as Boston, New York, Philadelphia, the Capes of the Chesapeake, Charleston, Jacksonville, Pensacola, Mobile, New Orleans, Galveston and Colon. On the Pacific coast are the ports such as Seattle and the other Puget Sound ports (the Straits of Juan de Fuca), Portland, San Francisco, Los Angeles, San Diego, Panama and the Hawaiian ports. . . .

"The fleet should never be tied to home ports through lack of means to advance overseas. If such an advance is made, convoys would be required for the service of supplying essential articles to the fleet. This requires cruisers for convoy duty. . . . This does not provide for escorts to convoys engaged in commercial pursuits. Such convoys will be required in both the engaged and unengaged ocean. In the unengaged ocean the presence of one cruiser with each convoy which is engaged in commercial traffic might be considered sufficient, but a single cruiser with a convoy in the engaged ocean would unquestionably be hazardous."

It is worthy of note that there is a very important difference between this statement of requirements and that made by Mr. Franklin Roosevelt at an earlier date. Admiral Hughes required security for the coastwise traffic, and "reasonable protection against enemy raiders" for the foreign commerce in the ocean. Mr. Roosevelt made a far wider demand. "Our national commerce must extend all over the Western Hemisphere, must go out thousands of miles to sea, must embrace the Philippines, *and over seas wherever our commerce may be* . . . we must create a navy not only to protect our shores and our possessions, but our merchant ships in time of war, *no matter where they go*." To protect shipping wherever it may go is, however, an unattainable object. As Britain could not protect her trade in the Baltic, where the enemy would always appear in superior force, nor would have been able to protect her trade in the Mediterranean against cruiser forces only, still less against flotilla forces, if she had possessed no bases in that sea, so the United States could not attain that desired degree of security in those waters where other Maritime Powers possess bases and she possesses none. Neither will any increase in numbers within the realm of practical possibilities enable her to do so, nor can size be a substitute: for small vessels are also needed in those areas where enemy flotillas of the three types are able to operate.

We thus possess a definite principle governing the cruiser strength. The strength is dictated by the number of points, fixed and moving, which require and can be given protection. It is not primarily relative to the number of cruisers possessed by other Powers, and hence the allocation of numbers upon a relative basis is incorrect. It is plain also that none of these services can be performed by aircraft, and that the existence of this new type of vessel cannot, at least for the present, either abolish or modify the need for what are called cruisers. Aircraft certainly are themselves cruisers, but they are not yet capable of performing this particular function of the cruiser. It would go far towards eliminating that friction which has been only too prominent in some of the conferences if all attempts to establish "ratios" in cruiser strength were abandoned.

If, however, there is to be stability in sea power, those ratios of battleship strength, which have been referred to earlier (whether they be those which have been illustrated, or any other) must not be liable to be upset by cruiser forces. The fear that an opponent might suddenly concentrate his cruiser forces with his battle fleet and thereby obtain a superiority seems to constitute one of the causes of the British opposition to a reduction in the size of the battleship. Speaking of the reasons why it is believed to be impossible for the "battleship" to be reduced to 10,000 tons, the First Lord of the Admiralty said that "there is one over-riding consideration, and that is that a battleship should be overwhelmingly more powerful than the next type of ship with which it is likely to come in contact."[12]

[12] *Hansard*, vol. 287, No. 54, Monday, March 12th, 1934.

Thus, the fear of strategical concentration would appear to be the only possible explanation of this, though it is not a factor which hitherto has ever governed the relation of size of the two types.

As a mere matter of historical fact, there never was a division between battleships and cruisers in the eighteenth century, though curiously enough history is occasionally called in to bear witness that there was an established proportion of size between them. History must not be made to give false witness. There were not two types, widely separated in size. Ships were "rated" in six rates of gradually descending size, and there was no overwhelming difference between the power of the ships of one rate and of those of the next.[13] Indeed, the ship of lower rate is not infrequently to be found engaging successfully a ship of a higher one. During the late nineteenth and early twentieth centuries the "cruiser" grew steadily and, to all intents and purposes, a new system of "rating" had come into existence by 1914 which might, without much straining of accuracy,

[13] From Derrick, *Memoirs of the Royal Navy*, London, 1806:

YEARS	RATES					
	I	II	III	IV	V*	VI*
1714	100	90	80 to 70	60 to 50	40 to 30	24 to 20
1762	100	90 to 84	80 to 64	60 to 50	44 to 24	30 to 20
1805	120 to 100	98 to 90	84 to 64	60 to 50	44 to 32	28 to 20

* The apparent discrepancy or overlap in these figures is due to administrative variations in rating.

be tabulated in the same way as the older rates.[14] Lord Fisher once asked the question: "When does a cruiser become a battleship?" and answered it with another: "When does a kitten become a cat?" and the table shows that there is no precise point of division.

Thus, it would be practically impossible to differentiate the ships called "battleships" from those called "cruisers." The third rates of the table were not fit to lie in the line with the first rates, though the Germans brought them into the line at Jutland. The fourth rates could lie in the line with the third rates, as they had done at Tsushima. A greater gap indeed lay between the different types of "cruisers" than between the so-called "battleships" and "cruisers." There was a marked difference in the strength of the fifth rates and the fourth, as the battle of Coronel showed; and between that of the second and the fourth rates, as was shown at the battle of the Falkland Islands.

These "rates" were swept away after the war. The armoured cruiser and the pre-dreadnought ship disappeared, and in their place new "rates" came into existence, the so-called "capital ship," the cruiser armed with 8-inch guns, and the cruiser with 6-inch guns.

[14] Rates.

I	II	III	IV*	V	VI
"Dread-nought" battleships 15″ to 11″	Battle cruisers 15″ to 11″	Earlier battleships	Armoured cruisers 9″.2 to 8″.0	Armoured cruisers 7″.5 to 6″	Unarmoured cruisers 6″ to 4″

* *Defence* (4–9″.2:10–7″.5); *Achilles* (6–9″.2:9–7″.5); *Black Prince* (6–9″.2: 10–6″); *Scharnhorst* (8–8″.2:6–6″).

The "8-inch gun cruiser," a vessel of about 10,000 tons, constitutes the real difficulty in making a satisfactory settlement of the cruiser problem on the lines which both experience and theory indicate as correct—namely, that each nation should possess as many cruisers as is necessary for the services of security. It is not irrelevant, therefore, to examine the purpose for which this type of vessel came into existence.

No need was experienced in the War for such a vessel in the North Sea or the Mediterranean. The scouting and subsidiary duties of the main fleets, performed in the past by the smaller frigates, were performed by the vessels called "light cruisers," of which the largest were ships of about 5000 tons, but many were smaller in both fleets. The circumstances that these were supported by battle cruisers does not alter the fact that all the scouting services could be efficiently performed by these vessels, and, if there had been no battle cruisers, would have been performed without them; as they were by similar ships, and even weaker ones, in the decisive operations of the Tsushima campaign. The armoured cruisers played no effective part at Jutland. Those which came under fire of the battleships—the *Defence* and *Warrior*—were sunk. They represented an intermediate type of ship which tends to come into existence in peace and to fall out of favour, and die out, in war, except in the particular circumstances of a weak navy which seeks to correct its weakness in numbers by individual size; the policy, for instance, adopted by the United States in the days of her weakness. "It was considered very important that all national ships should exceed in size and equipment those of the same class of the enemy: not merely that it should render victory more certain in single combats, but as it would put *hors de combat* all the ships of Great Britain of a similar size. If our sloops of war, frigates and seventy-fours were larger, mounted more guns, and fought more men than those of that nation, they would not cruise against us ship for ship."[15] This "bigger and better" policy was a natural one to follow, though it made no appreciable difference to the course of the war.

The experience of war points directly against the necessity for the big, or "intermediate," cruiser. Some figures will illustrate how she has fallen out of favour at two very widely separated dates:

CLASS	GUNS	1793	1810	+ OR −
"Heavy" frigates...............	56 to 44	30	15	−15
Frigates.......................	38 to 20	96	162	+66
Sloops........................	18 to 10	38	246	+208
Brigs.........................	14 to 10	0	144	+144

	AUGUST 1914	NOVEMBER 1918	+ OR −
Armoured cruisers...............	46	27	−19
Light cruisers...................	79	103	+24
Sloops and destroyers...........	260	558	+298
Armed escort ships..............	0	63	+63

During the war a new type of large cruiser of nearly 10,000 tons was built. When the ships were designed nothing had occurred to show that the 5000 tons "true" cruiser was lacking either in armament, speed or endurance. In all

[15] Dearborn, *Life of Commodore William Bainbridge* (1816), edn. 1931, p. 172.

those respects she had been equal to her work. She had escorted convoys from Australia to Colombo, had crossed the North Pacific from Yokohama to Vancouver. Ships of even a lesser size had accompanied Von Spee from the Marshall Islands to Chile; they had moved, without a base to break the journey, from the West Indies to the Falklands and had hunted in the South Pacific. There was no reason to suppose that they could not catch and fight any armed raider with whatever guns she might be fitted. Yet a new type of twice the size was brought into being, with over thirty knots speed. It was totally unnecessary.

As the creation of a new type is rarely confined to its creator, so other nations, later, followed suit; and, as so often has happened before, the idea grew in men's minds that ships of this size were indispensable, and every form of argument was produced to justify their existence. It was even said that a man-of-war would risk her existence if she should engage an armed merchant ship unless she was armed with 8-inch guns: in other words, unless the power of her individual guns were two and a half times that of the merchant vessel! The indispensability of the 8-inch gun was pressed into every discussion, yet without a shadow of proof in the form of evidence. Theory, in fact, not reason based upon experience, swayed the decision. At the same time, and not only with an equal absence of evidence but with all the evidence of the long passages made by the smaller cruisers, both British and German, during the War, it was said that the requirements of endurance could not be fulfilled on a lesser displacement than 10,000 tons. Instead, therefore, of the opportunity being taken, which the Conference at Washington afforded, to sweep away these anomalous vessels and at the same time of paving the way to that reduction which was foreshadowed in the Treaty of Versailles, the ships of this wholly unnecessary size were retained and adopted as the standard type. To-day, they constitute a definite obstacle to a reasoned policy of cruiser construction. The basis of all cruiser establishments is that numbers are needed and that the armed merchant ship is the criterion of size, renders the necessary number impossible.

A return to the old policy of small cruisers on the part of all nations would give all the number they needed and at the same time remove that particular hindrance to a reduction in the size of the battleship which arises from fear of a cruiser concentration upsetting the balance. If there be any doubt of this it is only necessary to recall some incidents in the recent war, to observe the vast gap in fighting power that divides the German 10,000-ton armoured ship from the 6000-ton cruiser, and to remember how much that wide gap could be further increased if so high a speed had not been given to the armoured vessel. Although strategy is not governed by the Rule of Three, one may ask this question: If four armoured cruisers, armed with 9.2-inch and 7.5-inch guns, were not strong enough to fight one armed with ten 11-inch guns, how many unarmoured cruisers, armed with 6-inch guns, would have to be concentrated to be equal to one armed with six 11-inch guns? It would indeed require a great deal of assurance to maintain that there could be any danger whatever of a concentration of such numbers of these smaller vessels as would affect the strength of a battle fleet composed of armoured ships with heavier guns. This fear of concentration never entered the heads of the Sea officers when battleships were actually of no greater tonnage than 10,000.

Two countries in particular are affected by these fears—Great Britain and Italy. One of the reasons why the former insists upon the retention of the great battleship of over 20,000 tons is in order to ensure that no concentration of the cruisers of an enemy can be made which will expose her to the danger of defeat of her "mass." The argument is that, while she, dependent upon commerce, must keep her cruisers scattered in many parts of the world, an opponent, who can afford to leave his commerce undefended—and, indeed, who finds himself unable to defend it—may suddenly call in all his cruisers, reinforce his battle fleet, and provoke an action under the resulting favourable conditions. The creation of superiority by strategical manoeuvre is nothing new. Those who are acquainted with the history of the wars of the past are well aware of the many schemes which were proposed and employed by the French strategists to divert British force from the theatre in which it was desired to establish superiority: and it is to be recollected that the ships which then formed the squadrons abroad, and with which these movements were made, were ships of the same types—64-, 74-, 80- and 90-gun ships—as those which formed the main squadrons in home waters. Movements were met by counter movements, and there are not many instances in which, even with the limited means and slowness of communication, a move by the enemy was not met by a suitable re-disposition of force.[16]

[16] The sailing of the Toulon squadron under d'Estaing in 1778 is such an instance. The reasons why the counter move was not made are familiar to students of that war.

To-day, however, though we have the most rapid means of communication, we are supposed to be unable to make such movements. Even, however, if this pessimistic view be accepted, it constitutes no reason for the very great ship upon which so much insistence is laid. The imagined danger would disappear if the limitation of size imposed upon Germany by the Peace of Versailles were adopted by all nations.

The other country affected is Italy. France has claimed, in virtue of her extended colonial empire, that she needs, for the protection of the interests connected with it, a greater number of "cruisers" than Italy. Italy opposes this demand for the reason that these might be drawn in and transform equality in the "mass" in the Mediterranean into French superiority by the reinforcement which the battle fleet would receive from these cruisers. That it would strengthen the cruiser forces must be admitted, but with the smaller vessels of both types the cruisers thus added to the battle fleet would not increase its strength: and so far as "cruiser" superiority is concerned, a lesson is to be learned from experience. The preventive to such a concentration lies in manoeuvre, in the use of diversionary force. The few commerce-destroying cruisers and armed vessels in the War of 1914–18 continued, up to the very end of the war, to occupy the attention of a far greater number of British cruisers.

There is, in fact, no strategical, tactical or technical reason for the retention of the very large cruiser which, as stated earlier, constitutes the real difficulty of solving the "cruiser problem" on the lines of common sense: which, in the end, are the lines of security, economy and international good will.

THE FLOTILLA

While it is possible to say that there are certain elements which dictate the quantitative and the qualitative factors governing the "battleship" and the "cruiser," it is far more difficult to establish similar governing principles regarding the flotilla forces.

The flotilla of to-day consists of three types of craft—those which navigate on, below and above the surface of the water. They have come into existence gradually. They react upon one another. They are vessels which invariably appear in large numbers in war, but, as has been remarked earlier, with the exception of the fireship in the seventeenth and eighteenth centuries, they have hitherto possessed no "battle value": for the reason that, with the exception given above, artillery was the only weapon which could affect the course of a battle, and the artillery which the flotilla vessel could carry was either so light as to be ineffective, or, if heavy artillery was mounted, as it was in bomb vessels with 13-inch mortars and in the Russian gun-boats armed with 8-inch cannon, the vessels were not mobile enough to be serviceable in a sea battle. For that reason, while these small vessels were used in many hundreds, the main part they played was that of fighting the guerilla craft which harassed communications, captured many vessels and were themselves captured in numbers, but without altering the course of the war except in so far as they produced a large diversion of effort and of force: a result not to be ignored by any means; but the diversion was never sufficient to affect the operations upon which the decision finally depended—the contest between the principal "masses" and their opponents. Communications were never severed by the guerilla. It was always possible to produce sufficient vessels to oppose them, both by hunting them in the areas in which they desired to operate, or by giving the protection of escorts to the larger bodies of shipping. The vessels themselves were inexpensive and could be produced in large numbers: private firms could afford to fit them out and to make profits out of their captures.

The flotilla of to-day differs in two important respects from the flotilla of the past. Two of the types of craft of which it is composed have a definite "battle value"—the surface and the flying torpedo craft; the submarine, at least at present, is lacking in speed: and two, the flying and submarine torpedo-boats, can themselves deal serious blows to the most powerful ships when cruising, the speed of the one and the invisibility of the other enabling them to approach close enough to fire their short-ranged missiles.

Thus the flotilla is an element in sea power which it never was prior to the invention of the torpedo. It has acquired additional importance with the very great increases which have been made in the size of the vessels, their speed, their endurance and the guns with which they are armed. The torpedo-boat has in actual fact become, in the process of development under the stress of competition, a light cruiser. The modern destroyer is a vessel far more powerful than the third-class cruiser of a generation ago.

Whereas it is possible to state the requirements of a vessel of the "cruiser" class, the speed, armament and endurance which will suffice to enable her to perform the duties of a detached vessel on the lines of communication, which same characteristics will enable her to fulfil all the duties which fall to her as a unit of a fleet,[17] this is not practicable in the case of the surface torpedo craft. We are met with one dilemma at the outset. The size of the modern battleship causes her to offer a very large target to the torpedo; the number of the battleships, owing to their size, is so small that each represents a considerable proportion of the strength of the "mass," so that the loss or disablement of one is a serious matter. She cannot be readily replaced, and, under the arrangements made at Washington, all that great reserve of older ships which have hitherto existed has been swept away. Hence the greatest precautions have to be taken to preserve these costly instruments, and one of these precautions is adequately to guard her by means of small vessels.

It is indeed one of the curious anomalies of naval policy that while any reduction in size is said to be impossible because of the danger from the submarine and the air, the great vessels which are in consequence produced have to be guarded by small ones. A further anomaly in the policy is that great size is said to be essential because of the great distances which the battleships have to go—that they would be unable to cross the oceans if they were smaller. Yet when they arrive in the waters where they are required to act, they have to be guarded by small vessels, which

[17] *Vide ante*, p. 114.

must therefore be able to cover the same distances, but, by the previous hypothesis, are unable to do so. The small protectors of the great ships are therefore required to be of such a size as will enable them to accompany their charges —which, as a practical matter of fact, does not call for any very great size—and numerous enough, so far as this function of theirs is concerned, to provide an effective screen against submarine attack.

While it might theoretically be possible—though this is doubtful—to fix a definite proportion of protective small craft according to the number of ships they have to defend, it is improbable in the highest degree that any standard of offensive flotilla strength in a battle fleet could be laid down, or if laid down, adhered to. A Power weaker in ships of the line will necessarily seek to mitigate its weakness by a strong flotilla. This possibility was visualised over forty years ago, and there can be small doubt that the attention which the German command paid to the development of their flotillas was due, in no small degree, to an intention to reduce the disparity in battleship strength by a powerful and well-trained torpedo flotilla. Even if, for example, the fleet torpedo flotillas—if such units existed— were established in the same ratio as the battleships, this would not remain permanent for one day in war unless it should happen to suit both parties. For torpedo craft could be called in, as we have seen that it is feared that cruisers could be called in, to strengthen the mass, and with these important differences: that whereas the cruisers would add little to the fighting strength, owing to the disparity in power[18]

[18] *Vide post*, p. 282.

between the cruiser and the battleship, a more numerous flotilla would constitute a definite increase to actual fighting power; and that whereas a concentration of its cruisers by one Power may be met by some counter concentration by the other Power, the degree to which a concentration of surface torpedo craft would be met is far less. Submarines, as an able French officer has pointed out, furnish a means of diverting force: and a considerable flotilla would be required for the protection of lines of communication against those vessels.

To this, however, there is one compensatory provision. No limit has been placed upon the number of small vessels of under 2000 tons, gun-armed, with which nations may furnish themselves. In that clause there are the germs of important possibilities. It embodies the sound principle which should govern cruiser strength, that cruisers should be as small as they can be consistent with the performance of their functions, and that their numbers depend upon the scope of their duties. The artificial limitations by guesswork and compromise which have been adopted in the cruiser are absent in this class of vessel. No objection has been raised to their unlimited numbers; or, to put it otherwise, to leaving each nation to decide what it needs. And why? For the reasons that the vessels are small and cheap, they have no complicated armaments, and, having no torpedoes, have no battle value. Hence, no concentration of these craft, however many of them might be brought into the "mass," can affect its strength.

Any one who advocates the abolition of any particular type of vessel, or limitation of some particular instrument must be prepared to be called academic, than which no more contemptuous epithet exists in the mind of the "practical man." Yet unless the general problem of sea power is subjected to a process of reasoning, the nations of the world must be prepared to witness a considerable growth in expenditure upon sea power; a growth which, like the one we of our generation have witnessed, will be unaccompanied by any increase whatever in security.

The "destroyer," originally a cheap little vessel costing some thirty thousand pounds, may now cost ten times that sum. With the continual craving for speed which is one of the characteristics of modern construction it is not impossible that the cost will increase. Is it then "academic," or is it severely practical, to ask whether the nations must for their security (which is the object of sea power) continue to furnish themselves with this particular type of craft? For what purpose did the destroyers come into existence? Do the same needs, or analogous needs, still exist? And is it only by means of vessels of this most costly type that those needs can be fulfilled?

If the answer to the last of these questions is that no other type of craft can fulfil the duties, let one thing be plainly faced: that the European maritime Powers are living in a fool's paradise so far as the safety of their communications is an essential element in their security. The late war gave an indication of the demands to which the security of the allied communications gave rise. To guard the sea lines of movement and supply by what proved to be the only effective measure—convoy—called for the services in the Atlantic, North Sea, Channel and Mediterranean of the destroyer flotillas of France, Great Britain, Italy and the United States, together with a small contingent from Japan. Of these Great Britain furnished over four hundred; in the Home Waters alone she employed over two hundred. The communications of the Mediterranean Powers were guarded by the joint forces of all the Allies. The present surface flotillas of the present destroyer type could not meet the requirements if an attack on similar lines were again to be developed.

Two questions arise: the first concerning the danger which the above remarks visualise, the second concerning the instrument with which to meet that danger.

It may properly be suggested that there is no need for numbers of submarine-destroyers (let us call the vessels by that name, as it is with that aspect of their work that we are at this moment concerned) on the scale of the War of 1914–18. These numbers were rendered necessary because submarines were employed in the attack of mercantile shipping, in a particular manner. The London Naval Treaty of 1930 has affirmed that certain provisions contained in Part iv, Article 22, "are accepted rules of international law." They have been mentioned earlier but may be repeated:

(1) In their action with regard to merchant ships submarines must conform to the rules of international law to which surface vessels are subject.

(2) In particular, except in case of persistent refusal to stop on being duly summoned, or of active resistance to visit or search, a warship, whether surface or submarine boat, may not sink or render incapable of navigation a

merchant vessel without having first placed passengers, crew, and ship's papers in a place of safety. For this purpose the ship's boats are not regarded as a place of safety unless the safety of the passengers and crew is assured in the existing sea and weather conditions, by the proximity of land, or the presence of another vessel which is in a position to take them on board.

The high contracting Powers "invited" all other Powers to express their assent to the rule above.

It will be seen that the submarine is not debarred from attacking commerce: she is forbidden to attack it in a certain manner. The destruction of the millions of tons of world shipping would not have been possible unless that manner of attack had been used, and it may be thought that the abolition of this would remove the danger and, therefore, the need for defence. This is partially but not wholly true. Five great Powers have assented to the rule, but there remain many minor Powers and some possible major Powers of the future, which have not. So far as those lesser and prospective maritime Powers are concerned, it seems permissible not to be unduly anxious as to their attitude, even if they should abstain from committing themselves to an unqualified assent. If any future naval convention is to be arranged in which the greater Powers take part, assent to this rule, and, it may be observed, the logical application of this rule to the flying torpedo craft, could not fail to figure among its essential provisions. And so far as the lesser Powers are concerned, such methods of warfare are not worth their while owing to the fact that they could not expect to relieve themselves from any severe maritime pressure by that means.

There is however the question—"Will these rules be observed in war?" An obvious reply is that if one is to assume that they will be broken, one sweeps away the whole structure of international agreements. In that reply there is obvious truth; but however greatly one may desire that international restrictions shall operate in all circumstances, one is not entitled to disregard the lessons of experience. The accepted rules concerning capture were as plain before the War as they are to-day. They were broken. The claim was made that old rules could not apply to new instruments, whose use would be hampered or even prevented by their observance; a plain and palpable sophistry. But such sophistries will always be forthcoming if defence of what appears to be a profitable line of conduct is required. Thus submarines were used in violation of custom so well established as to constitute law, mines were placed in forbidden waters, open towns were bombarded without notice, hospital ships were sunk. These episodes are not raked up to rekindle old feelings, but as reminders that, admirable as optimism is in international affairs, it may become indistinguishable from mental dishonesty.

This does not mean that it is not worth while to make such agreements. What it does mean is that there should be a means, other than moral probity, of preventing them from being broken. It must not be worth while, in fact, to break them. He who contemplates such a departure from his word hesitates—we will put it no higher—if either the defence is so strong that it is plain that the attack will be shattered against it, in other words, that it will fail to achieve its object: or if that departure will make the position worse, by bringing new enemies into line against him.

Both of these were considered by Germany. It was not believed that effective defence could be organised. It was recognised that new enemies might be created, but it was thought certain that victory would be achieved before the new enemies could intervene effectively.

Either one or both of these safeguards is the essential foundation for the observance of the rules in Article 22 of the London Treaty, and once more we are faced with the question of collective or individual action. If it could be assumed that a breach of the rules would, without fail, bring collective action into play against the offender, and if the force collectively available were both sufficient and ready, individual nations would be under no necessity themselves to make provision for security against this danger. But if, as these agreements presuppose, the nations have rejected as impracticable the conception of collective action against the breaker of the peace, it is not to be expected that they will be prepared to commit themselves to the obligation to enforce the rules of war, even if it were for no other reason than the difficulty of deciding who it was that first broke the rule. For it is common for such breaches to be justified on the plea that they are retaliatory acts, provoked and rendered necessary by prior breaches on the part of the enemy.

The logical consequence, therefore, of the rejection of the collective system of security in the greater issues is its rejection in the lesser; and, as individual sea power becomes necessary, in the absence of collective sea power, to ensure national security, so instruments of sea power are needed, in sufficient quantity and of appropriate shape, to deter an opponent from breaking any rules of war that may have been established, or, if they should be broken, to prevent his achieving the object at which he aimed.

If there is to be that confidence in the stability of security which is essential to prevent a recrudescence of competition, one characteristic is essential in the craft provided for this particular purpose. They should not be able to influence the tactical course of a conflict between the main masses. The only qualities which could give them battle value in this sense would be torpedo armaments and the speed necessary to bring torpedo armaments into action.

Speed is one of the factors affecting the efficiency of a vessel operating against submarines, and no one will pretend that a very fast craft is not a more effective instrument for this service than one of moderate speed; and, as it is quite impossible to place a limit upon speed, so the only practicable form of limitation is the size; and unless this should be drastically reduced there can be nothing to prevent such vessels being fitted in war with torpedo armaments, with all the consequential creation of insecurity. The vessels needed for security of the communications are, essentially and fundamentally, fast gun-boats whose armaments are designed for use against submarines—guns and underwater charges. Let it be remarked, moreover, that the destroyer of to-day is half as large again as the great majority of those of 1914–18, so that there is ample scope for reduction.

At an earlier stage of this discussion the question was asked whether it was practicable to obtain a designation of what dictated the qualitative and quantitative needs of the surface flotilla. Do those considerations affecting the submarine assist us to arrive at any conclusions?

It is suggested that they do. The growth of the surface flotilla was rendered necessary by the submarine. Article 22 of the London Treaty forbids that use of submarines which imposed the need for that flotilla, but the observance of the Treaty can only be relied upon if the disadvantages of breaking it plainly outweigh the advantages. A flotilla, the design of the units of which is strictly directed to the object of countering the submarine, is necessary. That portion of the duties of the flotilla which is concerned with the direct security of communications is one which can be fulfilled by comparatively small vessels. Like cruisers, which in their own sphere they are, their numbers are dictated by needs and cannot be assessed relatively.

The other duty of the flotilla is that which is related to the battle fleet. We are here brought back to the origin of the present-day destroyer.

The destroyer is the outcome of the torpedo-boat. When the torpedo was invented it was at once realised that it possessed capacities for attack on a battle fleet, and a flotilla of torpedo vessels became an arm of the battle fleet. The torpedo vessel developed along two lines. According to one school of thought, predominantly the German, she should be a pure torpedo carrier whose object was to attack the opposing battleships. This may be called the active or offensive school. In the British navy, the tactical theory was that the battle would be decided by the artillery, and that the object should be to ensure that the artillery should not be prevented from developing its full intensity; and the flotilla craft was developed as a gun-boat whose primary purpose was to prevent the torpedo craft of an enemy from delivering an attack which might oblige the fleet to suspend or diminish its volume of fire through having to alter its course in order to avoid an attack or evade the torpedoes. Hence, while one navy added constantly in size and number to its fleet-torpedo-boat flotilla, the other in reply added equally constantly in size and number to its fleet-torpedo-boat-destroyer flotilla. In the climax at Jutland there were approximately an equal number of torpedo boats and destroyers in each fleet. The German hope that an initial inferiority in battleship force would be compensated for by a flotilla was not fully attained for the reason that the counter was evolved in the form of the opposing flotilla. The numbers, thus, were not the outcome of some specific tactical doctrine of the proportion between the numbers of flotilla craft and of ships of the line, but of attempts to gain superiority by building larger numbers. It was the perfectly rational outcome of the policy of competition. The aim, and the unavoidable aim, things being as they were, was to attain superiority by outbuilding the rival.

Presumably no one desires to reintroduce the competitive system. If it is to be avoided, and if no collective measures are practicable, some basis of establishment is needed. It is idle to say that the force of destroyers depends upon the number of the similar craft in an enemy fleet unless one can also establish some basis to govern that number.

There is, however, one basis which appears to deserve serious thought, and is free from that objection.

A fleet of battleships, no matter if the ships be great or

small, requires defence against submarines, for even if the reduction to the size which was imposed upon Germany—10,000 tons—were adopted internationally the vessels would not possess the immunity which the small size of flotilla craft confers. The 2000-ton vessels which would be adequate for some purposes of trade defence would not be suitable for fleet purposes, mainly on account of insufficient speed, but also for other reasons. Faster vessels are needed for the security of a fleet than for the security of trading ships. This is not because the preservation of battleships is more important than the preservation of merchant ships, although that by itself would be a valid reason, since if the battleships are destroyed the trade ceases; but because far greater mobility, both in terms of endurance and of speed, is needed by those craft which form a portion of the fighting mass than by those which have to defend the trade in the more restricted areas in which it is most liable to submarine attack. For this purpose a vessel of the type of the present destroyer, which is largely the result of experience, is required.

If then there is a fundamental need for a screen of light craft it would not appear to be beyond the capacity of a body of sea officers to state in quantitative terms the needs of screening craft. Admittedly there will be differences of opinion; different officers may hold different views as to formations. But an approximation is possible. War is an art, not a mathematical science. To take an example which occurred many times during the War. Convoys had to be escorted by squadrons of British or American battleships across the North Sea. Was it impossible for the High Command to determine how many screening craft were sent with four ships, or with eight, or with twelve? Or a single battleship had been sent from her base to a docking port. With how many destroyers was it considered proper to guard her? The numerical strength of the destroyer flotillas, forming as they do an integral part of the main body, would be in proportion to the battleships. If, for instance, it should be determined that three escorts were needed per battleship—the number and the method of assessment are being taken purely in illustration and not as a considered statement of either—the battle fleets would each have their established proportion. To what tactical use commanders would put the thirty, or forty-five, or any other number of torpedo craft under their command, does not enter into the question. What is definitely germane is this. The number of battleships which the several Powers possess is now based, and still would be if the method of establishing the ratios were changed,[19] upon the strategical needs of security. That ratio represents the "mass," and it is essential to recognise that the mass is not composed of battleships only, but of all those vessels which constitute its fighting strength. It would be strictly and scientifically correct, therefore, that the established proportions should include the fleet flotilla.

It is not for a moment to be assumed that the adoption of such a principle would impose any limitation whatever upon the use which the High Command might make of these vessels. They would be no more bound to keep their flotillas with their battleships than commands in the past

[19] *Vide ante*, p. 259.

have been bound to keep their battleships concentrated. We have only to cast an eye backwards to the strategical conceptions of France in the time of Louis XIV, Louis XV and the latter parts of the Napoleonic Wars for innumerable examples of the use of detachments, in varying sizes, in the war of manoeuvre. That freedom must exist; and it would exist under the conditions of limitation of construction which have been outlined.

Passing next to the submarine. Is it possible to say what dictates either her size or her numbers? It was possible, as we have seen, to indicate a principle governing the size of the cruiser—that she must be large enough to do the duties which fall to detachments; and one governing her numbers—that they should be enough to supply the services with the fleet and to distribute to the many scattered points where she was needed. It was possible to indicate what dictated the size of the battleship. Under the conditions of the past, this had been purely the size of the battleship of the enemy: but when limitation of numbers by international agreement came into existence, and ratios, supposed to represent the relative needs, were rigidly fixed, it became necessary to ensure that the limitations should not be evaded by the construction of other ships, not coming within that limitation, but powerful enough to bring into the battle line and to upset the balance. If the size of the battleship relatively to that of the cruiser is such as will, within reason,[20] prevent one nation from being placed at a

[20] Within reason is a necessary qualification: for no one can say what novel use a fighting genius might be able to make of his lesser craft in battle.

patent disadvantage through his having to be strong in two places—his communications and his mass—while his rival has need only to be strong in one, she will be large enough.

The submarine cannot be assessed, either in point of size or of numbers. She is, in essence, a "cruiser," a vessel employed in detached duties. The detached duties of the surface cruiser are those of direct defence and attack of external lines of communications. The only grounds upon which the possession of the large ocean-going gun-armed submarine can be sustained is that she can be an effective commerce destroyer. She can be given a great endurance. She can be armed with guns which will enable her to overcome a merchant ship. Her powers of submersibility will enable her, so long as she is undamaged, to escape from superior force. But in respect of the other function of the cruising vessel, she is ill-suited to the duties. The protection of a convoy requires pre-eminently the power to stand up and fight, and this power the submarine possesses in a lesser degree than any other vessel. It is true that she can be armoured, that she offers a small target, and that she might be able to put up a good fight with an armed merchant cruiser; but she would be very unequal to opposing any regular cruiser, and defence against armed merchant cruisers can be more effectively and far more economically furnished by similar vessels, which impose no burden in times of peace; whereas the submarine not only imposes the burden of her cost and maintenance, but that burden is a constantly increasing one owing to the demands for improvement which must, in the nature of things, be made by

the technical authorities. How great this increase may be
can be realised from the example of the surface cruiser of
to-day and her forerunner of before the War. The cruiser
of 1912, mounting an armament of nine 6-inch guns, cost
£353,437. The cruiser which has taken her place in 1930,
mounting eight 6-inch guns, has cost £1,667,819: or four
and three-quarter times as much. The new vessel is larger,
faster, carries more torpedoes, though one gun less. The
demand for extra speed alone has added £300,000 to her
cost. But with all her extra speed and other improvements,
for all the fact that she is a more powerful instrument than
her predecessor, she is still a cruiser and can do no more
than her predecessor. So the same increases in cost will infallibly occur in the submarine cruiser. The same demand
for speed and for other qualities—the demands which Von
Tirpitz says he had to resist in his day for otherwise the
size of the ship would have reached 100,000 tons—will be
made under the stress of competition.

Those who would put forward the claim of necessity for
the large ocean-going submarine as an instrument of security by direct defence, find no support for their conten-
tion on the grounds of effectiveness or economy. Certainly,
the views expressed above may be challenged. It may be
said that the large gun-armed submarine can do that which
the escorts to convoys have always had to do, which is to
cover the escape of their convoy, to bar the way to the
attacker, drive him off or hold him up long enough to enable his charges to get out of reach of the attacker. It
will not be easy to demonstrate that the submarine possesses this capacity: and it will be less easy to show that, if

she is to possess this capacity of effectiveness, she can combine it with economy: in other words, that a corresponding degree of security could not be obtained at a lower cost.

As an instrument for attack upon commerce she stands in a different light. Undeniably she possesses power as an ocean raider. The effect of the ocean raider is to enforce the need of convoy on ocean routes, and the need of convoy increases the requirements of escorting vessels and slows up the flow of trade or increases the number of cargo carriers required. Thus, while it is possible to make some computation of the surface cruiser strength which a state needs, because there is a definite basis in the number of "points" which require defence, there is no logical means of computation of the number of submarine cruising vessels whose function lies so predominently, if not even exclusively, in the sporadic offensive warfare. But those who would therefore class the vessel as "offensive" must not lose sight of the fact, referred to elsewhere, that sporadic warfare is, for the weaker Power at sea, a diversion—a means of forcing his superior antagonist to dissipate his forces and render it more difficult for him to concentrate in the areas where he can most effectively bring pressure to bear.

Whether, taking the wider view, a particular Power will derive advantage from this weapon will depend upon circumstances. Though she may be a weaker Power than one possible adversary, she may be stronger than another whose external commerce is not essential. In that position it will by no means necessarily be an advantage that an equal or weaker opponent should possess the means of sending out its submarine cruisers upon the trade routes, and cutting up of the external communications. Cruisers would thereby have to be detached from the more important theatres where the major and decisive struggle is taking place.

It has been remarked by German writers that Germany's weakness at sea in the Franco-Prussian War of 1870-1 had one particular effect. France was able to import military stores and weapons from abroad with which to arm her new armies and thereby to continue her resistance longer than she could otherwise have done. Without going so far as to say that German submarines, if they had existed at that time, would have been able to prevent this importation, it can at least be said that they would have added in a marked degree to France's difficulties.[21] To-day Germany has no submarines. But one must foresee that if submarines are retained, she also will have them. There are pros and cons to all questions—this question of the retention of the submarine the cons appear most heavily to outweigh the pros, not merely so far as Great Britain is concerned, but also France. There are in fact three possible courses, apart from unrestricted competition: abolition, limitation on a basis of the needs of defence, and limitation to some figure, a figure which can only be purely arbitrary and have no strategical basis. If the first be rejected, and the second is impossible (which it is), we are driven back upon the third, a solution which is repellent to any one who believes either in economy or in clear thinking.

[21] "Even in 1870 a fleet which commanded the sea would have been of the greatest possible service, for it would have shortened the duration of the war by preventing the importation of guns from England and America into the French ports." Maltzahn, *Naval Warfare.*

CHAPTER IX

SEA POWER AND MODERN INSTRUMENTS

THERE are some who consider that sea power has had its day, admitting that it exercised the influence which Mahan attributed to it in the wars of the seventeenth and eighteenth centuries, and that this experience was repeated in the War of 1914–18, but stating that this will not again be possible. The principal reasons for this view may be broadly summarised under four headings:

(1) Sea power is slow acting. Wars in future will be short and sea power will not have time to make its effect felt.

(2) New instruments have come into use, principally under water and above the water, which deprive sea power of its capacity to control the sea.

(3) New means of communication have been developed on land and in the air which enable a nation to receive what it needs from over sea, irrespective of control at sea.

(4) Powerful neutrals will never again consent to any impediment being put in the way of their commerce by belligerents.

Reasons for differing from the view that all wars in the future will take this short and sharp turn have been given in an earlier chapter; but this does not dispose of the argument that there are conditions in which a decisive result would be obtained by direct attack upon the civil population, upon its means of supply, or by the disablement of the forces which have hitherto served to protect the people and their needs. But as the potentialities of this form of attack are undoubted, in certain circumstances, so it is equally undoubted that it is necessary to furnish the means of defence; and unless all previous experience is to be dismissed, these means can be developed. In one of his "Battle Studies" Ardant du Picq remarked: "At any time a new invention may assure victory. Granted. But practicable weapons are not invented every day and nations quickly put themselves on the same footing as regards armaments." Certainly if nations do not "put themselves upon the same footing," either by furnishing themselves with similar instruments or by developing means of nullifying the new instrument, they will suffer. The Allies suffered in the war when the submarine was used as a new instrument in trade attack, and their tardiness in adopting counter measures brought them very close to disaster. But when the counter has been developed, the instrument takes its place with all the other instruments. It has to fight for mastery, and no decision will be reached until it has mastered the opposition. The rise of counter measures—whether in the purely passive form of mere obstacles or in the most active form of a counter offensive—prevents that immediate decision. While this struggle continues, the other forms of warfare proceed, affected, according to circumstances, by the effects which this form of attack produces upon the whole conduct of the war.

It is worthy of recollection that anticipations of a short war have proved fallacious on many occasions; for man has a limited vision. Until he is faced with a difficulty he is unaware of his own resourcefulness, and he is as unaware of what sufferings he will stand as he is of the limits of endurance of a nation. Napoleon is said to have been more anxious about the temper of the people than anything else.[1] So it has often happened that statesmen of the highest ability and experience have been misled into the belief that some new instrument, some new strategical method or some economic influences will bring war to a rapid conclusion. In 1706 Vauban was sure that the *guerre-de-course* would force England and Holland to succumb in two or three years—a "short" time when wars dragged their length out over decades. Pitt was convinced that the war which began in 1793 would be short. He underestimated the driving power of the popular will, the sufferings which a united people were prepared to undergo, and the change which the substitution of a revolutionary for a royal government had caused. He overestimated the influence of lack of revenue. In 1801 Fulton told Napoleon that his submarine would destroy the British fleet, ensure the freedom of the seas, and end naval warfare by making it too terrible to contemplate. A century later the financial difficulties to which war would give rise were pointed out and the consequent impossibility of a war of long duration. Herr Bethmann-Hollweg was no less sure the war would be short: "It will be a violent storm but very short. I count on a war of three or at most of four months and I have organised all my policy on that assumption." The German sea-

---

[1] "Chaptal said of him (Napoleon) that he feared the slightest unrest among the workers more than a lost battle. His interest in industry arose partly from the fact that he wished to provide employment as an antidote to revolution. . . ." L. C. A. Knowles, *Economic Development of the Nineteenth Century*, p. 1231.

men, reasoning in 1916 as Vauban had reasoned two hundred and ten years before, persuaded their statesmen that the *guerre-de-course* conducted by submarines was a certain road to a decision in six months.

Each and all of these expectations were disappointed. The power of resistance, the inventiveness and the determination of man were all miscalculated. So, taking warning from these earlier experiences, we should be cautious in accepting these estimates of a rapid decision by action in the air, which are held to render sea power an instrument whose operations are too slow to exercise any influence in the future.

The second reason for the belief that sea power is no longer an influence, or less of an influence than it has hitherto been, is that new instruments have deprived it of its power. This, however, confuses sea power with one of its parts. It supposes that naval strength is the only element in sea power, which it is not; important and essential as it is, there are other elements.[2] And it visualises naval strength in terms solely of those ships which operate on the surface of the water.

Sea power is more than this. When we speak of its influence, what do we mean? In what has its influence consisted? It has consisted in the power to control movements at sea. Sea power is power in that form which enables its possessor and prevents his opponent from moving military forces by sea; which prevents an opponent from receiving, by way of the sea, the goods he needs, either for his people

[2] *Vide* chapter II: also, for a more extensive discussion, Mahan on "Elements of Sea Power" in *The Influence of Sea Power upon History*.

or his fighting forces, and sending across the sea in exchange the goods with which he pays for them. The shape or size of the vehicle which conveys force, its means of movement, or the medium in which it moves, are technical details. In whatever way the instrument moves or obtains "command," having obtained it by the only way in which command can be obtained—the disablement of the opposing fighting instruments—it is an instrument of sea power. The introduction of a new instrument capable of fighting at sea may affect an existing situation. If Fulton had been able to make his submarine effective, and therewith to sink the fleets off Brest and in the Mediterranean, and the transports carrying troops and their stores to the Mediterranean, it would not have meant that sea power was henceforward ineffective, but that sea power had passed into other hands. The pirates who operated from the coasts of Barbary, the Persian Gulf or Greece, and took toll of the merchantmen within the range of their vessels, were making use of sea power to fill their pockets: and sea power it still would have been (if they had survived) if they had exchanged their feluccas for frigates, their sailing vessels for steam vessels, their surface vessels for submarine craft, or their submarine craft for aircraft. Until it shall have become impossible to exercise any control over the movements of shipping at sea, sea power, which is the power of exercising that control, will continue to exist; and its influence will be measured by the extent to which the instruments are able to make that control effective.

The existence of new means of communication, enabling goods to reach enemy hands by way of the ports of neutrals, is said to have outflanked sea power, so that the blockade which closed the enemy ports is no longer an effective, even if it were a practicable, measure. Underlying this is the assumption, referred to earlier, that the method by which sea power exercised influence was blockade of the trading ports of an enemy. That such a measure was used on occasions is a fact. That it was the measure by which the Sea Power in the great struggles made its influence felt is incorrect. The trade which was conducted was carried by two agencies—the national and the neutral shipping. National shipping could sail only if it could be defended. While single ships or small convoys could evade capture, the volume of traffic of which they were capable was a trifle compared with the bulk-trade of the country. It was not blockade of the commercial ports which stopped the sailing, but observation of the major bodies of the enemy forces in a manner so effective that they could not put to sea with any large assembly of shipping, and the use of cruising forces which intercepted the detachments. The risk of sailing, not organised blockade, was the deterrent. Enemy goods carried by the neutral were subject to capture; as we have seen, that right has been abrogated, but, in the conditions which have arisen with the development of the new weapons, the effect of this abrogation is lessened. Mercantile ports may be made the bases of submarines, and if this should result in the laying of minefields to check the activities of these craft, there will be a danger to mercantile traffic.

Contraband goods raise a different question. The right to prevent such goods from reaching an enemy has been questioned by no one, though differences have arisen on

many occasions as to what goods may be treated as contraband. The fact that changes have taken place in the manner in which goods are carried does not in any way affect
the fundamental and acknowledged principle that it is
legitimate to prevent the enemy from obtaining the benefits of their use. Whether the goods go direct to the port, or
whether they go circuitously by one or several neutral
ports, is therefore not material. This principle of the con-
tinuity of a voyage, asserted in British prize courts in the
Napoleonic War, extended by the prize courts of the United
States in the Civil War, and practised by prize courts in
the War of 1914–18, can assuredly be said to be established.
Unless the new instruments of war at sea have rendered
impossible the interception, visit or search of shipping, sea
power remains capable of exercising its influence in the
sphere of its action.

Fears are expressed that any attempts made to interfere
with the commerce of an enemy in the future will be opposed by the United States, who are credited with a permanent sentiment in favour of the freedom of commerce.
No one can be unaware that this sentiment exists in spite
of Mahan's remark that "Public opinion in the United
States has great faith in war directed against an enemy's
commerce,"[3] and of more recent pronouncements by distinguished officers. Yet it cannot escape recollection that
it was largely by the use of sea power, including a very
great extension of the doctrine of continuous voyage and
blockade, that the United States preserved the Union in
the great struggle.

The War of 1812 is held up as warning against any act at

[3] *The Influence of Sea Power upon History*, p. 3.

sea prejudicial to the trade of the United States. It is assumed that that war was fought in consequence of capture at sea. Such assertions ignore the important part which was played by the impressment of seamen, and the further fact that the rights of capture and blockade were not disputed. What was disputed was the legality of the Orders-in-Council; even these had been rescinded when war was declared. Moreover, if a recent American historian is correct in his deductions,[4] a still further cause cannot be left out of account, in the desire of a strong section of the community in Kentucky to annex Canada, and of another in Georgia for the annexation of Florida from Spain, then fighting as the ally of Great Britain.

Still one further reason is expressed for doubting the value of sea power: it applies to the use of collective action. The supposition is made that if collective action were adopted against an aggressor, the method of its use would be blockade—that blockade would be rendered impossible by the United States, who would use their navy to break the blockade.

Two highly questionable assumptions inform this forecast. The first is that collective action must take the form of blockade. Blockade is merely a forcible means of keeping goods out of a country. Its object is to prevent the circulation of trade. If it is possible for nations collectively to agree to take common action, it would seem to be equally possible for the same nations collectively to impose an embargo. In actual fact, if a blockade should be declared, it must be accompanied by an embargo or by acts which for-

4 Julius W. Pratt, *The American Mercury*, October 1927.

bid trade with the nation concerned. An embargo is a far more comprehensive measure than a blockade. It closes both the land and the sea frontiers—the land frontiers are too often forgotten in these controversies, and the attendant fact that approximately fifty per cent. of the trade of a continental country moves across them.

The possibility of illicit trade is not to be denied, for corrupt persons are always to be found who will make profit out of the circumstance, however injurious to the community such behaviour may be. But it is not to be supposed that a trickle, or even a small flow, of illicit trade, would mitigate to an adequate degree the isolation caused by an embargo, accompanied, as such an act presumably would be, by its application to services as well as to goods. The national shipping of the offending country would find itself suspended except to such nations as stand without the agreement.

If, however, it should be deemed that an embargo would be an insufficient measure, more far-reaching though it be in its action than physical blockade, and that the act of blockade was necessary, either in place of or in addition to the embargo, the fear has been expressed that the blockade would be broken by the United States, standing, as she considers it in her interest to stand, apart from entanglements. This assumption appears highly unjust to that country. Apart from the declaration made by Mr. Stimson, there is the unmistakable fact that the United States has a high regard for law. On those occasions on which she has opposed the action at sea of Great Britain, her grounds have invariably been that the action was not lawful. Her opposition to the paper blockades of the Napoleonic Wars and to various of the acts in the War of 1914–18 were based upon what she considered their illegality. But on no occasion has she disputed the two fundamental principles of the use of sea power—the right of blockade and the right to prevent contraband goods reaching an enemy—and her actions when she herself has been a belligerent have been marked by a rigorous application of both measures, going even beyond what European legal opinion considered just.

But if blockade is to be used, it must be used in accordance with the law. Blockade is an act of war, it must be established in a certain form, be sustained by adequate force and conform to certain requirements. Even if Mr. Stimson had not made the declaration of policy referred to earlier, there is no reason to suppose that this great nation would so lightly regard her duties as a neutral, or treat the whole established system of International Law as though it did not exist.

If there is to be any satisfactory solution of the problems of sea power, and if collective action is not a practicable possibility in the world of to-day, the subject must be treated with a greater width of view than it has hitherto been. What is a "satisfactory" solution? It is one which is as stable as changing conditions admit. It must not be one that itself is based upon making changes, whether those changes are in the nature of territorial expansion, or, within limits as restricted as it is possible to impose, changes in design. For every new design brings with it a new need, calls for some antidote, calls for greater expenditure upon some particular quality. It must also achieve the object which it has in view in the most economical manner. The object itself must therefore be clear and must be interpreted in the same way by all nations. It is of little use to say that the object is security, if the interpretations of security differ, as they clearly do.

That every nation has a right to security cannot be denied: but that any nation has a prescriptive right to a greater degree of security than any other is inadmissible. What we have seen in recent years has been a series of claims for equality under the name of parity of naval strength. Parity of naval strength is not parity of sea power and still less is it parity of security.

Parity in the instruments which constitute naval strength is a mathematical possibility but a strategical absurdity, since it does not take into consideration the conditions under which those instruments have to be used, or the facilities which subserve their needs and without which they cannot be used. It does not represent parity in sea power, because geographical position, distribution of territory, and other elements referred to earlier, and treated at a greater length by Mahan in his first book, are constituents of sea power. And sea power itself does not represent total power, into which land force, natural resources, manufacturing and food-providing capacities enter.

Equality in power is impracticable if for no other reason than that the power of two nations is not comparable. Twelve years after Waterloo, when problems of the same nature as those which face the world to-day were under review, Macaulay pointed out the impossibility of comparing the powers of France to England. There was, he showed, no means of assessing them in a single general term: the chances that they were unequal were as infinity to one, but neither was endangered thereby. For some purposes, such as a campaign over sea, England was the stronger: for others—a campaign on the Danube or the Po—France was the stronger; while for some other purposes, neither had any strength at all. Neither had the power to bring the other under subjection for a month. This, he said, is the manly and sensible way of discussing such matters.[5]

What Macaulay then said of the strength of the Western neighbours in 1827 may be said with equal truth of the nations of the world of the twentieth century. No absolute comparisons of power can be made. Japan is stronger than America for a war in Northern Asia, but weaker for a war in the Caribbean. England is stronger than America for a war in the Indian Ocean, but weaker for one on the coasts of the Pacific. Any of the military states of the Continent is stronger than America, England or Japan for a war on the Continent. Is there not reason to suspect that many of our present troubles arise from refusal to recognise these facts? Are not the parallel growths of the fleets of the United States and Japan the result in some measure, perhaps a marked measure, of each trying to make itself stronger than the other in an area in which one possesses all the advantages of position? Growth in the size of ships to dimensions far exceeding any which are demanded by tactical or technical needs is due to the same cause. Ships larger than those of other Powers are believed to be neces-

[5] Macaulay on Mill's *Essay on Government.*

sary because they have, or are supposed to have, further to go. The length of a tiger is the same whether it is measured from the nose to the tail or the tail to the nose.

The only interpretation of the word Security upon which it is possible to build is security against the two forms of injury to which a nation is exposed at sea. That is not a narrow definition. It includes the mobility of armies which have to cross the sea to guard their country against invasion. It includes the defence of commerce in such areas as facilities exist for its defence: for where facilities do not exist, where men of war cannot find refreshment and supplies, or convoys may not assemble, defence is impracticable, and neither size nor numbers, unless carried to astronomical figures, will afford security in such conditions.

The purpose of policy which actuated the growth of the German fleet was perfectly clearly expressed. It was to render Germany secure by making others insecure. It made others insecure, and therefore stimulated growth, caused alliances, and made its contribution in this way to war. That policy, in different forms, has been responsible for the portentous growth in the size of navies, in the size of ships, in the development of new instruments, and in national expenditure. The questions, therefore, "What dictates the size of a navy?" and "What dictates the size of a ship?" academic as they may appear, are essentially practical: for if there is one unpractical thing to do it is to proceed upon any undertaking without having clearly defined one's object. Having defined the end, the means of attaining it become more clearly indicated.

INDEX

WORLD AFFAIRS: National and International Viewpoints
An Arno Press Collection

Angell, Norman. **The Great Illusion, 1933.** 1933.

Benes, Eduard. **Memoirs:** From Munich to New War and New Victory. 1954.

[Carrington, Charles Edmund] (Edmonds, Charles, pseud.) **A Subaltern's War.** 1930. New preface by Charles Edmund Carrington.

Cassel, Gustav. **Money and Foreign Exchange After 1914.** 1922.

Chambers, Frank P. **The War Behind the War, 1914-1918.** 1939.

Dedijer, Vladimir. **Tito.** 1953.

Dickinson, Edwin DeWitt. **The Equality of States in International Law.** 1920.

Douhet, Giulio. **The Command of the Air.** 1942.

Edib, Halidé. **Memoirs.** 1926.

Ferrero, Guglielmo. **The Principles of Power.** 1942.

Grew, Joseph C. **Ten Years in Japan.** 1944.

Hayden, Joseph Ralston. **The Philippines.** 1942.

Hudson, Manley O. **The Permanent Court of International Justice, 1920-1942.** 1943.

Huntington, Ellsworth. **Mainsprings of Civilization.** 1945.

Jacks, G. V. and R. O. Whyte. **Vanishing Lands:** A World Survey of Soil Erosion. 1939.

Mason, Edward S. **Controlling World Trade.** 1946.

Menon, V. P. **The Story of the Integration of the Indian States.** 1956.

Moore, Wilbert E. **Economic Demography of Eastern and Southern Europe.** 1945.

[Ohlin, Bertil]. **The Course and Phases of the World Economic Depression.** 1931.

Oliveira, A. Ramos. **Politics, Economics and Men of Modern Spain, 1808-1946.** 1946.

O'Sullivan, Donal. **The Irish Free State and Its Senate.** 1940.

Peffer, Nathaniel. **The White Man's Dilemma.** 1927.

Philby, H. St. John. **Sa'udi Arabia.** 1955.

Rappard, William E. **International Relations as Viewed From Geneva.** 1925.

Rauschning, Hermann. **The Revolution of Nihilism.** 1939.

Reshetar, John S., Jr. **The Ukrainian Revolution, 1917-1920.** 1952.

Richmond, Admiral Sir Herbert. **Sea Power in the Modern World.** 1934.

Robbins, Lionel. **Economic Planning and International Order.** 1937. New preface by Lionel Robbins.

Russell, Bertrand. **Bolshevism:** Practice and Theory. 1920.

Russell, Frank M. **Theories of International Relations.** 1936.

Schwarz, Solomon M. **The Jews in the Soviet Union.** 1951.

Siegfried, André. **Canada:** An International Power. [1947].

Souvarine, Boris. **Stalin.** 1939.

Spaulding, Oliver Lyman, Jr., Hoffman Nickerson, and John Womack Wright. **Warfare.** 1925.

Storrs, Sir Ronald. **Memoirs.** 1937.

Strausz-Hupé, Robert. **Geopolitics:** The Struggle for Space and Power. 1942.

Swinton, Sir Ernest D. **Eyewitness.** 1933.

Timasheff, Nicholas S. **The Great Retreat.** 1946.

Welles, Sumner. **Naboth's Vineyard:** The Dominican Republic, 1844-1924. 1928. Two volumes in one.

Whittlesey, Derwent. **The Earth and the State.** 1939.

Wilcox, Clair. **A Charter for World Trade.** 1949.